Nancy B

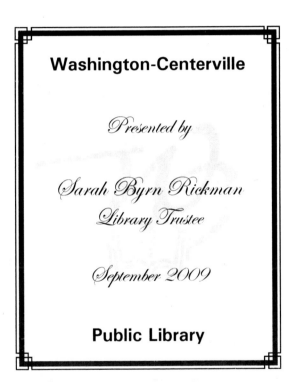

Fire Ant Books

Nancy Batson Crews on the steps of the King Air she copiloted for American Equity Insurance Company, 1999–2000. Photo taken by and courtesy of King Air pilot-in-command Chris Beal-Kaplan. This photo first appeared in *Alabama Aviation Heritage* magazine, 2006.

Nancy Batson Crews

Alabama's First Lady of Flight

SARAH BYRN RICKMAN

FOREWORD BY JANE KIRKPATRICK

[signature: S B Rickman]

THE UNIVERSITY OF ALABAMA PRESS

Tuscaloosa

Typeface: Goudy

∞

The paper on which this book is printed meets the minimum requirements of American National Standard for Information Sciences-Permanence of Paper for Printed Library Materials, ANSI Z39.48-1984.

Library of Congress Cataloging-in-Publication Data

Rickman, Sarah Byrn.
   Nancy Batson Crews : Alabama's first lady of flight / Sarah Byrn Rickman ; foreword by Jane Kirkpatrick.
      p. cm.
      "Fire Ant books."
   Includes bibliographical references and index.
   ISBN 978-0-8173-5553-1 (pbk. : alk. paper) 1. Crews, Nancy Batson, 1920–2001.
2. Women air pilots—United States—Biography. 3. Air pilots—United States—Biography.
4. United States. Women's Auxiliary Ferrying Squadron—Biography. 5. Women Airforce Service Pilots (U.S.)—Biography. 6. World War, 1939–1945—Participation, Female.
7. Birmingham (Ala.)—Biography. I. Title.
   TL540.C825R53 2009
   629.13092—dc22
   [B]
                                                                                    2009007965

Cover photo: Nancy Batson climbing into the cockpit of a North American AT-6 Army advanced trainer, ca. June 1943. This was the cover photo of *Air Force*, the Official Service Journal of the U.S. Army Air Forces, September 1943. Photo courtesy of the WASP Collection, the Woman's Collection at Texas Woman's University, Denton.

This book is dedicated to the most important people in my life—my family: my husband, Richard; my sons and their wives, Jim and Amy and Chuck and Susan; and my grandchildren, Katie, Alex, and James Daniel.

Contents

Illustrations

Foreword by Jane Kirkpatrick

It's said that place and space both border and define us. Historically this was true for women who typically found their place in the workings of the kitchen, the family, the near community. Within their life span, women often migrated only miles from the landscape of their birth. Though things changed rapidly for those coming of age during what we call the Greatest Generation, the stories we hear are more about men migrating from place and space than about women. Women's history is often relegated to stories of their leaving home only to fill the spaces of men gone off to war. When men returned, most women moved back into their traditional places and spaces.

But there was a cadre of women who defied those traditions and Nancy Batson Crews was one of them. What makes Nancy's story the more remarkable is that she never led a squadron the way her mentor Nancy Love did as founder of the WAFS; nor did she die the heroine's death in duty, as did her friend Evelyn Sharp. Nancy Batson Crews's place in the American experience peaks in the passion that filled her life and heart, soaring above the earth, maintaining aviation friendships across miles and years while earning her way for over six decades in an eclectic aviation career. How rare is it to be a woman doing what you love to do at eighteen and still being paid to do it at the age of eighty? That what Nancy loved to do was to pilot planes makes her story all the more amazing.

Yet *Nancy Batson Crews: Alabama's First Lady of Flight* is more than a story of one woman. Hers is the story of many women who fell in love with flight at a time when their country needed their willingness to risk winter snows, summer thunderstorms, western mountains, and active airport traffic to ferry planes men would fly in combat—freeing men from transport, so they could. These women performed with minimal fanfare and later fought for military recognition that they were even present, serving in that place.

What defines Nancy's story, however, is less that she helped lead that recognition but that when World War II was over, she continued to define her life in aviation whether it was towing gliders, teaching students, or increasing her own skills in whatever aircraft she could find to master. After the death of her husband, she went on to build a successful business in real estate, but always, the business of flight kept Nancy whole. The relationships she developed in those early years were the ones that sustained her through later troubling times. Those friendships defined a sisterhood of women among whom flight almost more than family marked their place.

I'd never heard of Nancy Batson Crews until I read Sarah Byrn Rickman's fine biography, which would have been my loss. But I've spent my life either counseling women to help them trust their dreams or writing about ordinary women who made places in their worlds worthy of remembering. As a pilot myself, Nancy's story resonated as we are shared adventurers. But flight for Nancy wasn't an achievement nor was it ancillary to some other occupation; it was not merely a way to move from place to place. Flight *was* Nancy. Her husband and children understood that without that time to soar, to wrap herself in flight plans, logbooks, weather reports, tending to the WAFS she never lost touch with, without that passion in her life, the wife and mother they came to love would have been bereft. She became untethered to this earth and needed flight as a balance to it in order to feel alive.

It's easy to see why Nancy trusted Sarah to tell this remarkable story. The compassion of this writer for her subject grows out of mutual respect and a desire to understand the complexity of this woman who never stopped taking risks and paid the personal price necessary to truly seek one's bliss. The author's care for truth, her ability to listen with her heart as well as her ears as children, friends, colleagues spoke of Nancy, gives those of us who never knew Nancy a deeper understanding of her life. Some of how that relationship grew between subject and biographer is shared within this narrative; some we speculate about because of the complexity of Nancy's life so tenderly unveiled.

Nancy's choices weren't always wise. The strength that drove her to succeed also pushed others away. Nancy was a product of the Old South. She harbored prejudices and later resentments from the war that pierced the bonds of her own flesh. Yet the author's compassion and admiration take us through these human frailties to meet a woman worthy of emulating, a woman who never stopped learning, never stopped discovering.

One cannot come away from reading of Nancy's life without profound respect and a deep sense of awe that during an era when married women were still not allowed to even teach in many places in the country, Nancy Batson Crews soared above such injustices. She made a remarkable life doing what she loved and met her obligations to family and community in extraordinary ways. Her story is a reminder to us all that we can dream and risk at any age. Looking back, Nancy surely could have agreed with the poet Mary Oliver that hers was a life "married to amazement" and that she "took the world into [her] arms." This fine biography shows us how to make those words our own epitaph.

Acknowledgments

Nancy Batson Crews's three children have worked with me, in full cooperation, throughout my research and the writing of this book. My heartfelt thanks to Paul Crews Jr., Radford Crews, and Jane Crews Tonarely. My thanks also to other members of Nancy's family for their help: her late sister Amy Batson Strange; her niece Elizabeth Strange Simpson; her nephew Luther Strange; and her cousin, Ken Coupland. Katherine Price "Kap" Garmon provided me with the written history of Camp Winnataska as well as personal memories of, and observations about, the camp Nancy loved so very much. In addition, several of Nancy's aviation friends in Birmingham have been enthusiastically supportive throughout the entire process: Chris Beal-Kaplan, Dr. James A. Pittman, Lt. Col. Joseph L. Shannon (USAF ret.), and Dr. Edward W. Stevenson.

I would also like to acknowledge assistance from the Southern Museum of Flight and the Alabama Aviation Hall of Fame in Birmingham; the Alabama Women's Hall of Fame located at Judson College in Marion; the International Women's Air and Space Museum in Cleveland, Ohio; and the WASP Collection, the Woman's Collection, Texas Woman's University in Denton.

Lastly, to the eight WAFS (Women's Auxiliary Ferrying Squadron) who survived Nancy—all of whom I met through her—my admiration, my respect, and my thanks: Bernice Batten (deceased 2004), Phyllis Burchfield Fulton, Teresa James (deceased 2008), Gertrude Meserve Tubbs LeValley, Barbara Jane "B.J." Erickson London, Barbara Donahue Ross, Barbara Poole Shoemaker (deceased 2008), and Florene Miller Watson.

Sarah Byrn Rickman

Abbreviations

AAF	Army Air Forces
AT	advanced trainer
ATC	Air Transport Command
ATP	Airline Transport Pilot
BOQ	Bachelor Officers' Quarters
BT	basic trainer
C.A.A.	Civil Aeronautics Authority (1938–1940) Civil Aeronautics Administration (1940–1958)
CFI	Certified Flight Instructor
CPT Program	Civilian Pilot Training Program
FAA	Federal Aviation Administration (1958–present)
IFR	instrument flight rules
IWASM	International Women's Air and Space Museum
NCAAB	New Castle Army Air Base
OTS	Officer Training School
PT	primary trainer
RAF	Royal Air Force
ROTC	Reserve Officer Training Corps
RON	remain overnight

TDY	temporary duty
USAF	United States Air Force
VFR	visual flight rules
WAFS	Women's Auxiliary Ferrying Squadron
WASP	Women Airforce Service Pilots
WFTD	Women's Flying Training Detachment
WSGA	Women's Student Government Association

Nancy Batson Crews

Introduction

Nancy Elizabeth Batson was number twenty to qualify for the Women's Auxiliary Ferrying Squadron (WAFS), which was made up of the first twenty-eight women to fly for the U.S. Army in World War II.

In September 1942, noted aviatrix Nancy Love was recruiting experienced women pilots to ferry badly needed single-engine trainer airplanes from the factories to the Army's flight training schools.[1] Love was working with Col. William H. Tunner, commander of the Ferrying Division, Air Transport Command, U.S. Army Air Forces. Tunner's need for ferry pilots was so critical to the war effort, he was willing to give competent women pilots a try. The women went on to fly far more than trainers.

In January 1944, Nancy Batson and eleven others became the first women pilots to graduate from pursuit school.[2] They were qualified to fly high-performance pursuit (fighter) aircraft. One hundred thirty-two women eventually qualified as pursuit ferry pilots for the Ferrying Division. They routinely ferried aircraft cross-country at speeds up to three hundred miles per hour, at altitudes up to four miles high, from one coast to the other—alone—in an era when most women hardly dared dream of driving the family automobile across the state line, let alone across the whole of the United States. Nancy spent much of 1944 ferrying P-47s from the factory to stateside embarkation points for transfer to the war zones.

Twenty-two when she joined the WAFS, Nancy Batson earned the nickname the Golden Girl of the Ferry Command.[3] Her prowess at the controls of an airplane, her absolute dedication to the job, her winning personality, and her engaging Southern accent all contributed to her acceptance by both the men and the women of the Ferrying Division.

Five feet seven inches tall and of slender but athletic build, Nancy was blessed with honey-blonde hair, gray eyes, finely sculpted features, and flawless skin. She was, unquestionably, a beautiful young woman. Her looks brought her yet another nickname—the Veronica Lake of the Ferry Command. Veronica Lake was a popular 1940s movie star whose long blonde hair fell seductively over one eye.

Nancy excelled early at horseback riding and school sports and later at golf. Her athlete's sense of timing and superb physical coordination carried over into her flying.

She tried out for cheerleader in high school—not for the popularity the role assured, but to prove she could do it. She campaigned for the highest elected office a coed could hold on the University of Alabama campus—not to impress others, but to prove her leadership skills to herself and to her father. Not surprisingly, she won both those competitions.

People liked Nancy. "Batson could charm the pants off a snake," said her good friend and fellow WAFS Teresa James.

Beneath the personable exterior was a woman with finely tempered hometown Birmingham steel in her backbone. She epitomized the Puritan work ethic and sense of right versus wrong—the latter to a fault. There were no shades of gray in Nancy's life. Typical of a young woman brought up in the pre–World War II South, she never questioned how she had been raised to think nor what she had been taught to believe. Who she was and how she was shaped by the socioeconomic, political, and racial realities of the South are an integral part of her story.

Nancy Batson's accomplishments and contributions as a WAFS are notable. So are her achievements in aviation before the war, and so too is what she did in her later years. She was born into a well-to-do upper-middle-class family, which gave her economic and social advantages, but she also was a girl-child born into the patriarchal South. Her personal mission—her passion—was to make her mark in a decidedly male profession: aviation.

She had the good fortune to have a mother who did not try to mold her into the traditional role of a Southern belle. Ruth Batson gave her daughter all the manners, social graces, and refinements one needs to get along in genteel society. But Ruth did far more than that. She didn't use those things to harness Nancy's energy and ambition. Nancy was allowed to grow up to be the person she wanted to be. Her mother gave her—to use our more modern-day expression—her space.

Nancy's father went along with this, willingly, paid the bills, and was proud of his daughter. When Nancy's brother died in the war, Nancy became his surrogate son. It was Nancy who worked with her father after the war, golfed with her father, planned real estate development strategy with her father, discussed politics with her father.

In her flying career, Nancy was a flight instructor, she flew commercially, and she ferried aircraft. The only thing she didn't do was fly for the airlines, but she did fly passengers. In 1944, she checked out in an Army twin-engine C-60 transport and flew her fellow ferry pilots from the docks at Newark back to the aircraft factory on Long Island so that they could pick up more P-47s and ferry them to the docks.[4]

In the 1960s, while in her forties, she built a flying business from scratch—just Nancy and her Super Cub. In a smart business move, she learned to tow gliders with her Cub. From there, she went on to learn to fly gliders. In her fifties, she became a glider instructor pilot.

Her parents taught her to "give back," so in order to serve her community, she took a stab at local politics at age sixty. She got burned. She switched her energies to land development and home building and was a success—this in her late sixties and seventies.

When Nancy Batson Crews was seventy-nine years old, she flew nearly eighty hours as copilot in a corporate turbo jet.

Nancy was a natural leader. The only time she tried to avoid that calling was in the war. She wanted so badly to fly the Army airplanes that she resisted Nancy Love's attempts to put her in charge of a small squadron, which would rob her of precious flying time. She did, however, serve frequently as a flight leader for the less experienced young women pilots as they qualified and came into the Ferrying Division.

She had her own private battles with racism—a legacy from her Southern upbringing—but far more telling was the impact World War II had on her gut-level personal beliefs and prejudices. It was not the black–white issue but the anti-Japanese, propaganda-fed sentiment that permeated this country during WWII that was Nancy's undoing.

She had few battles with sexism because Nancy was a woman at ease with men and men were at ease with her. Neither a flirt nor one to use her physical charms, she simply liked men, liked being with them, and they liked being around her. She learned early how to work with men and had more male than female friends.

By her own declaration, Nancy was not a feminist. Nevertheless, she was her own best advertisement of what a woman could do. She worked within the system and never took no for an answer. She believed in her abilities and made them work for her. When she needed help or advice, she sought the best she could get—usually from men. She paved her own way and simply did whatever she wanted.

She had a husband who loved her and supported her flying, though he had no personal interest in aviation. She was the mother of three children she adored. Nancy Batson Crews was a free woman, a rarity in the mid-twentieth century. This made her a fitting role model of what a woman can do if she has skills, determination, and drive. Nancy, however, never liked the label "role model," because she felt that she was given too much to begin with to be a realistic role model for young women who were not so fortunate.

Some would say she had it all, yet Nancy faced her share of personal tragedy, disappointment, and strife and was not always adept at handling the consequences. All told, Nancy and her personality redefine the meaning of complexity. Her life defies pigeonholing.

Nancy and I met in 1992. That meeting changed both our lives—mine to the greater extreme.

In January 1990, I had gone to work as a communications consultant for the International Women's Air and Space Museum (IWASM) located at that time near my home in Centerville, Ohio. The fledgling museum was (and is) a repository for papers, photos, and memorabilia of the early women pilots of Amelia Earhart's era and those who came after.

In November 1990, I helped IWASM launch a series of programs featuring pioneer women flyers to be aired for the cable television viewers in south-suburban Dayton, Ohio. We videotaped the women—sometimes panels, sometimes single speakers—before a live audience. We recorded their voices, images, and their stories for posterity, as a form of oral history.

IWASM Administrator Joan Hrubec and I worked with the Miami Valley Cable Council (now Miami Valley Communications Council) to produce the programs on MVCC's community-access channel. Between November 1990 and March 1994, we taped a dozen programs that still air on South Dayton's Channel 723.

The Women Airforce Service Pilots (WASP) are the other half of the equation when it comes to the women who flew for the Army Air Forces in World War II. In November 1942, famed aviatrix Jacqueline Cochran, with the backing of Army Air Forces Commanding General H. H. "Hap" Arnold, launched an Army flight training school for young women in Texas. The original purpose was to supply more women ferry pilots for the WAFS of Colonel Tunner's Ferrying Division—Nancy Love's group. As it turned out, not all the graduates could meet the Ferrying Division's exacting standards and Tunner refused to hire some of them. So Cochran turned to finding other wartime flight jobs the women might fill. The total number of women who flew in various capacities for the Army in WWII was 1,102.

Knowing that in 1992 the WASP—the name by which *all* the women who flew for the U.S. Army in World War II eventually became known—were coming up on the fiftieth anniversary of their founding, Joan and I decided to put together a WASP panel. We asked our Dayton-area resident WASP and a museum trustee, Nadine Nagle, to moderate the program and we asked nearby Springfield, Ohio, resident WASP Caro Bayley Bosca to be one of the panelists. Five more WASP, women who were trained to fly "the Army way" between November 1942 and December 1944, agreed to come to Centerville and be on the panel.

I suggested Nancy Batson Crews as the panel's representative original WAFS. I had just read about her in Sally Van Wagenen Keil's book about the WASP, *Those Wonderful Women in Their Flying Machines*. What Keil wrote about her assured me that Nancy would be a delight to have on our program. Nancy's desire to tell the WAFS' story led her to say yes, she would come.

Nadine and I picked Nancy up at the Dayton airport Sunday night, January 12, 1992. The taping was scheduled for Monday evening, January 13. As I got to know Nancy over the next two days, I was entranced. What I learned from her was that the existing WASP books told only part of the story. The surviving WAFS, and Nancy in particular, felt that their very different beginnings and service needed to be told in a separate account. The 1,074 women who earned their wings in Army training in Texas is one story. The other story is about Nancy Love and her twenty-seven professional women pilots who went straight into the Ferrying Division to ferry trainer airplanes as civil service employees beginning in the fall of 1942.

As Nancy and I became better acquainted, she decided that I was the person to write the story of Nancy Love and the WAFS. She convinced me and then she made it happen. My history of the WAFS, *The Originals: The Women's Auxiliary Ferrying Squadron of World War II*, was published in 2001 by Disc-Us Books, Inc. Nancy was the reason the book was written and published.

In this biography of Nancy Batson Crews, I tell the story of the writing and publication of *The Originals*, because it is part of her story. Ultimately, this volume you now hold in your hands is the third book to come out of Nancy's and my meeting, subsequent friendship, and collaboration. The University of North Texas Press published the second book, my biography of Nancy Love, *Nancy Love and the WASP Ferry Pilots of World War II*, in March 2008.

Shortly before she died, Nancy Crews said yes to my writing her biography. Her children and her friends have worked with me to tell her story. And thanks to The University of Alabama Press, it has become a reality.

1

Boys, I've Brought You a Real Lemon

The same Tuesday in November 1944 that Franklin Delano Roosevelt won his unprecedented fourth term as president of the United States, Nancy Elizabeth Batson of Birmingham, Alabama, tried to crowd FDR off the front page of the Pittsburgh, Pennsylvania, daily newspapers. She would just as soon have skipped the whole affair; she would have much preferred a quiet, uneventful delivery of her airplane to Newark, New Jersey, without all the fuss.

Nancy was a ferry pilot with the women's squadron, 2nd Ferrying Group, Ferrying Division, Air Transport Command (ATC), and she had orders to take a plane—destined for combat in Europe—from the Lockheed factory near Long Beach, California, to the docks at Newark.

"I picked up this brand-new, shiny P-38 in California and took off cross-country, made my last stop in Pittsburgh to refuel, and headed for Newark. About twenty minutes out of Pittsburgh, I noticed that the two engine coolant needles were oscillating—moving back and forth erratically instead of holding steady."

Too many P-38s already had lost engines. That was one of those vagaries for which the sleek, twin-engine Lightning was known. A lost engine on takeoff had killed fellow woman ferry pilot Evelyn Sharp the previous spring. Nancy knew that all too well. She had accompanied Evelyn's body home to Nebraska for the funeral.

No sense taking unnecessary chances. Nancy decided to return to the airport and let a mechanic check it out.

"I turned back to Pittsburgh, called the tower to get permission to land, and was cleared for a straight-in approach. I reached down, activated the landing gear handle, and listened for the hum of the wheels descending into the down and locked position. But the lights on the instrument panel showed that the nosewheel was not down and locked. The lights are in a tri-

Nancy fought for two hours to get the nosewheel down and locked on this P-38, November 1944. Photo courtesy the Woman's Collection at Texas Woman's University, Denton.

angle. The two at the bottom showed green, meaning that the main gear was down, but the nosewheel light was red. That meant it wasn't down and locked.

"Now the P-38 has these aluminum reflectors on the side of the two engine nacelles and they acted as mirrors—so the pilot can check and see if the nosewheel is in the down and locked position. This nosewheel was just hanging there.

"I called the tower and advised them of my situation.

"They asked me to do a fly-by—low—and raise my left wing so that they could see for sure that the nosewheel wasn't in the landing position.

"I did the fly-by and they looked and they determined that no, it wasn't locked in place. By then the coolant needles seemed to have stabilized. So I flew out away from the airport and away from traffic. I was going to try to pump the wheel down manually.

"The hydraulic pump, called a wobble pump, was there for the pilot to use to do exactly what I had to do, pump the faulty nose gear down by hand. Well, I started pumping. Then I stopped and looked out at the mirrors. That wheel hadn't moved. So I pumped some more. Nothing!

"The tower called periodically and asked, 'how are you doing?'

"I told them, 'I'm still flyin' over Pittsburgh and still pumpin' and I still have a red light.'"

Every airplane within earshot of the Pittsburgh radio frequency heard the exchange between Nancy and the tower. A woman—particularly one with a Southern accent—flying around in a P-38 wasn't exactly an everyday occurrence.

"I tried climbing to eight thousand feet and diving the airplane, to see if centrifugal force would push it down. I did that several times. It didn't work."

Nancy had one more tool in her flight kit. Under the pilot's seat in the P-38 was a button connected to a CO2 cartridge—there to aid a combat pilot trying to land a shot-up airplane with both a damaged hydraulics system and a useless wobble pump. The cartridge could be exploded as a last resort to force the nosewheel down.

"At the factory, they told us very emphatically not to use the CO2 cartridge because it might damage the landing gear. They told us that it was there to save some combat pilot's life."

Nancy figured the pilot whose life might need saving was the one currently flying the airplane. She wasn't flying combat, but she very definitely had a life-threatening situation.

"I could see that what I was doing wasn't working. I was all pumped out and by now the needle on the fuel gauge was telling me that I was getting low on gas. Now, I was going to have to do what I call creative flying. As a last resort, I decided to shoot off that CO2 cartridge. I climbed back up to eight thousand and dove the P-38 one more time, horsed back on the controls, pulled up sharply, pumped the manual pump, reached under the seat, and fired the cartridge.

"When the smoke cleared, there they were—three green lights! Then I looked down at the aluminum mirrors on the nacelles and that nosewheel was down and locked, just like it was supposed to be!"

Unbeknownst to Nancy, while she was flying around away from the airport pumping, the worried operations officer had called Nancy Love, commander of the women ferry pilots, to tell her of her pilot's plight.

"Who is it?" Nancy Love asked.

"Nancy Batson," he replied.

"Oh, don't worry about her. She'll be fine," said Love.

It was years later before Nancy Batson heard that story and learned the kind of confidence her commander, fellow pilot, and friend had in her.

"She never said a thing to me. Never called me or asked about the problem I had. I was a trained professional ferry pilot, doing my job. She expected us to handle situations as they came up. That's what ferry pilots do. We never knew what kind of plane we would be flying. All we knew was, they told us to take care of those planes so that they'd be in good shape for those boys to fly in overseas."

That same November afternoon, Nancy Batson's friend and fellow ferry pilot Helen Richey was inbound to Pittsburgh, also en route on a delivery to Newark. She heard the exchanges between the tower at the Pittsburgh airport and the woman in the balky P-38, and she recognized that Southern accent immediately.

The hour was late. The dusk of a November afternoon was beginning to leach the light from the airfield. Ferry pilots, as ordered, flew only in daylight hours. Helen landed, called her home base, and told them that she was going to RON (remain overnight) in Pittsburgh, which happened to be her hometown. She was going to spend that night with her sister and planned to take Nancy with her. Helen figured her friend would be in need of a good night's sleep while the mechanics looked over her airplane.

In the meantime, Nancy was ready to land. "I called the tower and told them the nosewheel was locked in place, but they said they wanted me to slow-fly by the tower so that they could see for sure if it was down.

"Shoot, by that time, I'd had enough of that P-38. Besides, I was really low on fuel! I told them I was coming in. They gave me permission to land. I decided right then and there that I was going to make this the best landing of my life.

"And I did.

"I was cleared for a straight-in approach and I greased it! I put that sick airplane in the proper landing attitude and touched down on the main wheels. Then I held that back pressure on the stick—back, back, back, all the way into my stomach—and kept that nosewheel up as long as possible. Then finally I let it touch down and did the roll out. I was pleased!

"As I was rolling down the runway, out of the corner of my eye on my left I noticed this Jeep running alongside, and this guy signaling me to stop. I thought, oh my golly, NOW what have I done?

"So I stopped. This guy jumps up on my wing. I push back the canopy. 'G-g-get out, I'll taxi it in.' He was kind of wild-eyed and nervous.

"I said, 'Well, no. I'll do it. I'll taxi it in.' I wasn't fixin' to get out at that point.

"When he got off the wing, I looked over my left shoulder and here came a couple of fire engines, an ambulance, several Jeeps—a whole line of vehicles, all following me.

"I taxied it on in, stopped, and cut the switch. Now here was a line of people waitin' for me—photographers, Red Cross ladies who said, 'we've been prayin' for you, honey,' airport officials, and lots of other people. That's when they took that picture that ran on the front page of the Pittsburgh paper the next morning—along with the news that Roosevelt had been re-elected.

"Then I turned the airplane over to the mechanics and told them what the problem was and they told me they would check it out.

"And there was Helen Richey waiting for me. She took me to her sister's to spend the night.

"I woke up in the middle of the night with this awful throbbing, aching pain in my right shoulder and upper arm. I had to wake Helen up and ask her if her sister had any aspirin. She found me some. I was OK the next morning.

"Two days later the airplane finally was ready. I flew it out of Pittsburgh and on into Newark. Coming in, I got my clearance from the tower to land and put the gear handle in the down position. Same damn thing! Two green lights and one red one.

"I wasn't gonna mess around anymore. I didn't think twice. I reached down and fired that CO2 cartridge. Fortunately, they had fixed it! The nose-wheel locked into position. Three green lights!

"I landed, taxied it up to the line guys waiting, cut the switch, climbed out, and told them, 'boys, this time I've brought you a real lemon!'"[1]

2

Daughter of Alabama

The young woman who "horsed back on the controls" in Pittsburgh that day and who "greased" her landing at the end of that harrowing flight came by her forthright approach to life and flying naturally. She came from hardy pioneer stock and she was, in her chosen profession—flying—a pioneer cast in their image.

Nancy's family roots ran deep in the Alabama soil. Her maternal grandparents were Jere and Mary Jane (Vandegrift) Philips of St. Clair County. Nancy's paternal grandparents were Nancy (for whom she was named) and Andrew Batson. Andrew, nicknamed Andy, was named for President Andrew Jackson. They were farmers from Jefferson County.[1]

Nancy Elizabeth Batson arrived February 1, 1920, the third of four children born to Stephen Radford and Ruth Philips Batson of Birmingham. Her older sister, Elinor, was born in 1914 and her brother, Radford, to whom she was the closest and with whom she played and competed, in 1917. Younger sister Amy came along in 1926.

Nancy's parents had an uncommonly positive effect on her life because they were so liberal with all four of their children and their upbringing. Nancy remembered them being criticized by friends and neighbors. "They give those children *everything!*" was the common complaint. The senior Batsons thought nothing of buying ponies for Radford and built Amy a playhouse—her heart's desire—in the backyard. A few years later, their father would buy Nancy her first airplane. Then tongues *really* wagged!

"When I was seven years old, my mother took me by the hand to the municipal auditorium in Birmingham to see Charles Lindbergh. We stood there on the sidewalk outside—it was October 1927, just a few months after he flew the Atlantic solo, the first man to do that. We watched as he and some of Birmingham's notables got out of a car and walked into the auditorium. That's all. But we saw him.

The Batson family in the early 1920s: young Radford, Elinor, Stephen Radford, Ruth, and Nancy. Photo courtesy the Crews family.

"My mother knew then that I had a yen for anything related to airplanes. When I was little, my bicycle was my very own airplane and I pretended it had a double set of wings to match the biplanes I'd seen. I didn't want to be a ballerina in a poufy pink dress, I wanted to wear jodhpurs, jacket, boots, and a white silk scarf. That's what all the flyers wore."

Nancy's parents also believed implicitly in education and saw to it that all four children went to the college of their choice. Ruth Philips knew the disappointment of not being allowed to go away to the school she desperately wished to attend. It colored her thinking for life—to her own children's benefit.

Mary Jane Philips was pregnant with Ruth in 1891 when her firstborn, also a daughter, died in her arms. Mary Jane was shattered by the experience and turned not only her hopes but also her fears on her second daughter. Consequently, Ruth grew up sheltered—unable to stretch her wings. A brilliant young woman, she was scheduled to go to Wellesley, the exclusive

Nancy in jodhpurs—her favorite outfit. Photo courtesy the Woman's Collection at Texas Woman's University, Denton.

women's college in Massachusetts. This was 1908, when most women didn't even graduate from high school let alone attend college. But her mother couldn't let her go. "I can't lose another child," Mary Jane said, and Ruth was sent, instead, to a small, "safe" teachers' college in Alabama, close to home.

Pretty and popular—truly a Southern belle—Ruth had lots of beaux. When Stephen Radford Batson met her, she was a young schoolteacher. He fell madly in love with her, pursued her until she married him in November 1912, and he never ceased to adore her. This scenario would be repeated a generation later by her daughter Nancy's husband-to-be.

Radford met his match in Ruth. She was a strong-minded, strong-willed lady. She had to be, otherwise Mary Jane would have smothered her with that consuming fear of imminent loss. This, in turn, colored Ruth's reaction to her own children. "She allowed us to be independent," both Nancy and Amy said. When Ruth's father died—not long before Amy was born—her mother came to live with them. They couldn't have two "Mamas" in the house, so Ruth became "Muddy" to her children and Mary Jane, their grandmother, became "Mama."

The family lived in Norwood, a "toney residential section of Birmingham," according to Amy. "Daddy bought the one-and-a-half-story house for cash money in 1926 when I was born." Their address was 1430 North 30th Street. The house is gone now, a victim of urban renewal. Industry built up and cut it off from other nice Birmingham neighborhoods and it started to go downhill.[2]

Nancy remembered the house with considerable nostalgia. A wide, balconied front porch graced one end and a similarly balconied sleeping porch the other. Five beds lined the sleeping porch and the family slept out there much of the year—not unusual in the hot, humid Southland. Besides, "Muddy was a firm believer in fresh air."

A log fireplace adorned the living room and one whole end of the room was windows. A sitting room by the back staircase boasted a tile-based fireplace that burned coal. To the left of the living room was the kitchen and a breakfast nook. To the other side of the kitchen was a huge dining room. A Victorian glass chandelier hung over the drop-leaf table that could seat twelve people. Left of the dining room was the sun parlor. Upstairs consisted of but two rooms. One was young Radford's bedroom. When he went to West Point, Amy moved into his room. The other room was Mama's. The girls and their parents had downstairs bedrooms.

Eventually, the house was modernized from coal to gas heat. It was built at the bottom of a hill with a steep embankment on one side planted with several dozen rose bushes. The garage in back was big enough for two ponies and a Cadillac touring car. Archie, the family chauffeur, kept it in excellent running order.

This was good because Muddy was a woman ahead of her time. She liked to drive and took her children on frequent automobile trips—opportunities to get out of the house and away from her anxious mother.

Stephen Radford Batson was a big man from a farming family. His business was that of a contractor/builder. "He built roads and bridges," was Nancy's description. And he did well. Her favorite story about her father comes from long before she was born. As she told it, Rad Batson didn't like farming. He wanted to go to college and, he thought, become a pharmacist.

Money was tight, but his father told him that whatever he could get from a watermelon patch he was raising, he could use for college tuition. Rad sold the watermelons and, with the proceeds in his pocket, went to Auburn to enroll in the university.

The president of the college was sitting outside under a tree enrolling students. "You look like an engineer to me," he told Rad, and promptly enrolled him in Civil Engineering, thereby setting him on a career path from which he did not deviate.

Rad was also blessed with good coordination and the tall, rangy build of an early 1900s-style football player. He was invited to join in a campus pickup game not long after matriculating and ended up as the center on the Auburn football team. His senior year, in the game against archrival Alabama, the score was six to nothing in Auburn's favor when Alabama scored on the last play of the game. The crowd roared. The teams lined up for the point after. The opposing center snapped the ball. As the kicker's foot met the pigskin, Rad unfolded his long body, leaped, reached for the sky with his long arms, and batted the ball away. Blocked kick! Final score six to six!

Students from both sides emptied onto the field and a free-for-all ensued. So bad was the postgame brawl, the university presidents banned the two teams from playing each other ever again. The ban lasted until after World War II.

Nancy told the story with relish.

Ruth wasn't the only one who liked to take driving trips. Radford enjoyed taking the family for what was, in the 1920s and 1930s, an American institution and a real treat—a Sunday afternoon ride in the car. "One day, Daddy said we were going to the airport to watch the airplanes take off and land," Nancy remembered. "Whooee! We sat up on the road and didn't get out of the car. We just watched the airplanes down there in that field. My parents were impressed!

"After I learned to drive, Daddy used to let me take him to the golf course on Saturday morning, leave him, and keep the car. Then I'd pick him up in the afternoon. The airport was on the way to the golf course. One day we drove by and planes were coming in getting ready for an air show. There was this silver biplane and a girl standing beside it putting on a helmet and goggles. That *girl* was going to fly that airplane!"

Summers from 1926 well into the 1930s, Nancy attended Camp Winnataska, an interdenominational camp operated from 1918 to 1986 by the Birmingham Sunday School Association. Camp Winnataska "grew out of the desire of youth-serving organizations to provide city children the opportunity to get out of the smoke and smog of the city during the summer months, and out into the woods with God."[3] Birmingham was, by 1918, a rapidly growing mining and mill town complete with the accompanying social and environmental ills.

For impressionable youngsters, the summer camp experience can be a defining one. So it was with Nancy. Elinor attended Winnataska and proved one of the most popular girls there and one tapped for leadership roles. When Nancy followed seven years later, she had her older sister's reputation to live up to—and she did. She learned self-reliance and experienced independence for the first time. She, too, drew accolades from counselors and fellow campers. She, too, was a leader. And she loved Winnataska and everything it stood for.

"I remember that first year. I was six. I went with a steamer trunk that slid under the iron bunk. I stayed in Elinor's cabin. They elected a chief of each cabin. I wanted to be the chief. That year, Elinor was named 'outstanding camper.' I wanted to be the outstanding camper. In 1930 when I was ten, I was elected chief. Then the last day of camp, after breakfast, the director announced that I was outstanding camper. My mother was surprised. 'Of the whole camp?' she asked.

"We had lots of competitions and from the beginning, I wanted to win the blue ribbons. But, even though I wanted to win and didn't like to lose, I also learned that you had to be a good loser—a good sport."

Sundays were special days. Everyone dressed in white and they all processed in a line from their huts to the chapel hidden among the pines. A camper carried the camp Bible. Flag bearers carried the United States and the Christian flags; a bugler played "God of our Fathers."

In the evening, following vespers on the hill at the Wayside Cross, the girls' camp held an after-dark Galilean service on Kelly Creek above the bridge. Campers watched as two boats—carrying the camp leaders singing "Jesus Savior, Pilot Me" and the Vesper Hymn—moved downstream toward the natural pool below the bridge. Campers placed lighted candles on the water and a wooden cross of lighted candles followed in their wake. As the flickering lights floated downstream and disappeared, the campers sang "Taps." The scene cast an unforgettable magic spell over the impressionable youngsters.[4]

Nancy never forgot it.

That environment had a profound effect on her. At Camp Winnataska, young Southern girls could run loose in the woods. "It was a release. It was freedom! We swam in the creek. But we also had Bible study and sang Bible and camp songs. It was training in religion, Christianity, Jesus, the Old and New Testaments. And it was so natural. As a child, I was interested in the religious outdoor stuff. But this wasn't forced on us. No one was trying to convert us. My mother and my father and my grandmother lived the Christian religion. They *lived* it. They were examples of living a Christian life. They weren't out trying to convert somebody else.

"My time at camp was mine; my parents had nothing to do with what I did at camp. Summer and camp, that's what I looked forward to all year. I was bored by school, but I did read—I went to the library and got books. My parents didn't insist that I make As. But I never flunked anything and I behaved."

Key words to Nancy Batson—"I behaved."

For Nancy, Winnataska provided anchors for her inner being and her soul that remained with her for the rest of her life. The camp experience made her aware of nature in the larger sense as well as giving her an appreciation of the outdoors. And the camp experience gave Nancy her very own personal take on religion that she never lost.

In 1930, Elinor was accepted at fashionable Goucher College and went off to school in Baltimore, where she pledged Alpha Gamma Delta sorority. Then Radford was granted an appointment to West Point. He would graduate Phi Beta Kappa in 1939. Nancy and Amy were left at home. By then Nancy was in high school and turning into a charming mix of athletic tomboy who loved to ride horses and attractive, blonde daughter of the South.

She spent her early years at Birmingham's Norwood Elementary School and was promoted from eighth grade to high school in 1933. She graduated from Birmingham's Ramsay High School in June 1937. Not the student that her older brother and sister were, Nancy elected to attend the larger, more socially oriented University of Alabama, where she, too, pledged Alpha Gamma Delta, following in her beloved sister's footsteps. The lessons Nancy took with her to college were not the academic ones, but those of pragmatic application. How to choose what you wanted and go after it. By then, both her mother and her father knew this about their unusual daughter—their "different" child.

"I majored in Southern belle at the university," Nancy loved to proclaim. That was the social Nancy—the Nancy who behaved, who "did the right thing" or what was expected of a girl of her position. But she had another side that was much truer to her inner nature—that little girl who liked to win. "Politics and power [were] what appealed to me."

Nancy learned her politics from her father. She listened to him, discussed the subject with him, and tagged along with him on his political forays when she could. Early on, Nancy was at home in the world of men. And men were at ease in her presence. At the university, she entered campus politics. In her junior year, she served as junior representative to the Women's Student Government Association (WSGA) and as house president of her dormitory, Colonial Hall. That same year, she was appointed to the Clarifications Committee of the Council of Clubs at Alabama. The university was trying to work itself out of a sticky situation with a vast number of social clubs on campus and was trying to regulate them through the student constitution. Nancy took on this challenge along with four young men and one other young woman. An editorial in the school paper challenged them to turn the "F" garnered by several previous years' committees into a "passing grade."[5]

Spring of her junior year (1940), Nancy took out a petition to place her name in nomination for president of the WSGA. And she was named to the YWCA Vespers Committee—yet another honor reserved for the top coeds of the school.

Politics did not detract in the least from her all-American girl/Southern belle image. She was chosen one of the attendants to the queen of the Cotillion Club Mid Winter Dances, February 1–3, 1940. Her escort was University of Alabama student Paul H. Crews.

Nancy was elected WSGA president on February 16, 1940, and took office April 1, to serve through March of her senior year. She became the twenty-sixth president of Alabama's WSGA and the first one elected through the use of voting machines. Two such machines were rented for that election and for the ensuing male student government elections. On May 10, 1940, she also was appointed to the AB Association, the successor to the Clarifications Committee, which had done its job (earning its passing grade) and rewritten the student constitution's club section.

A disintegrating scrapbook contains numerous photos and clippings of Nancy's college days, achievements, and honors. She was a lovely young woman with honey-blonde hair and gray eyes—aviator's eyes, far-sighted with that keen sense of perception—five feet seven and absolutely erect, which made her seem taller, slender but athletic in build and carriage. She was a rare mix of personality, good looks, and brains.

Her enigmatic, unsmiling college portrait photo accentuates eyes that seem to look beyond that classic middle distance—a foreshadowing of her WAFS portrait that would be taken some four years later. In the latter, her favorite, she wore a half smile. She called it her Mona Lisa look. She was a

WAFS and proud of it. But the younger photo, taken when she was nineteen, is unsmiling and telegraphs her depth of drive and determination through the forthright stare that says she is ready to take on the world. The portrait is strikingly different from the sweet, demure photographs of the other campus queens. These young women look into the camera with feminine guile and yet an innocence characteristic of the era. Nancy exhibits an outward yet deeper beauty and an inner restlessness. She's looking toward the future—that which is yet to come. Nancy isn't quite yet showing the world what she's got, but she's thinking about it.

"My mother always said that Nancy was her different child," Amy Batson Strange said in an interview on April 18, 2001, five months before her death and three months after Nancy's. "Muddy said Nancy never smiled as a little baby. When I came along, Nancy couldn't stand me. I was the "new" baby in the family. But Elinor and Radford played with me."

Nancy had been the adored baby girl for nearly seven years. Giving up that pedestal was not her choice. Nancy adored both her older sister and her older brother and didn't cotton to having a rival for their affection. She and Amy never really got along. But in the long run it was because they were so very different, not because of childhood jealousies.

Again, proof of the Batsons' willingness to send their children to the college of their choice, Amy, with budding artistic talent, went to the proper but avant-garde girls' school Stephens College in Columbia, Missouri. Several of Amy's paintings graced the walls of Nancy's house in Odenville, Alabama, in the 1990s. Amy rounded out her education at the University of Alabama, eventually earning a master's degree in history in her later years.

In her younger sister's eyes, Nancy was not born with that outgoing personality she later exhibited: "Elinor and I were the outgoing ones. Nancy made herself into an outgoing person." She saw the rewards a smile could bring and learned to light up the room with her charm—a charm that over time became more genuine than that acquired in Southern Belle 101.

"She made all the right moves," said Amy. "She was the child who got everything she wanted. Nancy could play our mother like a piano."[6]

3

Flight!

"'I have an announcement.'

"This girl had just entered the women students' dining hall. It was lunchtime. We all clinked on our glasses and shushed everyone at our table.

"'There's going to be a Civilian Pilot Training Program here at the University of Alabama,' she announced. 'They will take one woman for every ten men who sign up to learn to fly. Professor Fred Maxwell is the man you need to talk to if you are interested.'

"Well, I *was* interested! I couldn't wait to finish lunch and get out of the dining hall. I literally ran across campus to find Professor Maxwell. I was so out of breath when I got there, I could hardly talk. But he got the gist of what I was saying. I blurted out that I wanted to join the CPT Program, and paused for breath. He had a kind of crinkly face and he half smiled and told me I needed three things: permission from my parents since I wasn't twenty-one; forty dollars; and to pass a physical.

"That evening, my father stopped by to see me. He was building a road down in Greensboro and Tuscaloosa was on his way home. I saw him drive up—my dormitory room was on the ground floor—and ran out to the car to meet him.

"'Daddy, Daddy!'—I hardly said hello—'They're starting a Civilian Pilot Training Program here and they'll take five girls along with fifty boys. I've gotta be in that program, Daddy. I want to learn to fly.'

"'Sis, you're crazy,' he said.

"'No no, Daddy, I want to do this. I *have* to do this! This is my chance to learn to fly.' He could see I was enthusiastic. I was really selling.

"He got real quiet. I ran out of wind and shut up for a minute. He sat there—his hands on the steering wheel, his hat sitting square on his head—looking straight ahead. Finally he said, 'Well, I'll talk to your mother.'"

Amy, then a teenager who was still at home, later told Nancy what happened at the breakfast table the next morning when they discussed it. "Muddy just said to him, 'Well, write out the check and give it to me. I'll write the note and get it in the mail this morning.'

"Do you know that letter and check were in my post office box on campus that evening!

"I had two things that are very important to flying—a sense of adventure and good coordination. My mother had that sense of adventure and she passed it on to me. I got my good coordination from my football-player father. My mother encouraged me. She never tried to stop me, never told me not to do something because I'd get hurt."

Not long after, Nancy received a letter from Fred R. Maxwell, Director, University of Alabama Civil Aeronautics Authority, Flight Training Program, dated October 31, 1939.

> You have been selected as an alternate on the C.A.A. Civilian Pilot Training Program. It is your duty to continue in Ground School until the quota is entirely filled. Failure to do so will automatically remove your name from the list of eligible alternates. There is evidence that we will extend far down the list.
>
> The Ground School schedule is Tuesday and Thursday at 12:00 noon; Tuesday and Thursday at 7:00 p.m., in room 210 Engineering Hall. Alternates will be accepted in the order of the numeral list posted for Flight Training as rapidly as they become eligible.[1]

Nancy, of course, did qualify for the program and went on to become one of its early graduates.

President Franklin D. Roosevelt unveiled the Civilian Pilot Training Program in December 1938, when Nancy was a sophomore at the University of Alabama. It was a trial program of subsidized flying instruction destined for college campuses. CPT, the brainchild of the Civil Aeronautics Authority (precursor of the Federal Aviation Administration), was based on similar programs tried in Europe and was expected to provide pilot training for twenty thousand college students per year. The University of Alabama was one of the thirteen pioneering schools.[2]

Nancy and three other young women—Sue Clarkson, Virginia Richards, and Orene Putnam—were part of that first CPT class at Alabama.[3]

Nancy and airplanes were made for each other. She soloed March 20, 1940, and earned her private pilot's license on June 15, 1940.

"When I returned to the university the fall of 1940 to begin my senior

Four University of Alabama Civilian Pilot Training Program coeds: Virginia Richards, Orene Putnam, Nancy Batson, and Sue Clarkson. Photo taken during a photo shoot for *Mademoiselle* magazine, 1939. It served as the cover of the Summer 2002 issue of *Alabama Heritage* magazine, which featured an article on Nancy Batson Crews written by Sarah Byrn Rickman. Photo courtesy the Crews family.

year, one of the other flying students told me that they were going to sell a bunch of those J-3 Cub trainers for eight hundred dollars. Was I interested? Well, of course, I was. I called Daddy and told him that if I had one of those airplanes, I could continue to do my flying and earn my commercial certificate and then my instrument rating and get a JOB. Magic words.

"Well, that Saturday, here came Muddy and Daddy to look at the airplanes. This one fella took Daddy aside and told him, 'Mr. Batson, these things are pretty well wore out. But that guy over there is gonna be an instructor in the cadet program here and he wants to sell his airplane.' And Daddy went over to look at the J-4 Cub Coupe.

"Now the price was hardly comparable. The man wanted twelve or thirteen hundred dollars for the J-4 with a side-by-side cockpit instead of a tandem one. It hadn't been beat up by student pilots.

"I didn't ask for that plane. It just happened. Daddy decided that that was the airplane he was going to buy me. My parents were willing to *do* that!

That's how they were. Now I admit I did a selling job on them. But can you believe they bought me an airplane? I'm twenty years old, a senior in college. Other girls had automobiles. I had an airplane.

"Well, that year I flew back and forth to Birmingham—building time, working toward that commercial certificate. Of course, I was busy—being president of WSGA [Women's Student Government Association] and going to class and all my other activities. But I still got in a lot of flying time."

On June 2, 1941, Nancy completed the secondary section of the CPT Program. Also in June 1941, Nancy Elizabeth Batson graduated from the University of Alabama with a major in history. Then she set about making history. Back in Birmingham that summer, she became a fixture at the Birmingham Airport, where she hangared her airplane. "I was an airport bum—flying my J-4 Cub and working on my commercial."

She joined the Dawn Patrol, a group of local flyers who took off Sunday mornings and flew to meet other such groups for breakfast at a host airport. Nancy's mother joined her on one such jaunt. Fourteen men and women took seven airplanes on a Dawn Patrol flight from Birmingham to Chattanooga, September 28, 1941. A story and photo of the fourteen appeared in the *Chattanooga Press* the following day. Nancy also joined the Birmingham Aeronauts Club and, when it was established December 1, 1941, the Civil Air Patrol.[4]

Nancy got her commercial license on January 29, 1942,[5] promptly took the Cub to a nearby town, and hopped rides all one Saturday afternoon. People stood in line to fly with her at a dollar a ride. "I spent the night in this little country hotel. One of my passengers took me out to dinner. He thought I was some glamorous aviatrix and I think he had the idea he was gonna get further than dinner. Unh uhh! I flew on down to Tuscaloosa the next day where Paul was doing his ROTC training and told him I had made thirteen dollars giving hops."

Nancy and her mother flew to Tyler, Texas, to visit some of Ruth's family. "We flew into the airport there and they came out and picked us up. We had a good time, then we flew home to Birmingham.

"Mother flew with me a lot, but Daddy only flew with me once. He was building a road up in Huntsville. One day he said, 'Sis, I want you to fly me up to Huntsville.' He needed to see a man up there. So we flew up, he conducted his business and we flew back and landed in Birmingham. He was satisfied."

On December 7, 1941, Japan attacked Pearl Harbor and the United States entered the war against both Japan and Germany. After she had her commer-

Nancy, ready to graduate from the University of Alabama in June 1941. Photo courtesy the Crews family.

cial rating under her belt, Nancy went to Nashville, Tennessee, and tried to join the Ferry Command, soon to be the Air Transport Command (ATC), part of the U.S. Army Air Forces.

"I couldn't believe it when they told me they only took men.

"Well, I went home and earned my instructor's rating [granted March 24, 1942]. Then I applied for an instructing job with the flight school. The embarrassed looks I got from the director of flying preceded the news that they weren't currently looking for flight instructors. What he *didn't* say was, they weren't looking for *women* flight instructors."

Nancy and Paul with her J-4 Cub, January 1942. Photo courtesy the Crews family.

In spite of that discouraging news, things were looking up. The Birmingham paper carried a story about Nancy and two other local women active in aviation. The article said that young women were taking over the work of men just as they had in the days of World War I. The caption under Nancy's photo claimed she was the only Alabama woman to qualify as a flight instructor. The story didn't mention that she was unemployed at the time.[6]

The other two were Rosealee Bonner, a dispatcher for Southern Airways Corporation at Birmingham Municipal Airport, and Louise Powell, who was on her way to Miami to become a control tower operator for Pan-American

Airways. Louise had a private pilot's license and sixty hours. After taking an extension course in control tower operation at the University of Alabama and earning practical experience at the Birmingham Airport, she took the control tower operator's exam in Atlanta and made the highest score ever—man or woman. The job in Miami was her reward.

Nancy offered to fly Louise to Miami. Then, a few weeks later, Nancy got word from Louise that Pan-American wanted another woman in the tower. Nancy enrolled in a control tower operator's course and then she, too, left for Miami and a job with Pan-American. She was still awaiting her federal license when she went to work in May.[7]

Two weeks after she got to Miami, she heard from home that two new instructors—male—had just been hired at her old flying school.

"I got bored to death in the control tower and went to Embry-Riddle Aeronautical Institute in Miami and asked for a job instructing. Mr. Riddle liked women pilots." Nancy had the flight-instructing job by the end of July.

Twenty-two-year-old Nancy was heralded as the school's only female flight instructor, but she soon would be joined by two more, Helen Cavis and Mary Brooks. A newspaper photo showed her instructing another woman student who was a candidate for an instructor's license. But Nancy's biggest job was giving primary flight instruction to Army cadets.

"When the opportunity was at hand to instruct flying students, I leaped at it," Nancy told the reporter. "My mind had been set on it for a long time, especially since our entry into the war and the constant call for more manpower by the armed forces." In urging young women to take up flying, Nancy happened to mention to the reporter—presciently so—that the call of more and more men to active duty "means it will be the responsibility of women to fill the gaps, not only as instructors but in all probability as ferrying pilots."[8]

In less than two months, she would find out how right she was.

"In late September, a newspaper article caught my eye. The ATC—the ones who had turned me down in Nashville—was forming a woman's squadron to ferry airplanes. I told my boss at Embry-Riddle, 'that's where I belong.'"

By that time, Nancy Love, founder and commander of the Women's Auxiliary Ferrying Squadron, had sent eighty-three telegrams looking for willing recruits among America's elite professional or experienced amateur women pilots. Many of them had answered the call and already a dozen had qualified for the WAFS, part of the 2nd Ferrying Group, New Castle Army Air Base (NCAAB) in Wilmington, Delaware. Nancy Batson's name had not been among Nancy Love's eighty-three because she had not acquired sufficient hours to qualify at the time Nancy Love put the list together. Five hundred was the minimum. Nancy reached 503 hours on October 10, 1942, the same day she got her 200-horsepower rating, another WAFS requirement.[9]

The lack of that little piece of yellow paper from Western Union was no barrier to positive-thinking Nancy Batson. She resigned from Embry-Riddle, took the train home to Birmingham—she had already sold her airplane in Miami—repacked for a colder climate, and boarded the train for Wilmington and Nancy Love's squadron, unannounced. "It never occurred to me to wire ahead."

In mid-October 1942, Nancy Love was, by her own reckoning, behind in recruiting the first twenty-five of what was authorized to be a fifty-woman squadron. It had been over a month since she sent the now famous telegrams. Now, Nancy Love watched as a tall, very attractive blonde—dressed in a stylish brown herringbone suit, small matching hat, and brown leather high-heeled pumps—entered her office.

"Miss Batson? Please be seated." And she nodded toward the straight chair that sat facing her desk. Nancy Batson took the chair and handed the woman her logbooks, ratings, and three letters of recommendation.

For a few moments, neither of the Nancys spoke. Nancy Love carefully examined the papers. Nancy Batson tried to calm her flip-flopping stomach and remain cool and collected. Then Nancy Love excused herself and, carrying Nancy Batson's papers—along with her heart and her future—opened the door to the adjacent office, entered, and closed the door behind her. Nancy caught a glimpse of a uniformed man with dark hair and a black mustache sitting at a desk similar to Nancy Love's. The man, Nancy later learned, was Col. Robert Baker, the commanding officer of NCAAB.

After a few minutes, Nancy Love was back and she was smiling. She handed Nancy her papers and said, "Miss Batson, we need to arrange for a flight test and a physical examination. You can stay here on base tonight, in BOQ 14 where the women pilots are housed, and we'll take care of those two things in the morning."

Nancy Batson barely contained her shout for joy![10]

"When we all assembled in Wilmington, it was like we spoke different languages," said Gertrude Meserve, one of the women pilots accepted by Nancy Love and Colonel Baker. "Florene [Miller] with her Texas drawl, Nancy Batson and her even more leisurely Alabama drawl, Jamesy [Teresa James] with her slangy Pittsburghese, me from Baahston."

Not only did their speaking styles vary, but their backgrounds were vastly different—from Southern socialite Cornelia Fort to Evelyn Sharp, who was raised by adoptive parents struggling through the Depression years in rural Nebraska. Four were from prominent East Coast families: Barbara Donahue (Woolworth), Betty Huyler Gillies (Huyler Candies), Catherine Slocum (Luden Cough Drops), and Helen Mary Clark, whose husband was from a well-known real estate family in New Jersey. Betsy Ferguson and Bernice Batten hailed from the farming communities of eastern Kansas. Teresa James was the daughter of a Pittsburgh florist; Del Scharr, the daughter of a St. Louis police officer; and Barbara Erickson, the daughter of a Seattle publishing house executive. Aline "Pat" Rhonie was a divorcée who already had served with the British Red Cross Ambulance Corps in France before Dunkirk.

Most were employed in aviation as flight instructors. Dorothy Fulton and Esther Nelson were flight service owners. Esther was also a qualified interior decorator. Pat Rhonie painted aviation murals. Del Scharr had a master's degree in psychology and taught disadvantaged children in the St. Louis public schools until she married Harold Scharr. She was forced to quit because the schools wouldn't employ married women teachers. So she taught flying and ground school instead.

In age, they covered the allowed span—from Helen Richards, the youngest, at barely twenty-one, to Gillies, Rhonie, and Scharr, who were thirty-five or close to it.

Admission to the squadron required that they be high school graduates. However, the first six to arrive were products of finishing schools and the exclusive Eastern women's colleges—thus giving the false impression that the WAFS were all society girls. The first arrivals also tended to be older, most were married, and three had children. Then as the younger women and those from the Midwest and West arrived, the mix became more diverse— more democratic, as Nancy Batson liked to characterize the group.

4

The WAFS

"I was sitting there on the cot in my room in BOQ 14 wondering what to do next, when this tall brunette stuck her head in the door and introduced herself.

"'I'm Cornelia Fort from Nashville,' she said. Her voice was deep but with a distinct Southern drawl. 'Would you like to come down to my room and have a cocktail, then go over to the Officers' Club for dinner?'

"Well, I was so delighted to hear another Southern accent, I said 'yes,' even though we didn't have cocktails in our home in Birmingham. Ladies in Birmingham didn't drink cocktails."

Cornelia's room was down the hall from Nancy's on the second floor of the women's barracks. "I was fascinated by the array of liquor bottles lined up on the dresser. I felt quite sophisticated. When she asked me what I wanted, I said 'bourbon' like I had been drinking it for years."

During the first month of the WAFS' existence, while undergoing their Army indoctrination before they began ferrying, the earliest arrivals had established a ritual. Nancy Love, Betty Gillies, Pat Rhonie, Cornelia Fort, Helen Mary Clark, and Catherine Slocum gathered at 4:30 p.m. in Nancy's or Betty's room for cocktails. Cocktail hour was a time-honored tradition in the homes of these socially prominent women. Rum and Coke, also known as a Cuba Libra, was the odds-on favorite that year.

All but Cornelia were married and older, but Cornelia, at twenty-three, carried an elegant maturity about her, despite her youth. Pat was divorced, and Betty, Helen Mary, and Catherine had left children at home with their draft-exempt husbands and a grandmother or housekeeper. The next group of early arrivals—Teresa James, Del Scharr, and Esther Nelson (all married) and Barbara Poole—gravitated together and, as the even younger girls began to join the squadron, they, too, banded together.

Nancy Love, noting Nancy Batson's Southern birthright and wishing to make the young woman feel at ease, had asked her other Southern-born squadron member, Cornelia Fort, to look after her, to help her get introduced and made to feel one of them.

Cornelia's friendliness made an impression on Nancy. "She reached out to me—a newcomer, a stranger."

More WAFS wandered into Cornelia's room and Nancy was introduced to them. They walked over to the Officers' Club together for dinner. Now she saw that there were others her age. The women seemed at ease with themselves and at ease with each other. Nancy couldn't put her finger on why, but though they were all professional women pilots with the same patriotic commitment, hired to do the same job, each was distinctly different from the next.

That was when Nancy knew she had just entered a new and very different phase of her life. Though the group had all the earmarks of a sisterhood—a sorority of sorts—this was very different from the University of Alabama.[1]

The following morning, "they gave me one of those flight suits to put on, a helmet, goggles, and a parachute. Lieutenant Starbuck was my check pilot. We went out to a PT-19 (the single-engine Fairchild primary trainer—that's what *PT* stands for) and I got in the back seat and he got in the front seat. He told me what he wanted me to do. The Civilian Pilot Training Program instructors had taught me very well. I was ready."

Nancy taxied out, took off, and made climbing turns up to three thousand feet. After checking to see that no one was beneath her, "I closed the throttle, pulled the stick back real slow, held it all the way back, kicked the rudder, went into a spin, came out in two. I had learned how to do this. As you went around you counted a half, one, a half, two—you got out of the spin, came on out, gave it the throttle, came back up." She did one to the right and one to the left. "Then I did a chandelle. Close the throttle a little bit, stick the nose down to gain some airspeed. Then you put it into what you call a climbing turn. Pull on back. And what you do is when you get about halfway around you start what is a reverse turn. It's an advanced maneuver. They learned this in World War I flight, to get away from the enemy. Mmm, fun to do!"

Back on the ground, Lieutenant Starbuck went immediately into Nancy Love's office and conferred with her and Lt. Joe Tracy, who was in charge of training. Lieutenant Starbuck passed her. "Nancy Love came out, a big smile on her face. She shook my hand and congratulated me on becoming a member of the WAFS. My life has been different from that day since."

Once Nancy passed her Army physical, she became the twentieth woman admitted to the squadron and immediately began her thirty-day Army familiarization orientation.

Adapting to barracks life and Army living bothered some of the WAFS, but it came easy to Nancy, thanks to her days at Camp Winnataska. That experience alone made the rustic BOQ (Bachelor Officers' Quarters) easily acceptable. A sorority girl in college, she was used to dorm living. Being in close quarters with twenty or more females didn't faze her. Besides, Nancy was so enamored of flying Army airplanes, she didn't care where she lived.

Nancy Love already had chosen a uniform for the women in her squadron: a tailored, gray-green wool gabardine jacket with squared shoulders, straight set-in sleeves, and a detached belt of the same material, trimmed with gray-green brass buttons. The blouse (the Army name for the uniform jacket) had four patch pockets and was short enough that it would not interfere with wearing a parachute. The gored skirt for street wear and the slim-cut slacks for flying were of matching material. Shirts and ties were of contrasting tan broadcloth. Brown leather low-heeled pumps, a brown leather shoulder bag, an overseas cap, overcoat, and gloves completed the outfit. The WAFS would wear the command insignia—the civilian pilot wings of the Air Transport Command (ATC)—over the left breast pocket.

Nancy Batson knew from her interview with Nancy Love that the WAFS were to pay for their own uniforms. She also learned that they were required to wear them while on ferry duty or at their station in Wilmington.

For flying, the women were issued khaki flight coveralls (made to fit men and therefore far too large for most of them), a parachute, goggles, a white silk Army Air Forces (AAF) flying scarf, and leather flying jackets with the ATC patch.[2]

When the uniforms arrived and the women began to look and dress like soldiers, Colonel Baker decided the WAFS needed to take part in the base's weekly close-order drill. Nancy Love and her girls found themselves in for a challenge.

"Eight o'clock every Saturday morning, we marched in review," Nancy Batson recalled. "We had the band and flags, and the men all passed in review—hup, two, three, four—and the WAFS brought up the rear. And in order to do that, of course, we had to practice—every weekday morning from eight to nine. Nancy Love, as commander, had to lead the formation and give the commands, which was not one of her strong points. Occasionally, she would draw a blank on what command to give next."

Recalling one dreary morning in particular, Nancy Batson laughed. "We were drilling on an inactive runway. The squadron was marching smartly down the pavement. There was a drop-off of about ten feet at the end. As we approached the precipice, she didn't call out anything. What she was supposed to say was, 'To the rear—march!'

"Twenty-four girls, in close formation and roaring with laughter, went off the end—straight down the embankment and into the field, leaving her standing at the top, speechless.[3]

"Another time, I had picked up a bad cold, but it was Friday and the group was going dancing at Wilmington's posh DuPont Hotel. I couldn't miss out on that, so I went, and I danced away the night, had a couple of drinks, and thoroughly enjoyed myself. Of course, when I had to get up the next morning to march in parade review at 8 a.m., I could hardly drag myself out of bed."

She got her robe on, staggered down the hall to Nancy Love's room, and knocked.

"Come in." Nancy Love was already dressed for the review.

"Miz Love, I just don't think I can march this morning, I've got this *awful* cold and feel just lousy.

"'Didn't I see you out dancing at the DuPont Hotel last night, Nancy?' she asked me, straight faced.

"'Yes, ma'am,' I said. I knew what was coming.

"'Well then, Nancy, I think you can manage to march this morning.'"[4]

The Air Transport Command's tenet for delivering airplanes was "rapidly but with safety."

Ferrying Cubs (small single-engine liaison planes) and primary trainers (PTs) was not something that could be done rapidly. Cubs had a fuel capacity of twelve gallons, a sixty-five horsepower engine, averaged seventy-five miles per hour, and had to make frequent stops to refuel. They carried no radios and only rudimentary instrumentation, so they could only fly in good visibility known as VFR (visual flight rules). Consequently, bad, even marginal, weather grounded plane and pilot indefinitely. Winter weather made day-to-day flying conditions for light aircraft highly unstable.[5]

The 175-horsepower Fairchild PT-19 had more speed and power than a Cub, as well as a larger gas tank and therefore greater range, but still no radio and few instruments. And it was an open-cockpit airplane.

Even if the airplanes had been equipped with instruments, the WAFS, with one or two exceptions, were not instrument rated. That would come later. Besides, ATC ferry pilots, male and female, were restricted to flying between the hours of a half an hour after sunrise and a half an hour be-

Six Wilmington WAFS study navigation: Gertrude Meserve and Betty Gillies, kneeling; Nancy Batson, Esther Nelson, and Dorothy Fulton, seated; Teresa James, standing. Fall 1942. Photo courtesy the Crews family.

fore sunset. In wintertime, this didn't leave a lot of actual flying time; consequently trips cross-country could take several days.

Nancy Batson's first mission as a ferry pilot was to fly one of the first PT-19s to be entrusted to the WAFS to deliver. On November 22, 1942, eleven WAFS were assigned to ferry eleven of the trainers to fields in the South.

By late November along the eastern seaboard it was getting cold on the ground and colder aloft. Not only did the WAFS have to lug parachutes, they also had to carry bulky winter flying gear with them on the train to Baltimore and then on the bus to the Fairchild factory in Hagerstown, Maryland. They missed their bus in Baltimore by two minutes and, since there wasn't another one until seven in the morning, they had to sleep on benches in the station propped against parachutes and B-4 bags.

Their tardy arrival in Hagerstown brought the wrath of the Army down on them. "Where the hell have you been?" the captain in charge asked. "Everyone in the Army has been looking for you." Explanations fell on deaf ears. Then the weather closed in and they couldn't leave anyway, so they spent that night—and the next—in a Hagerstown hotel. One of the pilots, Del Scharr, became ill and had to be taken to the hospital.

Finally, on November 25—the day before Thanksgiving—the remaining ten took off. But the weather over Hagerstown was soupy and they couldn't see each other so Clark, Batson, Nelson, Sharp, and James returned. Gillies, Richards, Burchfield, Miller, and Erickson went on through—eventual destination, Union City, Tennessee.

The next day, Batson and the other four got off and turned their noses south as well. They RONed (remained overnight) that night at Morris Field in Charlotte, North Carolina, where the men made them feel welcome. The officers on base took them to the O-Club for drinks and a turkey dinner. They were lodged in the nurses' BOQ. The following day they flew on to Union City and delivered their airplanes.

The women returned to base just after midnight on November 28.[6]

"I was so tired after that trip, I thought I was getting sick. I wanted to curl up in my bunk and die. And the next morning, they told us we had to go right back out again. That was when I realized I had a problem. I might not be able to take this kind of schedule. But somewhere deep inside me I knew I had to do it and I knew I could do it. I'd just have to find a way."

With that, Nancy discovered a secret—the secret that would get her through twenty-six months of ferrying airplanes under all kinds of conditions. "I learned to fall asleep at a moment's notice. I just lay down on a bench or on my parachute and B-4 bag and conked out. That saved me."

Nancy Batson's ability to sleep anywhere under any conditions became legendary in the Ferrying Division.[7]

They were off again the next morning, the same crew—Clark, Gillies, Burchfield, Nelson, Batson, Sharp, Miller, Erickson, Richards, and James—only this time they were ferrying Cubs.

Colonel Baker took pity on them and flew them to Lock Haven, Pennsylvania, in the C-60 transport, but weather closed in on them en route and he had to go on instruments. The rest of the way they flew looking out the window at soup. On the ground, it was snowing. "I had never flown in snow," Nancy said.

The night of December 1, they were back at BOQ 14. "Nancy Love called and told us to pack. We were on our way to Montana."

The train trip to Great Falls—across the northern plains in winter—was an adventure with snow-blocked rails and breakdowns. Their assignment was to take primary trainers—not PT-19s but PT-17 Stearmans—from Great Falls,

Montana, to Jackson, Tennessee. Six WAFS and twenty-seven male ferry pilots were designated to make the deliveries. They flew thirty-three yellow, bi-wing, 225-horsepower, open-cockpit Stearmans twenty-five hundred miles in the dead of winter.

The planes were on loan from the United States to the Canadian RAF, which was using them to train their flight cadets. The open cockpits of the PT-17s made the airplanes almost useless in the wintertime over the mountains and high plains of Alberta, Canada. The solution—take them back to be used in a warmer climate.

Nancy Batson along with Teresa James, Florene Miller, Delphine Bohn, Phyllis Burchfield, and Kay Rawls Thompson made that unforgettable trip.

The ferry pilots picked up the planes in Great Falls, home of the ATC's 7th Ferrying Group. The temperature was zero degrees Fahrenheit on December 12, the morning the women took off. The engine oil had to be heated before it could be poured into the crankcases.

Clad in their Army-issue, bulky winter flying gear, the WAFS—looking like six giant overstuffed penguins—waddled to the flight line. Nancy recalled that the gear was a challenge to get into. The first layer consisted of long, scratchy woolen underwear and multiple socks. Over the long johns, they pulled on high-waisted, fleece-lined leather pants that zipped from the shinbone of one leg to the sternum and were held in place by suspenders. This was topped off with a fleece-lined leather jacket.

To this, they added leather flying caps with chin straps and goggles, fleece-lined leather gloves, and wool-lined boots. "We thought surely all this would be enough to keep the cold out, but it wasn't. Then to that we added a parachute with straps over the shoulders and around the thighs."

The women also were given chamois masks held in place by wide, black elastic bands. The masks were to provide at least some semblance of protection against frostbite since they would be flying another few thousand feet above the earth where the air was even colder. The WAFS had already learned that when flying in open-cockpit trainers a runny nose was a constant companion.

Nancy recalled that the entire landscape, as far as she could see, was white. Even though the airplanes were yellow, once they were in the air, it was hard for them to see each other against the white of their snow-and-ice-covered world.

Florene was navigating, but twenty miles out of Great Falls, the wind snatched her chart out of her hands. Now they were lost. Since they had no radios, all six had to land at a plowed out emergency field in the middle of nowhere in order to figure out where they were. It turned out they were only

The Great Falls six with their Stearman PT-17s: Kay Rawls Thompson, Phyllis Burch-field, Nancy Batson, Delphine Bohn, Florene Miller, and Teresa James. Wichita Falls, Texas, December 1942. Photo courtesy the Crews family.

ten miles off course. They took off and flew on to Billings to RON. The sun rose late in Montana in the wintertime and it also set early, so their daylight-flying day was quite short.

It took the six WAFS nineteen days and, at that, they beat all the men to Jackson. This, while enduring foul weather of all sorts, mechanical diffi-culties, bad gas that gunked up the engines, and illness—primarily the flu brought on, presumably, by flying in subfreezing weather in open cockpits at high altitude. Friends and family also threw a couple of parties for them as they RONed along the way, which may have led to a couple of hangovers, but those didn't slow them up.

They spent Christmas in Little Rock, Arkansas—the temperature there was eighty degrees with thundershowers. Nancy had originally planned to get to Birmingham for Christmas because Paul Crews was going to be home for the holiday as well. Realizing she wasn't going to make it, Nancy called him on December 24 from Little Rock. He promptly caught a train that got him into Little Rock at 5:30 Christmas morning. Florene's number-one boyfriend also arrived in Little Rock at 1 a.m. Christmas morning.

The WAFS flew on to Memphis on the twenty-sixth and were promptly grounded again by the weather. They finally delivered the planes to Jackson on New Year's Eve day, 1942.[8]

The hardships they endured and the flexibility that they developed in order to deal with the obstacles thrown in their way made better ferry pilots out of them. That they all made it safely may have been a miracle. But they all did make it back and in later years all told the story with relish and ever-growing fondness, and probably some embellishment along the way.[9]

The original WAFS in the order they joined were Nancy Love, Betty Gillies, Cornelia Fort, Aline "Pat" Rhonie, Helen Mary Clark, Adela "Del" Scharr, Esther Nelson, Teresa James, Barbara Poole, Helen Richards, Barbara Towne, Gertrude Meserve, Florene Miller, Barbara Jane "B.J." Erickson, Delphine Bohn, Barbara "Donnie" Donahue, Evelyn Sharp, Phyllis Burchfield, Esther Manning, Nancy Batson, Katherine "Kay" Rawls Thompson, Dorothy Fulton, Opal "Betsy" Ferguson, Bernice Batten, Dorothy Scott, Helen "Little Mac" McGilvery, Kathryn "Sis" Bernheim, and Lenore "Mac" McElroy. Among them, only Helen Mary Clark did not make a living flying.

The squadron would finally settle in at twenty-seven. Pat Rhonie left December 31 following a controversy with Colonel Baker. The story was, she spent an additional night away from base after the colonel told her to return. In an interview after the war, Nancy Love told AAF historian Lt. Col. Oliver La Farge that Rhonie was discharged: "This was done through normal civil service procedures. She [Rhonie] was given a hearing before a board first. Male civilian pilots were discharged in this way." Besides, Rhonie's initial ninety-day contract was up.[10] On January 3, 1943, Helen McGilvery and Sis Bernheim successfully passed their tests.

Catherine Slocum is not counted in the final twenty-eight because she never ferried, though she successfully completed her Army indoctrination and qualified to ferry. Alma Heflin McCormick never returned with her 200-horsepower rating. Pat Rhonie *is* counted because she ferried from October 22 to December 31, 1942.

Nancy Love flew into Romulus, Michigan (near Detroit), home of the 3rd Ferrying Group, on January 13, 1943. While there, she gave a flight test to Lenore McElroy, a woman from nearby Ypsilanti, wife of a Romulus ferry pilot and mother of three teenagers. A flight instructor, McElroy had thirty-five hundred hours. Nancy checked her out and, on January 23,

1943, accepted Lenore as the twenty-eighth and final member of the original WAFS.

On January 26, 1943, the office of the commanding general of the AAF, Henry H. "Hap" Arnold, sent a message to Ferrying Division commander Col. William H. Tunner—Nancy Love's boss—stating that, from that date, the Ferrying Division would employ only those women who had graduated from the Women's Flying Training (WFT) school in Texas. Arnold had backed famous record-setting aviatrix Jacqueline Cochran and made it possible for her to establish the women's flight training facility in November 1942. Women pilots were now being taught to fly the Army way.[11]

With the promise of more women ferry pilots—graduates of the Texas facility—the Ferrying Division had to get ready for them. Three more squadrons would be formed and the original WAFS would be divided among four locations. New squadrons were slated for Love Field in Dallas under the 5th Ferrying Group; Romulus under the 3rd Ferrying Group; and Long Beach, California, under the 6th Ferrying Group—to be activated in that order.

Florene Miller would command the Dallas contingent, which would consist of Helen Richards, Dorothy Scott, Betsy Ferguson, and Nancy Love herself.

Why did Nancy put Florene in charge? Nancy had bigger things in mind. She planned to check out on every available aircraft—to pave the way for her girls to fly any and everything in the Army's aviation arsenal. And she would be making trips to Long Beach, Romulus, and Wilmington to check on her deputy commanders and the squadrons there. Now she truly *was* senior squadron leader.

Del Scharr would command the Romulus group, consisting of Barbara Donahue, Barbara Poole, Katherine Thompson, Phyllis Burchfield, and newcomer Lenore McElroy. Leader of the Long Beach contingent would be Barbara Jane "B.J." Erickson and stationed with her would be Cornelia Fort, Evelyn Sharp, Barbara Towne, and Bernice Batten. The remaining eleven—Nancy Batson among them—would make up the Wilmington women's squadron with Betty Gillies now in command.

Life in the WAFS would never be the same.

5

The Best of All Jobs

"I developed an inferiority complex." Unlikely words to come out of Nancy Batson's mouth. "I was supposed to go to Dallas in January 1943, but Betty [Gillies] pulled me out and kept me in Wilmington. She never told us why the orders were changed. I thought I was being left in Wilmington because I wasn't any good. When I mentioned it to Betty, years later, she laughed and said, 'oh, no, I kept the good ones on purpose.'"

Del Scharr echoed Betty's comment when she wrote her memoir, *Sisters in the Sky*. Del claimed that Colonel Baker objected when Nancy Love "took all the cuties" for the newly formed squadrons and told her to leave some of them in Wilmington. So Betty—by then in charge at Wilmington—sent three others out instead and kept Batson, Gertrude Meserve, and a very unhappy Teresa James at Wilmington. Teresa's husband was stationed in California, Nancy had promised her Long Beach, and she wanted to go in the worst way.[1]

Teresa, characteristically, made the best of the situation. Ditto Nancy Batson, who may have felt the pull of disappointment and—in her words—"an inferiority complex" for a couple of days, but nothing kept resilient Nancy down for long if she was flying. "Besides, my older sister, Elinor, was living in Baltimore, so I didn't have a problem with Wilmington."

Nancy and her fellow Wilmington ferry pilots settled into a routine of assignments that consisted of ferrying PT-19s south from Hagerstown, Maryland, and PT-26s (PT-19s with canopies) north, often into Canada. This would be their life week in and week out through the winter and spring of 1943.

On January 13, 1943, Nancy Batson, Helen Mary Clark, Gertrude Meserve, and Delphine Bohn reported to the Fairchild factory in Hagerstown to check out in the PT-26. On the sixteenth, they began their journey north, each in a PT-26, bound for Toronto. First, they were weathered in in

Seven Wilmington WAFS arrive at the Fairchild factory in Hagerstown, Maryland, spring 1943, to ferry PT-26s. From left: Helen McGilvery, Teresa James, Dorothy Fulton, Sis Bernheim, Gertrude Meserve, Betty Gillies, and Nancy Batson visit with a Fairchild official. Photo courtesy the Crews family.

Williamsport, Pennsylvania. They headed north again on January 20 and got as far as Buffalo, where, once again, they were grounded by weather. "It was bad—snowy," the southern girl from Alabama remembered. They RONed (remained overnight) that night at Niagara Falls.[2]

The next day was Sunday and still bad weather. A number of male ferry pilots were weathered in as well and staying at the same hotel. Nancy recognized one of them from Birmingham. "He and I walked downtown to the picture show. When we walked back into the hotel later that afternoon, there sat the three WAFS in the lobby. You know how you sense something. I *knew* something was wrong.

"Helen Mary said, 'Nancy, you need to call your sister.'

"I said, 'Okay, I'll go up to the room.'

"Delphine said, 'I'll come with you.'

"Sitting on the bed, I called my sister Elinor in Baltimore. She told me my brother had been killed the day before. I remember saying, 'oh, poor Mother and Daddy.'"

Nancy's brother, Radford, an Army Air Forces officer, was in flight training at Ellington Field in Houston. His trainer had crashed.

The senior Batsons had called Elinor who, in turn, had called the base in Wilmington to find out where Nancy was. Betty Gillies had tried to reach Nancy in Niagara Falls and, since she was out at the movies, had talked to Helen Mary, the flight leader. "When I walked in that door, they already knew my brother had been killed," Nancy said. "Wasn't that thoughtful of Delphine to go with me to make the call—because she knew.

"After I talked to Elinor, I was told I had orders to get on the train and go to her in Baltimore."

Nancy's parents had heard about Radford's death Sunday morning. "My mother said that on Saturday afternoon she had gone with some friends to the picture show. And when she came out of the show something just hit her—something about her son. When she got home she tried to put in a call to him, but it didn't go through. She didn't find out until the next morning.

"My mother, my father, my grandmother, they were devastated. He was twenty-five years old. An only son. He was in the Army and had gotten out of the Philippines just ahead of Pearl Harbor. He was home and we thought he was safe.

"Radford was big, tall, handsome, big shoulders—smart! But he wasn't particularly well coordinated. Not like I was. He probably shouldn't have been flying airplanes. But airplanes held some of the same fascination for him that they did me. He and another cadet went up in this twin-engine trainer on Saturday afternoon (January 20) and it crashed on takeoff. He was killed instantly—burned. His wife was back in Columbia, South Carolina, at the base where they had a home. He had been sent to Houston for flight training. She was getting ready to have their first child."

Nancy paused in the telling—closed her eyes in the remembering. Then looked up again, characteristically dry-eyed.

"Mother and Daddy had gone immediately to Columbia to be with his wife. I got on the train and went to Baltimore to my sister's and then they came on up there. We all met at my sister's house. What could we do? We were all heartsick. We grieved—oh how we grieved—together. You never know what's going to happen." Radford's remains eventually were interred at West Point.

The WAFS did not expect Nancy to return. "The first thing Delphine said to me when I returned to Wilmington was, 'I thought your family would try to dissuade you—to keep you from flying.'

"But my parents never said one thing to me, not one thing. They never said, 'quit flying, please don't do it anymore.' Other people have told me that my mother used to brag on my flying. 'She does it so well.' And Amy told me Muddy told people, 'well, you know, she's never had an accident.'"[3]

Radford's son, Stephen, nicknamed Stevie, was born February 18. The senior Batsons persuaded Radford's widow, Orlens, to move to Birmingham so that they could help her raise their grandson. "My father tried to be, for Stevie, the father he didn't have."[4]

January, February, and March of 1943 left their mark on the WAFS—good and bad. Nancy Love, intent on proving that her women pilots could fly anything the Army built, went quietly about doing just that. Between December 7, 1942, and March 8, 1943, Love checked out in the C-36, AT-6, BT-13 and 15, C-53, and P-51 Mustang, the hottest pursuit plane (single-engine, single-cockpit fighter) the Army had. She also got her first opportunity to fly copilot in the twin-engine B-25—which she would later pilot—and an hour of instrument flight time as copilot in a four-engine B-24.[5]

Meanwhile, the girls in training down in Houston were already flying the basic trainers (BTs) and moving into AT-6s and some twin-engine advanced trainers. Love did not want her girls left behind—stuck flying only primary trainers. She wanted everyone on equal footing when the girls from the Army training facility joined the WAFS.

While Nancy Love was checking out in bigger, faster airplanes out west, back in Wilmington, Betty Gillies was transitioning into the P-47, the largest of the pursuit or fighter airplanes. She made her first flight in the big pursuit March 8, 1943.

Then tragedy struck again. This time it was one of the WAFS.

On Sunday, March 21, 1943, Cornelia Fort and six male Long Beach ferry pilots took off to deliver BT-13s to Dallas. Approximately ten miles south of Merkel, Texas, the landing gear on another BT struck the left wing of Cornelia's BT. The left wingtip of Cornelia's plane snapped off.

Cornelia's plane "suddenly broke off to the right as though on a snap roll," said one of the other ferry pilots. Then it spun, rolled, and went into an inverted dive, slamming vertically into the ground. The airplane did not catch fire, but Cornelia died on impact.[6]

The fellow Southerner who had reached out to newcomer Nancy Batson was gone.

But the women pilots were a resilient lot. If they couldn't deal with loss and move on, they would be useless to the Army, the war effort, and themselves. In spite of the deep sorrow felt and expressed by all the WAFS over Cornelia's death, her accident did not bring about resignations nor did it affect the women's desire to ferry airplanes. That went on without a hitch. The women stuck to their ferrying schedules, which speaks highly of the caliber of women they were, to their deep commitment and dedication, and to the fact that they were a well-adjusted bunch.

A letter went out on March 29, 1943, to all group commanders stating that no woman pilot was to be assigned any flying duties during pregnancy. That wasn't the bad part. At that point only Esther Manning Rathfelder in Betty Gillies' Wilmington squadron was affected and Betty had already addressed that dilemma. Esther, well into her pregnancy, was now Betty's operations officer and flying a desk. However, the rest of the directive was worse because it affected them all.

Women who had their menstrual period were not to fly—one day before and two days after. If adhered to, the restriction meant a wasteful eight or nine days of non-flying time a month per WAFS.[7]

That wasn't the worst. Just when women were beginning to fly bigger airplanes—like the BTs and ATs—on March 25, 1943, the women of the 3rd Ferrying Group at Romulus were blindsided. The commander there put out a directive repeating the original restriction of WAFS to light trainer aircraft only. The women in Romulus were not to be assigned to transition on any high-powered single-engine or twin-engine aircraft nor were they to fly as copilots on ferrying missions with a male pilot.

The directive went on to say that women were to be assigned deliveries on alternate days with the male pilots and, if at all possible, were to be sent in a different direction from any male flight. To that was added that no mixed flight or crew assignments would be tolerated. This meant women couldn't "build time" in different airplanes—work on transition—as copilots to male pilots other than instructors.[8]

Already the Air Transport Command (ATC) forbade the women to "hitch" rides in other military aircraft cross-country following a delivery. The men were encouraged to do this. The women rode trains and flew on airliners to get back to base. The primary reason for this was the Army's fear of scandal. But it wasn't that they didn't trust the women in their employ. It was the press the Army didn't trust. Already the press was pursuing the "lady flyers" and publishing stories about them—many of them based on misinformation. The Army didn't want idle gossip to start and spread and thereby tarnish their WAFS' reputations.[9]

But this from Romulus was too much.

Nancy Love objected strenuously to this directive. She felt it cast a slur on the morals of the WAFS. At that time there had been no gossip about the WAFS or moral lapses reported. It was an insult. She went over the heads of both Group and Ferrying Division commanders and appealed that directive and the one dealing with the menstrual periods directly to General C. R. Smith, Chief of Staff of the Air Transport Command about to become the deputy commander of the ATC.[10]

Love and Cyrus Rowlett Smith were, in fact, old friends and remained lifelong friends. Smith, the president of American Airlines before joining the ATC (and again after the war), knew Nancy and her husband, Bob, prior to the war. In going to C.R., Love risked Colonel Tunner's ire and she was indeed not in his good graces for a period of time after that.

In addition to being in the beginning stages of transition to more powerful airplanes, the WAFS had an almost perfect accident record. Cornelia was exonerated of any blame in her fatal accident. There was no pilot error on her part. And the only other accidents at that point had been a couple of bent propellers following ground loops.[11]

Still more change was on the way.

Colonel Tunner had four PT-26s that needed to be delivered to the Canadian RAF near Calgary, Alberta, before Easter. The Friday afternoon before Palm Sunday, Colonel Baker chose his women's squadron commander, Betty Gillies, to make this important mission happen. From her Wilmington cadre, she chose Nancy Batson and the two newcomers Sis Bernheim and Helen McGilvery, nicknamed Little Mac. She respected the flying abilities of both of them as well as those of young Batson.

"PT-26s have a cruising speed of about one hundred miles per hour. When Betty told us where we were going and how long we had to get there, we stared at her in total disbelief," Nancy remembered.

"I know, that's more than twenty-five hundred miles, but I promised Colonels Tunner and Baker we'd get them there before Easter," Betty said. Easter was only nine days away.

"That doesn't allow for any weather along the route," Nancy said, letting out a long, low whistle.

Betty nodded. "I know." What she didn't tell them was she had great faith in their abilities.

"Betty didn't say things like that. Neither she nor Nancy Love was loose with praise. The women under their command were professionals and were expected to perform at the top of their abilities. Praise for doing what was part of our job was not a side benefit.

"Very early Palm Sunday morning–April 18–we were in Hagerstown checking out our aircraft."

"Eeeeyow!" Nancy let out a Rebel yell as she climbed into the cockpit of her PT-26. "We're goin' back to Montana and on to Calgary, Canada!" The other three laughed. They were used to Nancy's enthusiastic outbursts.

"We left Hagerstown early, and headed west across Ohio, Indiana, and Illinois. We ran out of daylight in Joliet, Illinois, but not before we had flown an astounding 697 miles. And the weather was improving over what we had been having in Wilmington. Winter lasted forever in Delaware!"

Spring definitely was on the way. Besides, these airplanes had canopies so they didn't have to contend with wind in their faces and icicles forming on their runny noses.

"That night at the hotel in Joliet, Betty informed us that we would be up at four in the morning," Nancy related.

"'We're going to get an early start,' Betty said. 'I want to be sitting in our cockpits with the engines running when the sun breaks the horizon. Now get some sleep. Tomorrow's a long day.'

"Well, Sis and Little Mac began to howl. 'Today was a long day.' Sis said. 'We went seven hundred miles!' Little Mac said.

"'Four a.m.,' Betty said.

"I was on my way to bed when I overheard Sis and Mac grumbling," Nancy remembered. "They said there was no way in you-know-where that they were going to get up at four o'clock in the morning.

"Well, I listened to them bellyache for a few minutes and I got mad. Betty was putting her reputation on the line and here these two were saying they were too good and too tired to get up in the morning and get a move on and help get those planes out to Canada on time like Colonel Tunner wanted.

"So I marched into their room and gave them what-for. Well, when I got through, they just stared at me. Then I turned on my heel and walked out and went to bed. The next morning, I was in the lobby at four a.m., dressed and ready to go. And, you know what, so were they!

"We were sitting in our cockpits when dawn broke and we were off in a flash, headed due west again. This time our destination was North Platte, Nebraska, a six-hundred-mile flight. We crossed the Mississippi and pretty soon we were looking down on the cornfields of Iowa and later on the wheat fields of Nebraska. It was like I'd never seen corn and wheat fields before. We crossed the Missouri River below Omaha and kept on cruising until we hit North Platte. It was fun watching the ground rise up to meet us as we flew!

"We were beginning to enjoy ourselves by then. Here we were, three Easterners and a Southerner, and we were crossing this great big country of ours. This country we were fighting for. And, we were so proud of that fact. And, by golly, we were headin' west in the cockpits of sleek new Army airplanes and somebody else was paying for the gas!

"We were up at four again the next day and, that night, made Great Falls, Montana, a whopping 850-mile flight from North Platte. When we got there, Betty reminded us—rather proudly, I think—that we had just done it in airplanes that had an average ground speed of one hundred miles per hour.

"Before finding a hotel, Betty got all the Customs forms filled out. We were tired!"

Great Falls, Montana, is only one hundred miles from the Canadian border. During World War II, it was the home of the 7th Ferrying Group and the ferrying base from which planes were processed for Lend-Lease delivery to Canada and for aircraft bound to Alaska and, eventually, Russia. The WAFS' four airplanes, however, were bound for a Canadian RAF pilot-training facility somewhere in Alberta.

"The next day, up at four again, we flew along those majestic snow-capped Canadian Rockies. What we had seen the previous day was nothing compared to this."

The last leg was a short one—only 275 miles from Great Falls to a town named DeWinton. They had delivered the planes from Hagerstown in a record four days—and four days before the Easter deadline. Betty had done her job—so had the rest of them. And they had done it well.

"We talked a lot on the train ride back," Nancy said. "I think we took apart the entire women's flying program and put it together again. Much of the conversation centered around the news that Jacqueline Cochran's first class from Texas was destined to swell our ranks early in May. Betty had heard that they were to graduate April 24—day after tomorrow. The twenty-three graduates would be divided among the four existing women's squadrons."

The four were back on base by Friday night, April 23—Good Friday.

"Do you know what that sweet Colonel Baker did?" Nancy still liked to brag fifty-something years later. "He gave us all commendations—'for our efficient and prompt delivery which included not only flying of the planes but also the paper work involved in such deliveries, flight logs, gasoline reports, RON messages, etc.' I gotta tell you, I'm real proud of that!"[12]

Nancy's official WAFS portrait, 1942/43—the photo with
the Mona Lisa smile. Photo courtesy the Crews family.

What Betty Gillies, Nancy Batson, and the others had proved was what
Nancy Love already knew—that the women made excellent ferry pilots. Now
Nancy Love could point with pride to their accomplishment and tell the men
to whom she answered that there was a lot more where that came from.

Women were much more likely than were the men to take a plane directly
to its delivery point, because the men were apt to stop off en route—even go
out of the way—to visit a girlfriend or two. As of April 24, 1943, the WAFS'
stock was very high with the entire Ferrying Division—particularly their boss,
Colonel Tunner.

And it paid off.

Unbeknownst to the four ferry pilots, just before they left for Canada,
General C. R. Smith was in the process of addressing Nancy Love's appeal—
the one with which she went over the head of her commanding officer. In
an April 17, 1943, letter to Colonel Tunner, Smith stated that certain flight

limitations were being imposed on women pilots by the Ferrying Division without giving full consideration to the professional qualifications of the individual pilots; that the ferrying activities of women pilots were being restricted to trainer aircraft only; that women were being prohibited from acting as copilots on ferrying missions; that they were being prohibited from transition training on single-engine aircraft of the high horsepower class or twin-engine aircraft.

General Smith concluded his letter with the following statement: "It is the desire of this Command that all pilots, regardless of sex, be privileged to advance to the extent of their ability in keeping with the progress of aircraft development."[13]

On April 26, Ferrying Division Headquarters rescinded the letter of March 29 relative to WAFS' not flying during periods of "physical disability" (referring to monthly menstrual periods) and the letter of March 25 forbidding the women to transition into higher horsepower aircraft.[14]

A new directive stated that the WAFS would be transitioned on multiengine and high-powered single-engine aircraft under the same standards of individual experience and ability as any other pilot. However, still tiptoeing around the morals issue, the directive further stated that normally the WAFS would be given transition on cross-country checkouts by other fully qualified WAFS "when and if available."[15]

Now nothing stood in the way of the WAFS to move up the transition ladder. This was a high point for Nancy Love and her original WAFS. By May 1, they had been ferrying aircraft for the Army for a full six months. They had proved they could fly bigger aircraft than the primary trainers they were originally hired to ferry. They had proved their worth as ferry pilots who could get the job done safely and on time. And now they were about to grow in strength and numbers.

Transition into higher-powered and multiengine aircraft was, indeed, open to the WAFS. But more changes were in the air. Beyond lay events that would drastically alter the structure of the Army's women's flying program.

"Miss Jacqueline Cochran has been named Director of Women Pilots within the Army Air Forces and Special Assistant to Major General Barney M. Giles, the Assistant Chief of Staff, Operations, Commitments and Requirements," said the formal announcement from the War Department on July 5, 1943.

Also on July 5, the War Department announced the appointment of Mrs. Nancy Love as executive for WAFS on the staff of Colonel Tunner,

Ferrying Division, ATC. Cochran now had overall control of the growing women pilots' organization, but Nancy Love still worked for Tunner, who was promoted to brigadier general on July 12, 1943.

On August 5, the Women Airforce Service Pilots (WASP) came into existence. This so-named organization would take the place of the women pilots known up until then as WAFS and WFTDs. All the women pilots would now go under the name WASP.

"We went to bed WAFS and woke up the next morning WASPs," Betty Gillies said.

The early graduates of the Texas flight training school—the Women's Flying Training Detachment (WFTD)—were, for the most part, women who had just missed out on joining the original WAFS. By the time they had trained under the eyes of the instructors at Ellington Field in Houston, they met the qualifications laid down for the original squadron. However, Jackie Cochran began lowering the entrance requirements for her school, first to one hundred hours, then seventy-five, and in the spring of 1943 to thirty-five hours—the minimum required for a private pilot's license.

The newly graduated WASP would no longer have to have the equivalent of the three hundred hours required of male ferry pilots entering the Ferrying Division, let alone the five hundred required of the original WAFS. Because of this, Colonel Tunner did not want to accept these women carte blanche. If they couldn't meet Ferrying Division qualifications, Tunner wanted rights of refusal. Cochran insisted that the women be accepted under any circumstances.

A compromise, of sorts, resulted in Cochran assigning some of her graduates to other flight-related tasks within the Army Air Forces. And Tunner worked it out with the Training Command that the Ferrying Division would accept the top graduates of each class. It was an uneasy truce.

Cochran didn't like the WAFS' uniform. She considered it too drab. So she hired a fashion designer from New York's Bergdorf Goodman to design a new one for the WASP. The outcome was the now familiar uniform of what is known as Santiago blue—a sharp-looking, lightweight wool jacket, skirt, and slacks, accompanied by a matching beret and a pair of silver wings. Tunner didn't like the new uniform because his WAFS were being forced out of the uniform he knew they wore with pride. But Cochran won General Arnold's approval and Santiago blue carried the day.

All the WASP would wear the blues.

Nancy Batson loved her WAFS uniform, but she loved "flying those wonderful Army airplanes" even more. As long as they let her do that, she really didn't care what she wore. In April 1943, she began to get Link trainer time—which indicated that she was being primed for an instrument rating—and in June she began transition into the AT-6. She also began to get twin-engine time in a UC-61, UC-78, AT-9, C-56, and C-60, in that order.[16]

Something was up!

6

Women in Pursuit

By December 1943, the United States had been involved in World War II for two years. Warplanes were rolling off the assembly lines, in particular those swift, powerful single-engine, single-cockpit planes known as pursuits. The Army needed pilots to ferry those airplanes from the factory to the docks for shipment abroad. But General Tunner and the Ferrying Division had made an interesting discovery.

The way they trained their male ferry pilots, who made up the bulk of the division (eighty-five hundred pilots), was to transition them upwards in horsepower, number of engines, size, and complexity until they could handle four-engine bombers and transports like the B-17, 24, and 29 and the C-54 and fly them overseas. The one step up the ladder that was *not* needed to successfully train these men destined for the combat zones abroad, strangely enough, was pursuit. In concert with this, Tunner saw a slacking off in the production of the small single-engine trainer planes. The big manufacturing push now was pursuit. That meant the division would need fewer women ferry pilots—unless they could be trained to ferry something other than trainers.[1]

The answer, of course, was pursuit. Don't sidetrack the male pilots away from the job for which they were needed and waste valuable time when time and victory were of the essence. Train the best, most experienced women pilots to fly pursuit. Make use of your resources.

Nancy Batson and the other original WAFS, along with the earliest graduates of the Army flight training school—women who had nearly as many logged hours as did the "Originals"—were ready and itching to fly airplanes that, a year before, they could only dream of flying.

"All that twin-engine and Link trainer time the summer of 1943 was because Betty Gillies was trying to get us ready for pursuit school," Nancy recalled. "Pursuit school was going to begin the first of December 1943. The women pilots would be allowed to attend, but first we had to pass instrument training—flying under the hood, they called it.

"Now I liked to see where I was going. To me, that was flying—not instrument flying where you can't see the wonderful scenery and all the interesting things on the ground. But finally, in the fall of 1943, we started the real thing.

"Helen McGilvery and I had the same instructor and we traded off. She flew with him in the morning and I flew in the afternoon. He wore these horn-rimmed glasses and was kind of stern. We'd get in the airplane—a BT-13—and I'd be in the back seat and the instructor in the front. And he'd tell me to pull the hood up. The hood is this black cloth thing that you pull over your part of the cockpit so that you can't see anything but the instrument panel—nothing outside the cockpit.

"The instructor taxied the airplane out and got it lined up on the runway, then he'd tell me to set my gyro at zero. I'd take off from a dead stop, blind, climb into that highway in the sky, and fly to Philadelphia watching the instruments and following the beam. The beam—a radio signal—is a hum and you listened through your earphones. If you got off to one side you heard a 'dit dah.' If you got off to the other side, you heard a 'dah dit.' It told you if you were to the right or the left of the directional beam.

"Well, because I preferred flying VFR conditions—that means 'visual flight rules'—I guess I wasn't taking this instruction too seriously. One particular afternoon, I had been particularly bad. Helen knew our instructor off the field. I didn't. He and his wife lived in town and so did Little Mac and her husband, Charles McGilvery (Big Mac), who was a ferry pilot too. I think they got together occasionally as couples. Well, our instructor talked to her about me.

"The next day, Helen took me aside and told me that our instructor had told her I'd better 'do better' or I was going to flunk this course.

"Well, that afternoon, I was a different pilot! I loved flying those airplanes and I wasn't about to do anything to endanger my opportunity to fly them. Besides, pursuit school was coming.

"Finally, one afternoon, I guess I had done all right because the instructor told me he was taking the controls and [said] for me to push the hood back. We flew out and swooped down over DelMarVa, where Delaware, Maryland, and Virginia all meet. It's marshy, close to the coast. Turns out my instructor was a duck hunter and it was well into fall now—the colors were beautiful. He was thinking about getting in a little duck hunting and wanted to look over the territory.

"I sighed with relief. I knew I had passed! I had straightened up in time. Both Helen and my instructor were looking out for me.

"Well, in 1964, I was watching the Republican Convention on television and looked there on the screen and who did I see but my old instrument instructor from Wilmington. His name was Barry Goldwater. He was a senator from Arizona and he was about to be nominated to run for president of the United States!"[2]

When the second class of pilots reported to the Army's Pursuit Training School in Palm Springs, California, December 10, 1943, four women from Nancy Love's original WAFS were part of it.[3]

Nancy Batson and Gertrude Meserve shared one room in the barracks—two iron cots and a partition for a wall. Helen McGilvery and Barbara Donahue bunked right next door.

The four arrived just as the shock of losing one of their own was beginning to wear off. Dorothy Scott, the fun-loving, twenty-three-year-old WAFS from Washington State, had been killed the week before at the school. A P-39 entering the landing pattern overtook the BC-1 trainer in which Dorothy and her instructor were flying their final approach. The two airplanes collided at about two hundred feet and plummeted to the desert floor in a fiery heap.

With Dorothy Scott's death in pursuit training, the war moved even closer to the women pilots. Though they did not fly combat and never left North America, they did put their lives on the line every time one of them climbed into a cockpit. As fatalistic in their outlook as their male counterparts, the women never dwelled on crashes, comrades who had met their deaths, or what the future might hold. They never looked beyond the immediate mission. They flew for today.

Nancy Batson exhibited that attitude to a fault. She readily admitted to never looking beyond today, the next flight, the next mission. Having lived through her brother's death and coming back to active duty so soon afterwards was part of it.

Nancy flew her first pursuit school training flight with an instructor in a BC-1 (AT-6) on December 14. She immersed herself in the total learning process over the next several days, which included flying the BC-1 from the back seat to more closely simulate flying a taildragger pursuit with a large engine up front blocking forward visibility. By December 20, she was ready for her first flight in an actual pursuit. Since the pursuits were all single-cockpit airplanes, that meant the first flight was also a solo flight. No instructor riding along to help out if there was trouble.

Nancy climbed eagerly into the P-47, nicknamed the "Jug" because of its bottle shape. This was the biggest of all the pursuits. The rugged fighter weighed 17,500 pounds, was powered by a 2,300-horsepower engine, had a massive four-bladed prop, a wide landing gear, and a wingspan of more than forty feet.

The young woman from Alabama strapped herself in, ran her cockpit check, taxied the airplane out, called the tower for permission to take off, gunned it, and put it in the air with ease. As she did her climb out over the desert, she reveled in the whole exhilarating experience. This was what she had come to do. This was where she wanted to be!

Flying the P-47, she learned the flare landing, which she loved to describe to attentive listeners. "You're in this big heavy P-47. You're coming in and you're aiming at the end of the runway. As I'm coming in on my final approach I've got the nose right on there. The gear's down, the flaps are down. I'm holding a certain power and I'm holding my attitude and my nose is pointed right at the end of the runway and I'm doing 120 miles an hour. As you come over the fence here's what you do. You slowly close the throttle. And as you do, you slowly start raising the nose to come from level to a landing attitude. If you work it right and you plan ahead, as you come over the end of the runway you will sit down three point—the two main wheels and the tail wheel—and roll out."

Two magic words: "plan ahead." Nancy Batson lived her life by those two words. No wonder she made such a good pursuit pilot. It was ingrained in her nature.

In the next seventeen days, Nancy moved from the cockpit of the Republic P-47 Thunderbolt into the Curtiss P-40, known as the Warhawk and made famous by Claire Chennault's Flying Tigers in China early in the war; from there to the P-39, known as the Airacobra and built by Bell; to the Lockheed Lightning P-38 (the one twin-engine pursuit a few of the women learned to fly); and finally to the North American Mustang P-51.

But even with the serious business of learning to fly pursuit at hand, Nancy and her friends took full advantage of being in one of the country's most glamorous vacation spots. "I had never been to Palm Springs. By day I was flying pursuits and by night I was living the big high life, seeing movie stars. I got the biggest kick out of it.

"I dated one of my instructors—the one who checked me out on the flare landing in the AT-6. And there were some fellas there from Alabama. I dated them as well. We were in class with the men all day and then we'd go out dancing with them at the nightclubs in town that night. We got all dressed up in our uniforms to go out on the town. The stars looked like diamonds in that high, clear, black-velvet sky. The mountain was snow-capped and the sun shown on it from the east and it kept changing colors. Palm Springs was a beautiful place in December.

"Henry and Clare Boothe Luce were in Los Angeles for the holidays and they came out to the base to see what was going on. She came out on the field to watch us women pilots flying. I wanted to meet her. Somebody took me to her table that night at dinner and introduced me. She didn't gush over me, but I got to meet her.

"Then there was a big New Year's Eve celebration. They had taxied this P-38 out in front of the Officers' Club and had lights shining on it. And I knew I was going to get to check out in one. What an experience for a little girl from the South!"

The women pilots also weren't above high jinks to relieve the intense pressure they were under.

"One day at lunch, Little Mac and I were talking about how short we could land the P-47. It was a wonderful airplane, so easy to fly with that wide landing gear and all that power. Now mind you, we were experienced pilots. By that time we had been ferrying planes for the Army for more than a year. But occasionally, we had to have a little fun.

"Palm Springs had this one runway where, if you did everything just right, you could take the first turnoff to the taxiway.

"When you're landing a pursuit, you're doing 120 miles per hour and making a continuous descending turn to the left. The reason is, if the engine quits at that point, you have the runway made. You've planned ahead. As you come over the fence at the end of the runway, you can't see anything to the front because of that big engine, but peripherally you can see the white stripes on both sides and you know you've made it.

"You ease the stick back all the way into your stomach, close the throttle, and go to the flare landing. You set right down on the end of the runway. Then, if you put on just a bit of brake—mind you, we didn't use the brakes much, just a touch, 'cause too much and the tail would come up—you can make that first turnoff.

"Well, of course Mac and I wanted to see if we were good enough to do this. We set up a running contest between the two of us. We were getting a big kick out of trying to best each other landing as far back on the runway as possible and making that first turnoff.

"One day at lunch, some young guys at the next table overheard us talking about our little game and, not to be outdone by a couple of women, they decided to try it too. Well, those fellas didn't have the experience we women pilots did and one of 'em landed short, didn't make the runway. He hit the sand and the airplane flipped over on its back.

"Now, he wasn't hurt, but right after that, the order came down. 'No more short turnoffs.'

"Nobody ever said anything to us. Everything we did at the airfield was right out there in front of God and everybody. Our instructors were watching and so was the tower, we had no secrets, but after that incident, that order put an end to our fun.

"We were devils! But Little Mac and I didn't try it again—at least at Palm Springs."[4]

Nancy graduated January 10, 1944, with a Class IV-P rating.

The Class IV on her card meant she was now qualified to fly all twin-engine aircraft including high-performance airplanes like the P-38 and A-20 (DB-7). The *P* designation meant she was qualified to fly the single-engine, high-performance pursuits—P-39, P-40, P-47, and P-51.[5]

Pursuit school provided the affirmation Nancy sought. She had proved, beyond a doubt, that she belonged in this elite group of flyers—pursuit ferry pilots. She had made it!

Nancy, Little Mac, and Gert joined the rotation of Wilmington-based pilots up to the Republic factory in Farmingdale, New York, where the P-47s were built. As the pursuit-trained pilots came back from school in Palm Springs and later Brownsville, Texas, squadron leader Betty Gillies added them to the list. At first, only a few went, but as the contingent of pursuit ferry pilots grew, she could send eight at a time for two weeks of TDY (temporary duty).

To increase their efficiency, Betty had Gertrude, Teresa, and Nancy Batson checked out on the C-60 transport. They traded off flying the P-47 pilots back from Newark to the field at Republic. This way, each of the women could ferry four, maybe five airplanes per day, weather permitting.

"Betty Gillies was riding in the back of the C-60 one day when I was in the left seat. I've forgotten whether Gert or Teresa was copilot. We were flying out of Newark back to Farmingdale. All the other P-47 pilots were in the back as well. Well, I had to land in a crosswind and though I tried to hold it,

I still bounced the landing. 'God damn!' I hollered. Well, the cockpit door was open and everybody in the back heard me.

"Then I heard them all laughing up a storm over my bad landing and my bad language.

"Everybody else got out of the plane and then Betty came up to the cockpit. She looked at me—very serious—and said, 'Batson, I want to talk to you about crosswind landings. You've got to hold it straight with the rudder and get the wing into the wind and hold it there.'

"'Yes ma'am,' I said. I never bounced a crosswind landing again."

Gradually the women ferry pilots took over, allowing the men to be assigned elsewhere. On June 8, 1944, ferrying P-47s the fifty miles as the crow flies from the Republic factory on Long Island to the docks at Newark became an all-woman operation.

The life of a World War II ferry pilot could be considered close kin to that of a vagabond. They did not know from day to day where they would be sent next. One of Nancy's best friends, fellow Wilmington WAFS Teresa James, has been immortalized in several books and articles because of her famous four-week ferrying trip during which time she never got back to her home base. When she left the Republic factory on Long Island in her P-47 that first morning, she didn't even take her jacket. It was warm and, after all, she was only going to the modification plant in Evansville, Indiana. They promised her a P-47 back to Farmingdale. She'd be back before dark. Wrong!

Instead of a P-47 to Farmingdale, she got a P-47 bound for Long Beach and, from there, a P-51 bound for Fort Myers, Florida. That was only the beginning. Between long stretches of bad weather in Texas and the apparently urgent need to move one airplane after another, she was gone from base for four weeks. She covered eleven thousand miles and seventeen states in seven airplanes. Though her flight—or plight—seems to be the record-holder, others had similar if not as dramatic experiences.

Ferry pilots—male and female alike—lived a life of uncertainty. There was no such thing as a schedule. They flew when an airplane needed to be flown—somewhere. They got back to base when they could by whatever available conveyance. If they could, the ferry pilots ate in the Officers' Club on whatever base they had flown into. But he or she had to wear a uniform jacket, something Teresa didn't happen to have with her on her record-setting trip.

Usually, by the time the ferry pilots arrived back at base from deliveries, the mess hall was closed. Then, they had to be content with sandwiches and donuts in the canteens set up by the Red Cross at the various bases. Ferry pilots were always hungry.

"The good gray ladies of the Red Cross never failed us," Delphine Bohn wrote after the war. "With their soup, sandwiches, cookies, Cokes, coffee, milk, and millions of carrot sticks, they were our saviors."

Sometimes the women ferry pilots spent the night in the nurses' quarters—if there were nurses' quarters on that particular base—or in the WAC's (Women's Army Corps) barracks. They might end up being sent into town to a hotel when they RONed. Sometimes the hotels were nice, but not always. Betty Gillies recalled sleeping on the couch in the lobby of a hotel that had no rooms available and being awakened in the morning to the sound of a vacuum cleaner being pushed nearby by housekeeping. WASP Ann Hamilton recalled sleeping on her parachute bag under the wing of an airplane when a group of them got stranded overnight at a desert base in California. One WASP spent the night in a whorehouse when no other lodging could be found for her.

Ferry pilots—male and female—who flew pursuit were alone in a seventy-thousand-dollar (1940s' dollars) piece of Army equipment, for which they were totally responsible while flying it three miles high in the sky, from coast to coast, with two mid-continent stops for fuel. Yes, they wore specially fitted oxygen masks. Yes, they had prescribed routes. They had to watch for the weather reports on each and choose the optimum way to get where they needed to go.

They did this as casually as we, today, point our GPS-equipped SUVs west—or east, or north, or south—on a four-lane interstate highway. The ferry pilots had their trusty charts and they had their eyes and their compasses. But there are no highways in the sky and no mileage markers or directional signs. However, they only flew daylight hours—sunrise to sunset, a Ferrying Division rule.

A ferry pilot was self-contained and her own boss while in the air and making decisions that would result in the safe delivery of the airplane as well as the preservation and safe delivery of her own hide. Every night she had to check in with her home base. Notify the operations officer where she planned to RON. Nightly, the map in each Ferrying Group office had pins stuck in it representing pilots housed in sleeping quarters from the west to east coast and from north of the Canadian border to the Mexican border.

What they had was freedom—freedom like most women had never known before. Famed 1930s record-setting aviatrix Louise Thaden, who, born in

1905, was two years too old to join the WAFS in 1942, wrote: "Perhaps flying is the only real freedom we are privileged to possess."[6]

When Nancy Batson climbed into a pursuit aircraft, taxied it out, charged down the runway, and pulled the wheels up seconds after lifting off, she was on her own—for thousand-mile stretches of thin air above the varying terrain of the American continental landscape. As easily as a young woman her age back in Birmingham would hop in her automobile and drive to the corner drugstore, Nancy hopped in her airplane and flew across the country from one coast to another. And while she had possession of that airplane, she was completely responsible for it and what happened to it.

"I loved it," she exclaimed. "It was my life! I could get in anything and fly it anywhere. I was trained and had the experience. I was the right age, at the right time, at the right place."

Life and World War II had brought Nancy Batson to the pinnacle of her existence.

"I was in the Alert Room at the Republic factory in Farmingdale, waiting to take a P-47 over to Newark, when Helen Mary Clark told me Evelyn Sharp had been killed. I was stunned. Evelyn was such a good pilot. Of course, we later learned what happened.

"Helen Mary said, 'you have orders from Nancy Love to return to Wilmington, immediately. Then you are to go to Harrisburg [Pennsylvania] to pick up Evelyn's body from the undertaker and accompany her home on the train to Ord, Nebraska.'"

That was April 3, 1944. Fifty-six years later, Nancy Batson Crews remembered the events like they had happened yesterday. "Nancy Love never attended a funeral after Cornelia's. We think she was so broken up over Cornelia [Fort], that she couldn't face another one. She sent Florene [Miller] home with Dorothy Scott. And she sent me with Evelyn.

"I hadn't seen Evelyn since she and I roomed together on a trip to Hagerstown to pick up PT-26s. That was early in February of 1943, and we were on our way to Toronto. I remember it was late and I was sleepy, but Evelyn wanted to talk. She told me that she had recently learned that the woman she had always known as Aunt Elsie was, in fact, her real mother. Right after that trip, Evelyn left for Long Beach and I never saw her again."

Dressed in a Santiago blue WASP uniform—the new uniforms, by then, had been issued to the original WAFS as well as to the Texas graduates— Nancy left Wilmington with two hundred dollars collected from the WASP who were members of the 2nd Ferrying Group. "My instructions were to give it to Evelyn's parents when I arrived in Ord. I also had with me the letters that Evelyn had been carrying, unanswered, in her purse.

"That was a long, lonely train ride," Nancy remembered. "Oh, it was crowded all right. Lots of people around. Trains and planes were jammed during the war. But all I could think of was Evelyn lying in that wooden casket in the baggage car."

Nancy Batson never thought she'd live out the war. After her brother died in the crash during Army cadet training in Houston, she was convinced she would go the same way. Unlike fellow Southerner Cornelia Fort, who constantly wrote letters to friends and family members, Nancy didn't write a single letter during her twenty-seven months in service. She preferred to drop in while on her way through Birmingham on a ferrying trip. And she did that frequently—often to show off the latest hot airplane she had checked out in.

"I wasn't scared. I loved doing what I was doing. But a lot better pilots than me were getting killed. So, I didn't take things too seriously. Didn't answer my mail. I didn't think I'd live out the war." Nancy had no sense of her own future beyond the war. If her number came up, it came up—just as Evelyn Sharp's number had come up on April 3, 1944.

Nancy shed no tears during the train trip west. All she could think of was the waste of a good friend, a good pilot, a young woman who should have had a bright future ahead of her.

Ord and the surrounding communities turned out en masse for Evelyn. The Eastern Star, of which Evelyn's mother, Mary, was a member, officiated at the funeral at the Ord Methodist Church—the church in which Evelyn had grown up. The American Legion conducted the graveside service. Flight students of Jack Jeffords, the man who taught her to fly, served as pallbearers.

One man asked Nancy Batson if he could drape Evelyn's casket with an American flag.

The WASP, of course, had not been militarized. As Nancy stood there beside her friend's casket, that heated debate was raging in Congress. Brave young women like Evelyn and Nancy had become a political football. The WASP carried no insurance, had no government benefits, no burial subsidy, and certainly were not in line for official military honors even when they died serving their country. That had become painfully clear with Cornelia's and Dorothy's deaths and with the deaths of several WASP student trainees in Texas as well as others on active duty. The classmates at Avenger Field or the women in the various ferrying squadrons or other duty posts kicked in the money to send their friends home in coffins.

But this thoughtful, grieving man wanted to put the American flag on her friend's coffin. Nancy could think of nothing more appropriate.

"Of course you can," she said, in her warm Southern voice.

Hundreds came to pay final tribute that Easter Sunday morning, April 9, 1944. The love of the citizens of Ord for Evelyn was painfully obvious to Nancy. "I saw it in their red-rimmed eyes and heard it in their voices. So much grief! But when they saw me, a young woman like Evelyn in uniform, they straightened their backs, held their heads a little higher, and offered their hands with a grip that showed respect, pride, and gratitude."[7]

Evelyn took off at 10:29 that fateful morning, April 3, 1944. She had to have known, immediately, that she didn't have full power. The grounds crew saw the black smoke pouring from the left engine. They watched as the pilot and the airplane tried to fly. If she turned right into the good engine, she would be headed over Harrisburg and a potentially deadly, destructive crash in a populated area. Straight ahead was Beacon Hill, 150 feet higher than the airport. To the left, but uphill, were only a few farmhouses.

Evelyn obviously made a split-second decision. Even though the rule when flying a twin-engine airplane is never to turn into a dead engine, she began a shallow, climbing bank to the left—as seen clearly by the men on the ground.

"Keeping the towers on top of Beacon Hill in her view, she pushed the right throttle forward and eased up a bit on the right rudder. The crippled P-38 yawed, and skidded to the left. Watchmen on duty at the Radio Range Station watched her plane go by, barely missing the tops of the 150-foot towers," the *Harrisburg Telegraph* reported on April 4, 1944. The P-38 stalled, hung for a moment in the air, caught a cluster of trees with the left wing tip, and hit the ground in a flat position. It skidded broadside about ten feet. When it stopped, the Plexiglas canopy lay upside down a few feet ahead of the right prop. The clock on the instrument panel had stopped at 10:30.[8]

"Years later, Betty Gillies told me that she also lost an engine in a P-38, in the very same place as Evelyn," Nancy said. "But the wind was blowing the other way, so she was taking off on the opposite runway. Going that direction, the ground sloped downwards and she flew out over the river. She was able to get her plane up enough to go around, come back, and land safely.

"Nancy Love was waiting for me at BOQ 14 in Wilmington when I got back from the funeral. 'How did it go?' was all she said, and I told her."

Both Nancys did their crying in private.[9]

A generation gave its youth to The War. Many also gave their lives. Lost were many of the best and the brightest—young women like Evelyn and Dorothy and Cornelia, and countless young men. But those who survived had a gift they could give to the postwar world. In giving their youth—the years 1939 to 1945 elsewhere, 1942 to 1945 in America—they had defeated the untenable philosophies of Nazism, Fascism, and Japanese Imperialism and hopefully given the world back its reason. Surely that generation's yet-to-be-born children would be the beneficiaries. Nancy Batson was one of those whose mettle was tested by the fire of war, shaped by the march to victory, and who lived to make of her life and her gifts what she would.

7

The Question of Militarization

Militarizing the women pilots had been the plan from the beginning. The question was, how? And why militarize the women pilots? Because military status would give them military insurance, death benefits, hospitalization, and pensions. And continuity of their service would be ensured.

Nancy Batson didn't care one way or the other. As long as she could continue to fly those military airplanes, she was happy.

On September 30, 1943, Congressman John Costello of California introduced a bill in Congress calling for the militarization of the WASP. The bill went to the House Committee on Military Affairs for study. Subsequently it was amended to include the appointment of female trainees at Avenger Field in Sweetwater, Texas, as aviation cadets and was reintroduced on February 17, 1944.[1]

General Arnold had overestimated the number of pilots he was going to need, which had been based on earlier British RAF losses. Surprisingly, pilot casualties on the battlefronts had been far fewer than anticipated. On January 15, 1944, the Civil Aeronautics Authority terminated its War Training Service program for training flying personnel and the Army Air Forces (AAF) began to cut back on its own pilot training program.[2]

Now, rather than a dearth of male pilots, there was a surplus. A year earlier, as Nancy Batson and her fellow WAFS were just beginning to stretch their wings and ferry airplanes—albeit single-engine trainers—the demand for more pilots was loud and insistent. The women were needed. Now, as a result of the cutbacks in pilot training, the WASP became increasingly aware that, suddenly, their presence was not looked on as the saving grace it had been.

Paraphrased, what the Costello Bill said was: "For the duration of the war, women would be commissioned as flight officers or aviation students in accordance with existing regulations. No woman would be appointed to a grade above colonel and there would be no more than one officer of that grade. Female flight cadets, upon successful completion of the prescribed course of training, would be commissioned as second lieutenants in the Army of the United States. All commissioned women would receive the same pay and allowances as male members of the Army and they would be entitled to the same rights, privileges, and benefits according to their rank, grade, and length of service."[3]

The hearings began in March 1944. When the news of the WASP bill reached the streets through the nation's newspapers, congressmen began to receive angry protests—from civilian flying instructors now out of jobs and threatened with the draft; from the American Legion and other veterans' organizations; and from mothers of boys who had been transferred from aviation cadet training to the infantry. Congress was far more interested in the plight of the male trainees and instructors who at this time were being released by the AAF than it was in a handful of women pilots. The anti-WASP forces made far more noise, and politicians pay attention to the squeaky wheel.[4]

In order to prepare the WASP for the militarization she expected to come about, Jacqueline Cochran had opted for officer training for her girls. Women pilots already on active duty were to attend Officer Training School (OTS) at Orlando, Florida.

The course was four weeks and the women selected had to have been on active duty at least ninety days. A new class would begin every first and third Wednesday of the month, first with twenty-four students and later with fifty students. A total of 460 women pilots graduated from OTS before the school was closed to women in the fall of 1944.

The first class reported April 19, 1944. It was made up of squadron leaders and the women pilots who had been on duty the longest and included many of the original WAFS—Nancy Love, Betty Gillies, Barbara Donahue, Del Scharr, B. J. Erickson, Delphine Bohn, Florene Miller, Bernice Batten, and Nancy Batson. Evelyn Sharp had been destined to attend as well.

"We attended class six days a week. We studied military discipline, courtesy, and customs, and we also learned about the organization of the army and staff procedures. Like they said, we were learning how to be officers. A fun part was memorizing aircraft silhouettes. Every kid in America was doing the same thing by then. And we had to practice air–sea rescue and jungle survival, which meant catching, cooking, and eating a whole bunch of creepy crawly things.

"It was the first time some of us original WAFS had been together in more

Fourteen members of the first Officer Training School class, Orlando, Florida, April 1944. Delphine Bohn, Betty Gillies, and Nancy are in the front. Nancy Love is directly behind Gillies. Photo courtesy the Crews family.

than a year. I had hardly seen B.J. or Florene since they left for their new assignments back in the winter of 1943."

The timing couldn't have been worse, public relations–wise. The Congressional hearings were on, debating the WASP's fate—would they be militarized—and the press was having a field day at the WASP's expense, criticizing them at every opportunity. And here were the women being treated to a four-week training session to make them officers when their militarization was in question. To add to that, this was when the Ferrying Division desperately needed every pursuit ferry pilot it could lay its hands on and could ill afford the loss of several of them for four weeks. Though it wasn't publicly known then, D-Day was just over a month away.

Nancy Love and her women pilots had several visitors in Orlando—columnists from east-coast newspapers among them. Jacqueline Cochran herself flew in to greet the first class and invited Nancy Love, Betty Gillies, Delphine Bohn, and others to dinner. Another to call on the first attendees was the chairman of the House Civil Service Committee, Representative Robert Ramspeck, who also extended an invitation to dinner.

Congressional debate on militarization continued and the press coverage, most of it against the WASP but some decidedly in their favor, continued to churn.

"The day we graduated, Nancy Love took B. J. Erickson, Barbara Donahue, and me aside and told us there were three combat-weary DB-7s there in Orlando that needed to be delivered to the West Coast. Would we three like to ferry them? You know what the answer was. I was thrilled! A big twin-engine, single-seat attack bomber!

"That afternoon, Nancy drove the three of us out to the base. It was warm, and on the way out I fell asleep in the car. I think that impressed Nancy because I wasn't nervous. She gave us each a cockpit check and we took off and went upstairs to fly around and practice. Well, I was right at home. By that time I had had a lot of twin-engine time and of course I had already checked out in the P-38. Anyway, I loved it! I think I was the last one to come in. And there was Nancy waiting for us with a big smile on her face.

"The next morning, right after sunup, we took off for California. I can't tell you how good it felt. Biggest thing I had ever flown."

The three wrote and mailed a group postcard to Nancy Love from every fuel stop. They had to RON one night en route, but delivered their aircraft to Salinas, California, the following day. "B.J., the squadron commander at Long Beach, saw how much I liked flying that ol' shot-up DB-7 and gave me a brand-new A-20—same type airplane—to take back east to Savannah.

"En route, I landed that A-20 in Meridian, Mississippi, stepped on the brakes and, *whomp*, they caught and pulled to the left. I tried again, same thing. By the time I got that thing stopped, I had burned out the brakes. Well, I started looking for help. In the chow line, I ran into Joe Shannon, an old friend from Birmingham. I asked him if he could help me get the brakes fixed on that A-20.

"Joe said he was acting maintenance officer and he'd sure see what he could do. He called the superintendent on the line and told him, 'This young lady is an old friend of mine from Birmingham and she wants to know if we can help her get her airplane fixed.'

"Do you know what that guy said to him?" Nancy said in her best Southern accent, her gray eyes twinkling. "'How long do you want to keep her here?'"

Joe, according to Nancy, very patiently explained to the man how it really was. Besides, Joe was due to leave for overseas on a transport later in the day. More than fifty years later, the two still entertained their friends with that story at aviation gatherings in Birmingham.

Nancy's description of her favorite airplane was almost poetic. "The A-20 was such a powerful, wonderful machine. I loved it. Twin engine. Single cockpit. It was like the wings came right out from my shoulders. It was mine, all mine. I was alone in it and it felt like a flying Cadillac. See, I get the feel of an airplane. My god, it was something. I knew that I could have gone to war in the A-20. When I flew that A-20, that was the first time I realized that I could have been a fighter pilot and strafed railroads and dropped bombs.

"To this day, I think Nancy Love was saying to me, 'you've done a good job.' Choosing the three of us to deliver those airplanes was special. That was her way of patting us on the back and saying thanks for all your hard work and dedication. Nancy Love didn't say things like that to you in person. She expected you to do your job—the job we were hired to do, fly airplanes—and to do it right, no questions asked. She was a wonderful person to work and fly for."[5]

On June 5, 1944, the day before D-Day, the Ramspeck committee presented its report to Congress. The WASP program was "unnecessary and unjustifiably expensive" was the verdict. The committee was opposed to militarization and recommended "the recruiting of inexperienced women and their training as pilots be terminated immediately."

On June 21, fifteen days after the Allies landed in Normandy and began the push that would end the war in Europe eleven months later, Congress voted down the WASP bill. Militarization was denied.[6]

That did not mean, however, that the WASP were out of a job. Not yet anyway.

8

The Best and Worst of Times

Nancy's memories of the assignments in Farmingdale throughout 1944 are her fondest from the WASP years. The small contingent that went up there each month was like family. Between July 24 and September 12, 1944, Nancy, Gertrude, Teresa, and Sis Bernheim more often than not were stationed in Farmingdale flying P-47s to Newark daily.

"Sis had this little house on Long Island, not far from Farmingdale. She also had a car—a yellow Buick convertible, she loved Buick convertibles—and she would drive Gertrude, Teresa, and me out to her house and she'd cook dinner for us. It was a chance to get away from spartan hotel living at the Huntington.

"She had this cute little bar with an airplane theme. I was so impressed that someone had a bar right there in their house. Sis loved her rye whiskey, which she drank with Coke. I had never had rye whiskey before, but I tried it. Sis was such a good friend with a great sense of humor. We all had such a good time together."

A typical day at Farmingdale meant downtime between flights.

"The bus would pick us up at the Huntington Hotel and take us to the Republic factory. We'd get to the Alert Room at eight in the morning. And then we would wait—wait for them to bring the planes over to us from across the field. After a test pilot had put a few minutes on them, the ground crew would taxi them over to our side of the field. But the waiting was boring. We'd sit around and talk and smoke and read. Some of the gals would write letters. Sometimes I took a nap.

"One time, after lunch, I lay down on the couch and loosened my trouser belt and, wouldn't you know, some colonel came visiting and all the WASP stood up at attention immediately, except for me. I was still waking up and fumbling with my pants and my belt so I could stand up and not lose my

The WASP crew at Farmingdale, ready to ferry P-47s, July 1944. Nancy is on the left. Photo courtesy the Crews family.

pants. After that an order came down that we were to remain fully dressed at all times in the Alert Room.

"Anyway, we were always looking for things to do to relieve the boredom. I loved that song "Tico Tico," so we'd sing that and dance around. I brought in a bat and ball and we organized a game and played ball outside.

"But when the planes arrived, we were all business. We'd get our orders, climb in our plane, and take off, one right after the other, headed for Newark. We'd call the tower and get permission to take off. Then we'd fly west, cross north of New York City, turn left at the Hudson River and head south toward Newark. Then we'd call the Newark Airport and ask for permission to land.

"We parked 'em, sold 'em—that's what we called it when we turned the paperwork over to Operations—then we headed for the C-60 that had followed us over and was to take us back to Farmingdale so we could bring another batch of planes over. Before Betty had Gert, Teresa, and me checked out in the C-60, one of the men would fly it over, pick us up in Newark, and fly us back. On a good day, without weather or haze, each of us could bring four or five planes over. We called it the 'gear-up, gear-down' run. Thirty minutes in the air.

"What happened to the planes after we delivered them? They removed the wings and pickled them to withstand the salt spray from the ocean. Then they loaded them on ships and sent them to Europe. Sometimes I'd be assigned to take a P-47 to Long Beach and then they'd give me a P-51 to bring back to Newark."

Nancy climbing into a P-47, August 1944. Photo courtesy the International Women's Air and Space Museum (IWASM), Cleveland, Ohio, the Teresa James Collection.

Rumors of possible deactivation of the WASP began to build in August 1944. Jackie Cochran had issued a report to General Arnold in which she "recommended that consideration be given either to disbandment of the WASPs or to another attempt at militarization. General Arnold made her report public in a War Department press release. The suggestion was heralded in the newspapers as an 'ultimatum' on the WASP question."[1]

Allied troops retook Paris on August 24, 1944, setting off a celebration on both sides of the Atlantic. The march to victory was on.

The assignment that Nancy disliked the most was that of squadron leader. In September 1944, Betty Gillies placed her in charge of the newly established sixteen-woman squadron at Republic's P-47 modification center in Evansville, Indiana. In doing so, Betty and commander Nancy Love were showing their faith in young Batson's abilities and recognizing her leadership potential, two things of which she was most proud. But during the war, Nancy was interested in one thing—flying airplanes. She considered everything else an impingement on her potential time in the air.[2]

"Sixteen members of the Women Airforce Service Pilots arrived at the Evansville Air Transport Command headquarters this week to expedite Thunderbolts from the ATC [Air Transport Command] to ports of embarkation," said the September 15, 1944, story in the *Republic Aviation News* (Indiana Division).

The women were the first contingent to arrive in Evansville for this temporary duty. Most of them, including Nancy, came from the 2nd Ferrying Group in Wilmington, Delaware, but a few came from the 3rd Ferrying Group in Romulus, Michigan. This group was to stay four weeks and rotate back to their respective home bases, to be replaced by sixteen more women ferry pilots. A total of eighty-five WASP were scheduled to take part in the program. Original WAFS Helen McGilvery and Sis Bernheim accompanied Nancy to Evansville.[3]

"Nancy Love rented this little house there in town and put Army bunks in it, upstairs and downstairs. That was our BOQ," Nancy said. "I couldn't stand it! I tried, but I had to stay there on the ground and do paperwork while the other girls got to fly every day! All I wanted to do was fly those airplanes. Then Helen Mary flew a P-47 in and I broke down in tears in front of her. She went back to Wilmington and told Betty Gillies how unhappy I was.

"Betty didn't like that. In her eyes, I was not holding up my end of the bargain. But I hated it! I asked for a transfer and, finally, Betty gave it to me. But she was mad at me for awhile. My punishment was having to fly a bunch of war-weary airplanes, the shot-up ones coming back from overseas. The WASP ferried a lot of those the last months of 1944.

"I got my share of war wearies to take to the boneyard. We all did. Other than the pursuits, that was what the Army needed ferried the latter half of 1944. Sometimes you wondered if it was really worth risking life and limb to move some of those planes to a graveyard. Some of them were real scary to fly, all sorts of things wrong with them. One dog of a P-38 I flew had parts falling off of it.

"One day six of us from Wilmington—Jill McCormick [WASP Class 43-5] was one of 'em—went over to Baltimore to pick up these worn-out trainers. We were to take those planes up to Reading, Pennsylvania, to the boneyard.

"I was the flight leader so I took off first—right out over the water—and the others were supposed to follow me. We were going to circle until everybody got off and then fly up there in loose formation. Well, I take off and I'm looking behind me, counting 'one . . . two . . . three . . . four.' Then, out of the corner of my eye, here comes a boat tearing along the shore. I looked down and there sits Jill McCormick, perched on the wing of her airplane and the airplane is sitting in the water off the runway. Her engine quit on takeoff and she couldn't get it stopped in time. She went right off the end of the runway into the water.

"Well, I kept on flyin'. The rest of us went on to Reading.

"And it turns out my compass didn't work. Amazing what you can do when you look at the ground and watch the section lines. I had my good ol' trusty chart. I set up a course and flew by the seat of my pants and I found it. I was pretty damn good navigating cross-country like that when I had to.[4]

"Finally, I got back to Farmingdale, and when I did, I flew the C-60 a lot."

On October 2, General Arnold announced the total casualties suffered by the Army Air Forces (AAF) since the outbreak of the war. They were far fewer than the numbers for which the Army had planned. General Arnold was able to state, positively, that the AAF now had sufficient pilots for present combat needs. The following day, he announced that the WASP would be disbanded on December 20, 1944.[5]

In retrospect, his move was not as cold hearted as it sounds. He had a war to win and the situation abroad was changing rapidly. The Army historians who pieced together the history titled *Women Pilots with the AAF, 1941–1944* reached the following conclusion: "To a casual observer, unacquainted with the course of military events during the summer of 1944, the AAF would appear to have made an about-face on the WASP question. In June, General Arnold was pleading for the induction of women pilots into the Army as a military necessity. In October, he was stating that unless the program was deactivated these pilots would be keeping men out of the air. The explanation for this rapid change in view apparently lies in the phenomenal military successes of the intervening months and in an AAF attrition rate much lower than had been expected."[6]

In his letter to each of the WASP, which accompanied a letter from Jacqueline Cochran, Arnold told the women how proud he was of them and explained his decision to shut down the program. And he added: "The situation is that if you continue in service, you will be replacing instead of releasing our young men. I know that the WASP wouldn't want that."

The letters notifying them of deactivation were delivered on October 8 to all active WASP—those with the Training Command and those on duty with the ATC's Ferrying Groups. No one was exempt. The approximately 125 women ferry pilots now serving the Ferrying Division so well and with

Nancy climbing into a P-38, November 1944. Photo courtesy the Crews family.

such dedication—ferrying two-thirds of all pursuit aircraft manufactured in the United States and so desperately needed to keep those aircraft moving to embarkation points for overseas—were being released as well.[7]

The WASP were stunned. They didn't agree with that final sentence in Arnold's letter. They thought they had earned the right to stay on active duty.

Between October 8 and December 20, the WASP on active duty put their hearts and souls into their jobs. The ferry pilots in particular could not believe they were being released when they were still needed. The men they were ostensibly keeping out of the air would have to be retrained—at taxpayers' expense—to ferry those hot, temperamental pursuits. But the inevitable was at hand.

It was during this time (November 1944) that Nancy made her now famous flight in the P-38 with the balky nosewheel.

The day the WASP were released—December 20—B. J. Erickson observed sixty-three P-51s sitting on the runway in Long Beach that would not be delivered that day because the women who could have performed that task had been sent home.

As the final day drew near, farewell parties were planned at the ferrying bases and many of the other bases where WASP were stationed.

Seven of Nancy Love's original twenty-eight were still actively flying out of Wilmington. These seven plus Nancy Love herself were joined by the rest of the 2nd Ferrying Group's women's squadron the evening of December 19 at the New Castle Army Air Base (NCAAB) Officers' Club for "The Last Supper." Smartly dressed in their blue WASP uniform jackets, skirts, and wings, the eight sat at the head table with Betty Gillies, squadron commander, and Nancy Love in the center. To Nancy's right were Nancy Batson, Helen McGilvery, and Gertrude Meserve Tubbs (Gertrude had married fellow pilot Charlie Tubbs in the spring). To Betty's left were her assistant squadron leader, Helen Mary Clark, Teresa James, and Sis Bernheim.

Nancy Batson always felt that Nancy Love purposely placed her on her right hand. She took it as further proof of her commanding officer's approval of the job she had done.

The rest of the squadron, thirty graduates of Houston or Sweetwater, sat at tables down each side of the head table, making a horseshoe. The menu was chicken à la king, sweet potato croquets, fresh fruit, chocolate éclairs, and rare French wine to help with the toasts, which were sometimes long and often teary. Nancy Love had come from Ferrying Division Headquarters in Cincinnati to join them. She was there to enjoy herself and share the pleasure of being back with friends. They all smoked, drank, laughed, and reminisced.[8]

Finally, the thirty-eight weary WASP—including the eight original WAFS—found the exhaustion of emotion too much, said goodnight for the last time, and went back to BOQ 14 to finish packing.

Not long after that, a male voice outside shouted, "Fire!"

Out they went, some clad in bathrobes, others in coats, into the cold December night. The women joined the crowd of male officers outside the Officers' Club that had been their haven for twenty-seven months and where they had just eaten their last dinner as active-duty ferry pilots.

Nancy Batson watched the building go down in flames. She wondered if she was watching her future burn with it. For the first time she could think beyond today and beyond tomorrow's flight and that was a strange, quite foreign feeling. Her passion—her need to fly those hot airplanes—would have to be channeled elsewhere. For a brief moment she was very, very tired. She knew she needed to readjust her life's goals. Not start over, but start fresh. Tomorrow she would go to her sister's in Baltimore, where the family was gathering for Christmas.

A modern-day Scarlett O'Hara, a heroine of a different war and a different time in history, Nancy would think about her future later—when she got home to Alabama.

"Let it burn!" she hollered, and added a Rebel yell. "Let it burn!"

9

Beyond the War

Life Goes On

Nancy Batson and Paul Crews may have known they were destined for each other when the war separated them for four years, but Nancy had no romantic strings attached to her while she was in the WAFS. As one who enjoyed the company of men, she dated throughout her service career and enjoyed the mixed-company social life that went with being stationed at a large Army Air Forces base and moving around the country as a ferry pilot. However, there was someone special for awhile. She met Charlie Miller in 1944 when he was stationed with the Air Transport Command in Wilmington.

"I liked Charlie a lot—he used to call me 'Baby Doll'—but he wanted to get serious. I was serious about flying airplanes and Charlie was getting serious about me. And he was a Catholic."

The Catholicism bothered Nancy. That the Protestant South was ingrained in her was not surprising—certainly not in 1944. When Nancy was growing up in the 1920s and 1930s, the South was still cut off from the rest of the country, insular, immersed in its own way of life and fiercely proud of it. For a young woman raised in that atmosphere—even with a progressive mother and indulgent father—to consider marrying a Catholic was a leap she had trouble reconciling. But Charlie was oh so attractive—and he was quite persistent. He was in love and he was *there*, whereas Paul was in England from 1943 through 1945. Nancy and Charlie saw a lot of each other in the summer and fall of 1944.

"One time I flew a P-51 to Florida and he was ferrying a B-26. We flew along together, then I dropped off my P-51 and flew on with him to Miami where the B-26 was going. We RONed—separate hotel rooms. Everything was on the up-and-up. No hanky-panky. Charlie was very moral. [Nancy neglects to say it, but so was she.] The next day we went to the horse races and then we took an airliner back to base.

"He came over to Aberdeen, Maryland, one time to pick me up after I delivered a beat-up P-38 to the target-practice area there. Charlie knew the guys in the Aberdeen control tower and told them to call him in Wilmington when I landed, that he'd come over and get me. He also came to see me when I was stationed in Evansville. He knew how unhappy I was there.

"But I wasn't ready to let any man get between me and those airplanes.

"When my mother and sister were at Columbia [University] that summer of 1944, since I was stationed out on Long Island, I used to come up to the city on weekends on the train to stay with them," Nancy remembered. "We went to plays, and to the opera. Charlie had a friend in New York. He knew I was there visiting Muddy and Amy so he came up to New York, too. He got his friend to take Amy out and the four of us double dated and went to some of the New York nightclubs. Then the next day we were going up the Hudson to visit some kinfolks and we took Charlie with us. We also went down to Wall Street and he showed me where his New York Life headquarters were."

Charlie had been an insurance salesman in his civilian days.

"Our mother really liked Charlie," Amy recalled. "The fact that he was Catholic didn't bother her. But it bothered Nancy. Muddy thought Nancy was crazy."[1]

"I think the family was very happy with Charlie," said Nancy's niece Liz Simpson. "From what I've heard, everybody loved Charlie. He was gregarious and fun and seemed the perfect match for Aunt Nancy. There was something charismatic in their two strong personalities. Of all the men she dated during her wartime service, his name was the only one ever mentioned."[2]

When Nancy and Charlie both were in Wilmington, they occasionally would sneak off in the afternoons and go to the horse races in nearby Dover. But their relationship was a companionable one, though Charlie obviously considered Nancy wife material and would have liked for it to have gone further.

"Charlie had looked around. He told me he always went with nice girls. He was pretty high minded, but a lot of fun. We were good friends. One night we pulled into the parking lot by the BOQ and there were other cars around. I don't remember the exact words, but Charlie told me he'd like to be more, you know, amorous. I said no, and then I said, 'I've got to go in,' and got out of the car."

Some of the other women ferry pilots and their dates were in those other cars and they overheard the exchange. "When I opened the door and got out, they laughed. They thought it was funny. And they went and told on me. You see, it goes around who is saying what and doing what."[3]

Late in the fall of 1944, fate stepped in and put a halt to their budding relationship. Charlie was assigned to the China Burma India (CBI) theater of war. He was being sent to fly supplies over "The Hump," the legendary five-hundred-mile corridor from the Army bases in eastern India over the Himalayas and the jungles of Burma to Kunming, China. Nancy faced the impending WASP deactivation on December 20. So the romance was put on hold—like so many wartime encounters.

Tragically, any future Nancy and Charlie might have had together— whatever plans or commitments they made, if any—died with him January 19, 1945.

First Lieutenant Charles Preston Miller was killed in the crash of his four-engine C-54 transport in China. A yellowed copy of the article that appeared in the newspaper on Saturday, January 27, 1945, was in Nancy's wartime papers and personal effects when she died. A picture of Charlie, hatless, handsome, and wearing his fleece-lined leather flight jacket, accompanied the article, which said that Charlie was twenty-nine, a graduate of Catholic High School in Memphis and a 1938 graduate of Spring Hill College in Alabama. He left his job at New York Life in July 1941 to enter the service with the Army Medical Corps at Camp Lee, Virginia. He later transferred to the Air Forces and received his commission at George Field in Illinois. His first mission was to fly to Greenland with the famous Norwegian-American flyer Col. Bernt Balchen,[4] where he took part in the Battle of the Arctic.

Charlie was then assigned to fly transport planes between the United States and Africa. By the time he got to India in late 1944, he had flown around most of the globe with the Air Transport Command. His last letter home, written on January 17, 1945, said that he had received the Distinguished Flying Cross and the Air Medal.[5]

Charlie was the son of Mrs. Charles P. Miller and the late Mr. Miller of Yazoo City, Mississippi. Charlie's mother called Nancy, by then back home in Birmingham, to tell her the news. Nancy was devastated.

"I was grief stricken. That was one of the lowest points in my life. My mother said that I should go visit his mother. I had never met her before, but I went. She was a charming Southern lady, but of course she was in shock. She had lost her only son. Her only child! I stayed a couple of days and then came on back home."

Nancy, too, was in a state of shock. Her grandmother had died December 30, 1944. She had lost her brother two years earlier and being home now, knowing she had survived the war and he hadn't, was eating at her. And then to lose Charlie—two years after her brother, almost to the day—added to her separation from the life she had known as a WASP and was almost more than she could bear. For twenty-seven months, she had flown increasingly complex and faster airplanes. She was, of necessity, on alert and ready to go daily. Today, we would say she lived on the edge. Now, she was home and idle and bored. Going out to the airport to fly Cubs didn't interest her. Not much of anything interested her. "It was like being in a black hole."

So spring 1945 and the news of impending victory in Europe found former Army ferry pilot Nancy Batson at loose ends. Life in Birmingham had moved on during the three years she had been gone—dating back to when she left for Miami in May 1942. All the boys had gone to war. The girls were married or had gone to live elsewhere. No one really understood what she had been doing—most didn't care—and she didn't want to explain it anyway. It hurt too much.

"My cousin wanted me to show her how to fly, but my heart wasn't in it. One of the men had bought a PT-19 and I flew it a couple of times, but after the war, things were just different. It was terrible. It was a lot easier going in than coming out—emotionally, psychologically."

No one knows where Nancy and Charlie's relationship stood by the time he left for The Hump and she left the WASP. Admittedly, Nancy was *not* ready to get married as long as she could fly those Army planes. Entanglements with the opposite sex were not the only relationships she avoided. The fatalistic belief that she would die in an airplane crash before the war was over haunted her. Throughout the war she never ceased to live one day at a time, never planned for the future. And that was unlike the old Nancy who always planned ahead. Her refusal to write letters home or to friends was part of her attempt to keep everyone and everything at arm's length. For her, it was self-protection.

Much of Nancy's unhappiness in those early months of 1945 was directly related to Charlie Miller. Whether she had decided to marry him when—if—he came home, no one knows. She never confided in her sister Amy, and if she talked to her mother about her relationship with Charlie, Muddy never told. If Nancy told Elinor, she, too, kept quiet. Knowing Nancy for who she was, it is doubtful that she confided in anyone. Likewise, it is doubtful that Nancy made a commitment to Charlie either way. Nancy kept her emotions in check, under control—as evidenced when she took Evelyn Sharp home to be buried. Ruth Batson never let her emotions show either, and Nancy had learned her mother's lessons well.

What we do know is that Paul Crews *did* come home.

Slowly Nancy began to climb out of the desolation she lived with during the early months of 1945. She spent the balance of that year working with her father in his construction business. "Daddy wanted me to come work in the business with him, so I did, and I enjoyed that. He and I spent a lot of time playing golf together that year. I was just waiting around for the war to be over—or something."

Paul, now a lieutenant colonel, came home in January 1946. He had been stationed in North Africa and then in England with the Inspector General's office. "We both were ready to get married," Nancy said. The wedding—"an intimate affair with just close friends and relatives invited"—took place in the Batson home at 1430 North 30th Street on February 1, 1946, Nancy's twenty-sixth birthday. "Paul said it would be easier to remember that both my birthday and our anniversary were the same day. It was also when he could get leave." Shortly after they were married, Paul was discharged from the Army.

"Daddy wanted Paul to come to work for him at S. R. Batson Construction because his office manager had quit. Paul didn't want to go back to school, so it just worked out. You see, life went on."

Nancy's flying tapered off after she and Paul were married, though she did ferry a couple of airplanes for Helen McGilvery. After the WASP were disbanded, Little Mac moved to Annapolis, Maryland, where she became part owner of a flying service and manager of the Annapolis airport. She was one of the few women airport managers in the country. Much of her time was spent giving flight instruction to young men using their GI Bill benefits to learn to fly. But she also brokered airplanes and she asked Nancy to go to Dallas and pick up a Luscombe for her and ferry it up to Annapolis.

Helen happened to come through Birmingham on May 12, 1947—her thirtieth birthday. "She was on her way to Dallas to ferry another Luscombe back to Maryland and stopped in to see me. My mother baked her a birthday cake and we had a big celebration at my parents' house. That was the last time I saw her."

The afternoon of August 25, 1948, the trainer in which Helen and a student were flying collided with another small airplane. Witness accounts varied. One said Helen's plane burst into flame upon impact. Others said it ignited shortly after it hit the ground. Helen and her student died in the crash,

Wedding day, February 1, 1946: Nancy and Paul with her parents, Radford and Ruth Batson. Photo courtesy the Crews family.

as did the two men in the other plane.[6] Once again, tragedy had struck close to home for Nancy. Little Mac had been one of her closest friends during her WAFS days. Helen was the first of the original WAFS to die after the war.

Nancy and Paul set up housekeeping in a small house on her father's farm in Rocky Ridge outside of Birmingham. Nancy's parents raised beef cattle on that farm and a tenant farmer cared for the land and the animals. Paul Jr., born September 25, 1948, remembers the farm as his first home.

Like the entire generation of World War II veterans, Nancy and Paul Crews settled down and settled in. The war had stolen their youth—those normally carefree early twenties years—and they were tired of fighting. They wanted things to return to normal. And they did for a few years—until

June 25, 1950, when North Korea invaded South Korea and the United Nations authorized aid to South Korea. The United States was off to war again—though it was called a police action.

Paul was in the Reserves and was called back into the new U.S. Air Force. Hap Arnold had made good on his dream—a separate service founded September 17, 1947. "We were so poor—struggling young marrieds—I told Paul he'd have to borrow money from the bank to buy his uniform. They sent us to Warner Robins over in Georgia. I liked it. They had a good Officers' Club and a nice swimming pool and a golf course. It was fun for me. I had this wonderful little boy and we were going to have a second child." Their second son, Radford, named for Nancy's father and her brother, was born October 25, 1951, while they were living in Georgia.

"We made more money than we had as civilians, Paul liked his job and they liked him. Then they sent him to Washington, D.C., to the Inspector General's office and we moved to Kensington, Maryland, which was nice because I could see my older sister in Baltimore."

Paul traveled abroad a good bit with the general in charge and he was promoted to full colonel. They stayed in Washington for four years. "We thought for awhile they might send us to Japan, but that fell through. They sent us to California instead. Would you believe we went to live in Anaheim, near Disneyland? We had this little house on what had been an orange grove with an orange tree in the front and the back yards."

The Crews family lived in the shadow of Disneyland for eight years. Paul Jr. and Radford recall an all-American childhood with a decided Disney flavor. "Anaheim was a nice growing-up period for us," Paul Jr. says. "It was a time when kids could run free in the streets and fly their kites and model airplanes and feel safe. The neighborhood was full of children. We even went to Walt Disney Elementary School. I remember when Walt Disney invited all the students at the school—and their families—to the park for a special day, FREE!

"Surfing was popular for California kids. Our father bought a surfboarding kit and we—mostly he and Radford—worked on it. Then he piled us and our friends in our green Rambler station wagon and took us surfing." Always attuned to activities the whole family could take part in, Paul bought an RV and they took weekend excursions to the beach, the mountains, the desert, wherever their wanderlust led.

A year or so after the move to California, the general for whom Paul worked was hired by Northrop Corporation. The company invited the general to bring his staff with him. Northrop offered Paul the position of di-

Family portrait, summer 1956, with Paul Jr., 8, and Radford, 5. California, here we come! Photo courtesy the Crews family.

rector of personnel. He quit the Air Force one day and went right to work in the aerospace industry. Nancy and Paul's daughter, Elinor Jane—named for Nancy's sister and maternal grandmother—was born August 27, 1958.

Nancy had given up flying when she was expecting Paul Jr., so by the time Janey was born, Nancy had been out of the cockpit for ten years. She hadn't completely forgotten about flying, but life and her family responsibilities took over and she moved on. During those years, Nancy found her role as wife and mother a reaffirmation of her roots, her heritage, and her destiny. It was what women did, and Nancy enjoyed the role—to a point.

At this stage in her life, her days as a WASP were fond but distant memories. In spite of that, after moving to California and before Jane was born, Nancy got word that the women who had lived in BOQ 14 were planning a reunion. "I just had to go. I begged Paul to let me go. I took my children with me to Baltimore and left them with Muddy at Elinor's."

Nancy was getting restless.

10

The Pain of Change

Paul Crews Jr. remembers when his mother caught the flying bug all over again.

"We had this RV and we used to take it on weekend family trips all over southern California. One day, we were going by the Palm Springs airport and they were offering airplane rides. 'Oh, please, Paul, can I go up?' she asked my father.

"When she got down, she went right back up again and this time she took Radford and me with her. My brother and I were in the back seat. My mother was in the front with the pilot. She told him she had flown in World War II and he let her fly the plane while we were up. That poor woman got hooked all over again."

Nancy turned forty on February 1, 1960. She was the mother of two healthy, active sons, nine and twelve years old, and a beautiful 18-month-old baby daughter. But a month after Jane was born, Nancy had suffered yet another devastating loss. Elinor, only forty-four, died from breast cancer.

"When Elinor died, I went into a depression. It nearly killed me." In spite of the six-year age difference, Nancy and Elinor had been close. Nancy had looked up to her sister and tried to emulate her—beginning with her desire to, like Elinor, be named "outstanding camper" at Camp Winnataska and then following her into Alpha Gamma Delta sorority. And Nancy had seen a lot of Elinor and her family when she was stationed in Wilmington during the war. The bond they had shared in getting through their brother's wartime death had grown even stronger over the years.

Now, suddenly, Nancy was forty years old, and two of her three siblings were gone. Then in November 1961, her father died. Nancy's support system was seriously diminished. But as time healed the loss of both her sister and her father and her grief subsided, Nancy began to reexamine who she was and what she wanted. Always goal oriented, she realized it was time to get on with the rest of her life.

"My mother raised her daughters to be homemakers, but not house-keepers," Nancy said. "And keeping house did *not* appeal to me." Though she was a typical 1950s stay-at-home mom when the boys were young, by 1960 that homemaker mantle no longer sat well on her shoulders. Inside, she was still a pursuit pilot. When she was a young woman, flying had been her ticket out of a comfortable but potentially stifling existence and Nancy had uncommon aspirations.

"I wanted an opportunity and my parents gave me that. We were in-dulged, but my parents enjoyed our doing things. We were spoiled, but my mother also spanked the hell out of me. She was the disciplinarian. My mother was an idealist. If you achieved, you were rewarded. The standards were there. You behaved!

"I knew as a child I wanted to *be* somebody. But I was a girl in the South. Getting married and keeping house did not appeal to me. Boys had adven-tures and made money and played games. They had *fun*. I liked being with boys and they liked me to be with them. It was grand!"

But Nancy, too, wanted to have adventures, make money, play games, and have fun.

"I had this inner drive, this inner motivation that came from the envi-ronment my parents created. When I got to college, I already knew I was a leader, but I didn't know what I wanted to do. I didn't know what I wanted to do until I started flying." Then Nancy Love, Colonel Tunner, and the Air Transport Command gave her the opportunity to fly the fastest and the best airplanes the Army had to offer. Those memories may have dimmed a bit by 1960, but they were far from forgotten.

In the 1950s and early 1960s, athletic, game-loving Nancy played a lot of golf—club championship quality—and enjoyed the active, outdoor, southern California lifestyle. But she found it wasn't enough. Her temporarily dormant inner drive was returning. As much as she loved Paul and her children—and, as Jane emphasized, "my mother loved us fiercely"—Nancy knew she was cut out for something more than a domestic life and prowess on the golf course.

When Nancy went after something, she did so with a vengeance. Com-petitive by nature, she sometimes let that drive get the best of her. "If she had a bad day on the golf course, she brought it home with her," Paul Jr. said. "She'd be in a snit around the house—'snit' was her word—and she was hard to live with. One day my brother asked her to stop."

Though Paul remembered the incident well, Radford did not. But he admitted that as a kid he had a way of coming up with smart remarks out of the blue.

Nancy's quest to be a golf champion subsided.

"Shortly after that, she took up flying again," said Paul.

On February 26, 1964, Nancy took to the air at Orange County Airport—as a student flying with an instructor, this time in a Piper Colt. Not surprisingly, she was a quick learner. She earned her private pilot's license on June 12, 1964. She had accumulated only thirty-six new hours.

Paul researched her old logbooks. Between 1940 and 1945, she had accumulated 1,224:15 hours. He added the hours in her old logbooks to her new ones (by then her 36 had grown to 43:30 hours) and she showed a total of 1,267:45 hours of flight time.[1]

The biggest airplane she was credited with flying was the A-20 attack plane (twin engines, 1,600 horsepower each)—her all-time favorite. Now she was back in 100-horsepower trainers. It didn't matter. She was flying. And Paul, though he had no interest in flying himself, supported her desire to fly.

The summer of 1964, the family moved from Anaheim to Inglewood. Paul Sr. worked long hours. He was never home. The long commute to Northrop was getting to him, so they made the move to put him close to his workplace. In October 1964, Nancy started flying out of nearby Hawthorne Airport, building time and working on her instrument rating, which she earned on April 14, 1965.

That July, she competed in her first air race, the Powder Puff Derby (All-Woman Transcontinental Air Race) sponsored by the Ninety-Nines.[2] Another woman flying out of Orange County wanted to fly the race and needed a copilot. Nancy, with her ferrying and cross-country experience, was a natural.

"The Powder Puff Derby intrigued me. B.J. [Erickson London] and Betty [Gillies] were running the race for the Ninety-Nines back in those days. We flew a 235-horsepower Cherokee across Texas and finished in Chattanooga. I had fun on that trip."

On August 20, 1965, she earned her commercial rating and began work on her Certified Flight Instructor (CFI) rating. Then on November 3, 1965, flying with Federal Aviation Administration (FAA) inspector Ralph Thomas, Nancy completed her work for her CFI. He signed her off. She joined Rose Aviation at the Hawthorne airport as an instructor and began to put her flying skills to work part time, once again earning a paycheck. During that time, she took fourteen-year-old Radford up for his first lesson.[3]

"He ate it up!"

Janey was now in school all day, so Nancy could throw herself into instructing. Jane didn't realize that what her mother did "at work" was very different from what the other mothers were doing—not until Nancy started competing in air races. Then it became apparent to Janey that her mom was not exactly like other moms. Her mom flew airplanes.

In May 1966, Nancy entered the All Woman's International Air Race, also known as the Angel Derby. She left Hawthorne for Yuma, Arizona, on May 21, flying a Cessna 150—a single-engine, two-seater, high-wing trainer airplane like the one in which she had been giving flight lessons. The race route took her to El Paso, across Texas to Laurel, Mississippi, and on to the terminus at West Palm Beach, Florida, where she touched down on May 27. She flew this race solo—just like she did when she was a ferry pilot. "I'm in it for the sheer fun. But I wouldn't take anybody along. That's extra weight."

She left West Palm on May 29 and headed for Birmingham. There, on May 30, she took her brother-in-law Luther Strange, Amy's husband, and their two children, Luther Jr. and Elizabeth, each up for a half-hour flight. The next day her logbook simply says "Muddy." Nancy and her mother flew back to California together. Her logbook shows a succession of stops for fuel at small Texas airports along the way. They left May 31 and arrived at Hawthorne on June 1.

"Mother and Aunt Nancy were getting worried about Muddy," Amy's daughter, Liz, recalled. "She still lived in the house in Norwood, alone, and the neighborhood was changing. Aunt Nancy took her out to California to see if Muddy could live out there with her, but Muddy didn't want to live in California. She was fiercely independent and she and Aunt Nancy didn't get along very well. And Aunt Nancy was gone a lot. Muddy didn't know the neighborhood and felt shut away. I think they both decided that it wasn't going to work. When Muddy came back to Birmingham, she decided to come live with us. Mom had been working on her to do that.

"Aunt Nancy had been handling Muddy's finances. But later, mother needed to have women come in to help take care of Muddy as her illness got worse. [Ruth Batson was a victim of Parkinson's disease.] Mom and Nancy became co-executors because they had to draw on her estate to handle that. Of course, anything Mom and Aunt Nancy did was contentious. They just didn't get along. So after that, they went through some strained times."[4]

The years in Anaheim, 1956 to 1964, were the last of the gentle years—brought to a shattering halt with the assassination of President John F.

Kennedy, November 22, 1963. On that day, America—and all of its people old enough to remember where they were when they heard—lost its innocence.

The world began to change and the Crews family was not immune to those changes. The move to Inglewood would bear that out. "We had been used to the laid-back Orange County lifestyle," Paul Jr. said. "The Watts riots broke out not long after we moved to Inglewood. They were only about five miles away. Radford and I sat on the roof and watched the fires."[5]

After that, changes seemed to come rapidly. Civil rights and the Vietnam War became the two big issues in everybody's lives—in California and throughout the country.

Each member of the Crews family dealt with the changes differently. Nancy threw herself into flying. Paul Sr., in the limited time his job allowed him, focused on the family, on woodcraft and building furniture, on leather craft, on music—he played the organ—and he shut out the outside strife. He also was dealing with a growing and pervasive tiredness that puzzled him. And it puzzled Nancy. Paul turned fifty in 1965 and it was becoming increasingly obvious that his health was, for some reason, deteriorating.

Radford became interested in cars and girls. Paul Jr. turned to music.

"Soon after we moved to Inglewood, our parents bought Rad a guitar and me a drum set," Paul said. "I really got into music and I made new friends." Paul graduated from high school in 1966, enrolled in California State University Long Beach, and continued with his music. "I had found a way to put myself through college." He played music four nights a week and worked at Northrop thirty-six hours a week—all while attending college. He graduated with a bachelor of arts degree in 1971.

Janey was too young to really notice any difference in the atmosphere surrounding the neighborhood and in general, except that all her friends' parents seemed to become more guarded about their children. "I remember Paul walked me to school a lot. So did Mom and our German shepherd, Patsy. But Mom said it was because she needed the exercise."

Civil rights affected Nancy differently than it did most Californians because she had grown up in the pre–World War II, traditional Old South. "Aunt Nancy tried to be a Southern lady in California, and it didn't work," Liz recalled.

For her, what was happening asked for a total and immediate reversal of her ingrained heritage. This was the dilemma that affected so many people in and from the South. They were expected to unlearn, overnight, a lifetime of living in a system that they had never heard questioned—had never thought to question.

Nancy had been raised on states' rights and the racial strictures of the Old South. For her to go counter to that, someone was going to have to prove to her that she had been taught wrong. And Nancy believed in and honored her heritage. Her ambivalence over Charlie Miller's Catholicism was an early clue that she would have a problem going counter to her White Anglo-Saxon Protestant upbringing—a WASP of a totally different origin and meaning than the WWII WASP she had been.

Old South or not, and raised in a racist society, Nancy considered herself the most democratic of individuals. She was not a social snob. Nancy believed what you did with your god-given talents and skills was what was important, *not* who your family was or how much money your father made. In her thinking, each individual must earn his or her own way; make his or her own choices. No one else can do it for you. She had neither sympathy nor empathy for anyone who did not understand that. Nancy took people for what she saw inside them and what she thought they were made of—not who they were outside or who they professed to be.

"In the WAFS it didn't matter who your mother's family was or what your father did for a living. What mattered was whether you could fly those airplanes. It was the most democratic organization I ever belonged to."[6]

She suffered no fools and countenanced no whiners. If she was convinced she was right, she gave no quarter. This was a lifetime trait seen unmistakably in the young Nancy. The twenty-three-year-old Nancy had read out her fellow WAFS Helen McGilvery and Sis Bernheim—both several years older than she—and told them to obey their leader Betty Gillies and be ready to fly at 4 a.m. She never abandoned that stance. What was right was right—black and white, no shades of gray. This stance was to cause her considerable grief along the way. But that was Nancy.

She learned her politics at her father's knee and Nancy adored her father. He had been a Jefferson County commissioner under Alabama governor Bibb Graves (1927–1931 and 1935–1939). Her foray into running for office in college was part of proving herself to her father, all the while testing her own mettle.

George C. Wallace, who became a four-time governor of Alabama, had been a friend and classmate of Nancy at the university. They had danced together at the Cotillion Club dances that were so popular before the war. At one point, Wallace was a candidate for president of the Cotillion Club, though he was not elected.[7] Nancy liked and admired Wallace because he spoke his mind. Didn't pull punches. She was cut from that same cloth.

When he ran for president in 1968 on the American Independent Party ticket, she supported him and campaigned for him in California.

Politics, the saying goes, makes strange bedfellows, and their connection was a case in point. He was a rough-cut boy from the country, honed by the hardscrabble rural life of the Depression years. She came from a privileged, gentile, urban family. He was a hothead and a brawler. She, a cool, level-headed patrician.

Nancy took George for the man she knew and who she sensed he was. She followed her instincts—what she felt Wallace offered as a candidate and as a man, not what the world labeled him.

Nancy also was loyal to a fault and, when committed to a cause, she was passionate in her advocacy. Her loyalty to Nancy Love and antipathy toward Jackie Cochran—in the years long after the WASP deactivation, when she felt that Cochran was getting all the glory and recognition for launching the WASP—was unrelenting. She blamed Cochran for the closing down of the WASP. She felt that Cochran's interference from the beginning was what caused the disbanding—this when the women flying for the Ferrying Division were still vitally needed.

Likewise, she was loyal to her Alabama classmate, Wallace, in his quest for political power and the presidency.

Sis Bernheim was Nancy's first Jewish friend. Prior to Sis and the WAFS, Nancy had little interaction with Jewish people as individuals or a group. Nancy and Sis established a lifelong relationship and mutual admiration society. Nevertheless, Nancy felt their friendship was the exception to the rule.

"You talk about two different people, one from the North, the other from the South, that was Sis and me. She was definitely a Yankee—a New York Jew. She looked it and she had this loud, rather raucous voice. Her personality kind of put you off at first. But, when you really got to know her, she was so real and so warm. She was a wonderful person. So versatile. So intelligent. She and I both enjoyed doing things like going to the opera and to plays. Me, being from Alabama, she really made me feel at home in and around New York. I really enjoyed Sis's company."[8]

Here again Nancy could overlook perceived differences on a personal level, but she could not quite escape the prejudices of the culture in which she was raised.

Nancy acted on her ingrained instincts. When one of her sons wanted to date a Jewish girl in high school, her disapproval was palpable. That pushed the limits of her tolerance. But Paul Jr. was the one who took her over the edge when he announced that he planned to marry a Japanese girl.

Nancy's generation bore the brunt of World War II. December 7, 1941, would never be forgotten. Our war against Japan had been a racist war. The anti-Japanese propaganda during the war made that very clear. Nancy lost her beloved only brother to that war. She lost friends like Charlie Miller; three of her fellow original WAFS; and countless other friends, classmates, and acquaintances. Americans were taught hatred of the Japanese from 1941 to 1945. When it was all over and the healing began, it didn't come quickly to everyone and it never came at all to some. Nancy was one of those. In this instance, the word *acceptance* was not in her vocabulary.

Nancy was aghast even though she had welcomed the girl into her home as Paul's friend. The young woman had stayed with the Crews family when she visited from Japan. But extending the Southern hospitality ingrained in her versus accepting a daughter-in-law were two entirely different matters with Nancy. She was dead set against the union and verbally forbade Paul to marry the girl.

Nancy went to her minister. "He told me that nowhere in the Bible does it say you have to accept a daughter-in-law." That was all the reassurance Nancy needed.

"She would not accept a Japanese daughter-in-law," Paul Jr. said, "nor, when the time came, would she recognize a mixed-blood grandchild." That was, in reality, what she objected to—the mixing of the races.

Paul went against his mother's wishes and the couple married in September 1971. The result? "My mother divorced me from the family."[9]

So there it is. All of the foibles and strengths of humanity wrapped up in one very strong, outspoken, charismatic woman. To truly know her is to walk a mile in her shoes. We are all the sum total of our heritage, our birthright, our environment, and our own destiny. Paul Jr. and his mother were estranged for almost thirty years. But life went on for both of them.

The Vietnam War was on everybody's mind. Paul, knowing that he would be drafted after graduating from college, chose to enlist in the Navy in 1971. He became a hospital corpsman and thought he would be assigned to the Marine Corps and sent into combat in Vietnam. Instead, he was sent through the hospital corps to neuro-psychiatric technician school and then on to San Diego to the Naval Drug Rehabilitation Center as a staff therapist. His wife joined him there and their son was born while they were stationed in San Diego. Paul served his entire enlistment in California. When he got out of the Navy in 1975, he had found his career in medical technology and administration. He earned his master of science degree in 1977 from San Diego State University.

Radford graduated from high school in 1969 and went to college for a semester because it was the thing to do. But he dropped out. "I got nailed for drunk driving and that didn't go over too well at home. I joined the Air Force in 1970. I served as a missile mechanic in South Dakota, but cross-trained to be a clerk. I was assigned to Vietnam toward the end of the conflict there, but I was based with the Army. I worked in the office during the day, but had to pull guard duty on the perimeter one night out of four. We went through rocket and mortar attacks. You feel the concussions. They are alive. I wasn't prepared for that.

"On February 11, 1973, I was on perimeter duty. The cease-fire was due to begin at 8 a.m. At 6:30 we started getting rocket fire. We were scared. We thought they were waiting for the last moment and that we would be overrun. We were expecting to get it. We took fire until eight and then it stopped. That was the last of the American involvement.

"I was fortunate, I saw something of war and experienced the fear of losing my life, but I wasn't hurt or scarred emotionally. I was among the last one thousand American soldiers to leave Vietnam after the cease-fire. I went from there to Thailand, then was sent home and discharged in October 1973."[10]

Nancy said of Radford after Vietnam: "When he came home, he had been through the fire and it had made him steel."

11

Gliding

Better than Sex!

B. J. London, Nancy's friend from WAFS days, and her business partner, Barney Frazier, operated Barney Frazier Aviation at the Long Beach airport. B.J. bought and sold airplanes and provided that service for several of her WASP friends over the years. She also belonged to the Ninety-Nines chapter there in Long Beach.

"Early in 1969, B.J. invited me down for a program her Ninety-Nines chapter was having on gliding up in the high desert country. The speaker was Fred Robinson of Crystalaire—he had a glider operation up in the Mojave Desert. He talked about his place and gliding—or soaring, as he called it. B.J. and Barney had a Piper dealership and she had sold Fred a Super Cub. I was intrigued with him and his place and the whole idea. Then B.J. said if I bought a Super Cub, he'd use it up there in the desert to tow gliders. 'You can go up there and fly and make some money, at the same time,' she said.

"Wow! A good excuse to do some more flying. I talked to Paul about it, and he agreed that it was a good idea. So we bought a brand new Super Cub—4425 Zulu. The plane cost seventy-five hundred dollars. I took out a loan through Northrop and made monthly payments on it."

On April 4, 1969, Nancy went to Long Beach to pick up the Super Cub from B.J. That very afternoon, she flew the Cub to Pearblossom airport up in the high desert country northeast of Los Angeles—a forty-minute flight. She began transition into glider towing on April 19, and on April 27, Fred checked her out as a glider tow pilot. Nancy had a new airplane and a new career. She moved over to the Crystalaire airport on May 17 and began doing glider tows there.[1]

"We had the RV, so in May, we began spending our weekends up at the glider field. It was a two-hour drive—up Saturday morning and back Sunday night. Paul enjoyed it. Janey had a dirt bike that we carried on the side. It

Nancy and her new Super Cub, N4425Z, purchased April 4, 1969.
Photo courtesy the Crews family.

worked out great. I was back in a taildragger and I was in hog heaven." Nancy did anywhere from nineteen to sixty tows a day.

Pearblossom and Barney Frazier Aviation sponsored Nancy and the Super Cub in the 1969 Powder Puff Derby (PPD). Janey, now eleven, took part in her mother's preparation for the big race. "I flew down with Mom along the beach to San Diego and Dad drove. We stayed in a hotel. I remember it was fun. I helped her wash and wax the airplane. Because I was little, I could get underneath and wax and polish the belly.

"My mother flew the only taildragger in the race. All those other women had Bonanzas and other big planes—and copilots—and she had a stick and was flying alone."

Nancy liked to tell another story on herself in that race, which got underway on the Fourth of July from Lindbergh Field in San Diego, where they took off out over the ocean.

"I'm one of the last ones to take off. Fran Bera [seven-time winner of the PPD] was to take off right before me. I'm sitting there on the end of the runway and I'm thinking, I'm gonna make this a racing takeoff. So I stood on the brakes like we used to do in the Ferry Command in the P-47s and got that Super Cub all revved up. When they gave me the flag, I poured the coals to it, but I held the plane just a few feet off the runway, gaining a lot of airspeed.

"The rules were to make a turn when you got to the water and start circling to get on course to go east. As I cleared the runway and saw the water, *wham*, I hauled back on that thing, did a chandelle, and cut inside Fran Bera. I came back around over land and headed east for Las Vegas, our first stop. Paul told me the people in the stands jumped up and hollered, 'look, look, that Cub is passing Fran Bera.' Isn't that a hoot. I think Janey and Paul got a kick out of what I did."

In a timed, handicapped race, the feat meant little, but it was spectacular to watch and doing it gave Nancy a real charge. "It tickled the fire out of Betty Gillies."

The race was to end in Washington, D.C. The women competing were invited to the White House to meet President and Mrs. Richard Nixon. "Before I took off, I asked Janey if she had a message for Mrs. Nixon. Janey said to tell Mrs. Nixon 'hi' for her.

"Well there I was, standing in the receiving line waiting to meet Mrs. Nixon, and I started thinking, 'what am I going to say to her?' Then I remembered, she's got two daughters, I'll tell her about Jane. So I told Mrs. Nixon that my eleven-year-old daughter, Janey, had helped me get the plane ready and that she said to tell her 'hi.' And Mrs. Nixon smiled—she had the most beautiful smile—and she took my hand between her two hands and said, 'well you tell Janey hi for me.' She was such a lovely person."

Flying back from that race, July 12–16, Nancy retraced the route the Army ferry pilots used to fly—heading down to Knoxville, then Birmingham, west across Texas, through Guadeloupe Pass to El Paso, across southern New Mexico to Tucson, and into California. Then she took the Cub home to Crystalaire.

The family had been anxiously awaiting her return. She and Paul had bought an old beat-up Taylorcraft with the idea of rebuilding it in their garage in Inglewood. "They found it in a cotton field somewhere," Paul Jr. re-

C. G. Taylor, whose name was synonymous with Taylorcraft in the early days, wishes Nancy and Paul Crews "many happy flying hours" in their rebuilt red and white Taylorcraft, N96921, January 12, 1971. Photo courtesy the Crews family.

membered. "It was a fabric-covered airplane. My father found an old rat's nest in it. They had a guy who came and helped them work on it."

The project took a couple of years, but now it was ready to fly. On July 26, 1969, Nancy, Paul Sr., and Radford took their antique Taylorcraft out for its second "maiden" flight. "We were really proud of that airplane. It had been a basket case, but it looked brand new when we finished with it," Radford recalled. They hangared it at Compton Airport, not far from where they lived. Nancy's first flight in the Taylorcraft was only fifteen minutes. Then on September 2, she took it for a real test flight—3.8 hours in duration. "My mother and I flew it together after that."

Nancy's initial interest in gliding was strictly business-related. She was, after all, a professional pilot for whom towing gliders was a livelihood. But one day, quite by accident, she discovered how exhilarating soaring—flying without power on air currents and thermals—could be. The realization hit her like a bolt of desert lightning and changed her personal flight path.

"I was getting ready to tow this guy's glider. It was about 10:30 in the morning and it's starting to warm up. I took off and took him up. He was hardly a thousand feet above the ground level when he released.

"When a glider releases, the tow plane goes left and glider goes right. So I went left and came back around and landed thinking he'd be right behind me. He wasn't. Well, I kept towing all day long, looking for him. He didn't appear. Nobody said anything. Dark came and he still hadn't come back.

"The next day is Sunday and I'm towing again. Sunday afternoon, he comes driving up with his glider on a trailer.

"'Where have you been?' I asked him. I was really curious.

"'Oh, I went over to Arizona.'

"'You mean you can go cross-country in these things!' And he told me that, if conditions are right, you could have a driver keep in radio contact with you up in the glider, and pick you up where you come down. At that point I thought, *wow*, I've got to get into this glider thing.

"I started taking lessons in a glider and I felt a sensation like I've never felt before. Better than sex! Up until then aviation, for me, was power. Now, here I was in some wing thing without a prop, without a throttle, and one little wheel under the belly. It was another world. Well I studied, and I took the written exam." On February 26, 1970, Nancy earned her commercial glider certificate.

Thoroughly taken with this new mode of transportation, Nancy convinced Paul that if she bought a glider and leased it to Fred Robinson, her company could make more money. Besides, her competitive side had kicked in and she wanted to earn soaring badges. It would be cheaper, she figured, if she could do it in her own plane. The Schweitzer Company in Elmira, New York, built gliders. She purchased a two-place 2-33 glider from Schweitzer for about six thousand dollars.

While she was working on her gliding, she leased her Super Cub out to other tow pilots. And she could give rides in her glider, too.

The Silver Soaring Badge was next. The requirement for the Silver Badge included an altitude gain of three thousand feet—which meant she had to use the thermals to rise three thousand feet from her release point. Then she had to stay up five hours. After that came the cross-country. She had to go thirty-one miles away from the airport.

"This was SCA-REEE—'cause you've gotta get away from the airport. See, big coward me, I'm spending all my time gliding right over the airport. Then one day a bunch of fellas said, 'you follow us, we'll get lift.' Well, east of the LA basin are the San Gabriel Mountains—twelve thousand feet. These fellas said they could get up there on a good day. Keep in mind, the elevation of the field was thirty-five hundred feet. [The highest summit of the San Gabriels is Mount San Antonio (10,064 feet in elevation), but the San Bernardino

Mountains immediately to the east are topped by 11,499-foot-high Mount San Gorgonio.[2]]

"So here I am. I'm gonna attempt to go cross-country. I had my own glider with a radio in it. And I've got oxygen. Everything going for me. It was the middle of the day, good conditions. I thermaled up and got to the top of the San Gabriels, then went a little further. I was just sitting up there at fourteen thousand feet. Ellendale is straight across the desert—thirty-one miles. I knew I had to do it, but it was like going over Niagara Falls in a barrel.

"I was scared, but I knew I was going. Oh lord, the whole Mojave Desert is nothing but hot air coming up. I got down to 13,500 and came right back up. In no time I'm over top of Ellendale at 14,000 feet.

"I could have gone to Las Vegas!

"Finally, I called them back at the field and said send a tow plane for me. I flew around, had a great time, and finally went in and landed. The tow plane came in front, picked me up, and towed me back to the field. I was gone two to three hours.

"That's how I got my Silver Badge."

12

Paul and the WASP

Paul Crews was not an Alabama native; his family came to Birmingham from Elgin, Illinois. His father, Fristoe Givens Crews, was a store manager for Sears, Roebuck & Co.—but he was a specialist at what he did. He had the skills to improve the profitability of a store and he was sent to Birmingham in the 1930s to do just that. Fristoe's family came from the Missouri Ozarks. Paul's mother, Lala Bell Silvernail—whose grandmother was an Indian princess—was from Michigan.

When Paul and Nancy met at a fraternity–sorority mixer at the University of Alabama, Nancy already knew who Paul was. She and his sister, Cleo, had gone to Ramsay High School together. Both girls entered the university as freshmen the fall of 1937. Cleo told Nancy that her brother was enrolled as well. When Lambda Chi Alpha fraternity invited the young women of Alpha Gamma Delta for a dinner at the fraternity house that fall, Nancy met Paul for the first time. "We had something to talk about since I knew both his sisters."

Paul Hubert Crews was born October 13, 1915, in Hastings, Nebraska. Graduating from high school in the Depression years, he went directly into the workforce. When he entered college, he was twenty-two, more mature than the boys just out of high school, and far more serious about his studies. He was enrolled in the School of Commerce and worked as a grader for one of the professors. Medium tall (five feet, eleven inches), he had black wavy hair and wore glasses that did not hide his intelligent brown eyes. He was quite handsome in a scholarly sort of way.

Like many college men of his generation, he joined the Reserve Officer Training Corps (ROTC). Following graduation, Paul entered the Army Reserves as a second lieutenant and was teaching ROTC at the University of Alabama when war was declared December 8, 1941. He was activated immediately in the Army Air Forces.

Assigned to the 9th Air Force, Paul was sent first to Egypt and, later in the war, to England. He was there at the time of the Normandy invasion. He rose steadily in rank and completed his World War II service as a member of the Inspector General's staff. He was released from the Army in early 1946 with the rank of lieutenant colonel. When the Korean War began in June 1950, he was called back into the United States Air Force—now a separate service from the Army.

In 1952, Paul was sent to the Pentagon, and once again he was with the Inspector General's staff. The Pentagon job frequently took him abroad to Africa, Europe, and England. "He brought back boxes of toys," Paul Jr. recalled, "things nobody else had, like a pair of camel saddles. We used to sit in them and watch television."

The Crews family had one car then and often Nancy and the boys drove Paul to work in the morning and picked him up in late afternoon. While waiting for him, the boys played on the steps of the Pentagon. Living in Kensington, Maryland, they had to drive through Washington, D.C., to get to the Pentagon. "We saw a lot of buildings and monuments. We were right in the middle of American history," said Paul Jr.

Paul Sr., promoted to full colonel in 1952, opted to stay in the Air Force and in Washington after the Korean Conflict. Then in 1956, he was assigned to southern California. The Crews family made the move west to Anaheim into a fun, cross-country, summer camping trip. When, less than two years later, he left the Air Force to take the job at Northrop, Paul began several years of a long, arduous LA-style commute.

In 1964, the family moved to Inglewood so that he would be closer to the plant. There was, however, more to the story. Nancy was growing increasingly concerned because "Paul didn't feel good, he began losing weight, and his whole nature changed." Paul was on his way to a possible vice presidency with Northrop when, in 1965, he was diagnosed with diabetes.

The diagnosis came about as a result of a medical situation that surfaced, seemingly, out of nowhere. "We were at the beach in Laguna and he was unable to negotiate the stairs," Paul Jr. recalled. "He had to stop halfway up. He knew something was wrong. Also, he got very badly sunburned—in a very short time."

"He lost the sensation in his legs," Radford remembered. "My mother insisted that he go to the doctor." Not only did he have diabetes, but Paul was found also to suffer from arteriosclerosis with major blockage of the arteries to his legs. He was not getting an adequate flow of blood to his legs. Surgery was recommended to clean out his arteries. "The operation almost killed him," Radford said.

After that, he couldn't handle the stress of the high-powered corporate life. But Northrop liked him and kept him on, though he was no longer on the track to a possible vice presidency. He took a less stressful job.

Finding himself with leisure time, Paul got more involved with family projects. This was the time of the rebuilding of the Taylorcraft. And as Nancy got into glider towing and subsequently flying gliders herself in the late 1960s, Paul took on the support role for her. She had become, once again, a professional pilot. It was Paul who helped Nancy make a business out of her flying skills. Nancy also took a job as a receptionist at Northrop to supplement her aviation business. And on weekends, Paul, Nancy, and Janey drove the family RV to the high desert country, where Nancy towed gliders with the Super Cub.

"My father didn't like to fly, but he encouraged Nancy to fly," Radford said.

Something else Paul encouraged Nancy to do was get involved with the WASP organization. In fact, he pitched in and helped. She had gone to that one WAFS reunion back east, but had never been involved in the WASP organization known then as the Order of Fifinella—named for the winsome lady gremlin mascot Walt Disney had designed for the WASP during the war.

With the end of their active duty approaching, December 20, 1944, the WASP who were *not* a part of the Ferrying Division began to talk up, among themselves, an organization of their own. They put together a roster. They also tried to convince the women in the Ferrying Division to join them.

Clara Jo Marsh, WASP Staff Executive, headquarters, Eastern Flying Training Command, wrote to Nancy Love asking for a roster of the women in the Ferrying Division. "Many WASP . . . have felt a strong need for maintaining contact with each other, personally and professionally," she explained. The group was establishing an unofficial newsletter. Marsh continued, "Many of us in the Training Command have felt isolated from the ATC WASP. We've not wanted to be. A newsletter should keep us informed about our friends in any situation."[1]

Nancy Love chose not to join and the other Originals, including Nancy Batson, followed her example. They still resented being placed under Jackie Cochran's authority and having to give up the WAFS uniforms they wore with pride. They believed that if Cochran hadn't meddled in the work they were doing for the Ferrying Division, they would not have been looking at deactivation and the loss of their jobs. They never switched loyalties from Nancy Love to Jackie Cochran.

WASP who were not flying for the Ferrying Division founded the Order of Fifinella. They held their first reunion in 1946 at Lock Haven, Pennsylvania. William Piper, of the Piper Company, sponsored the event. Many of the WASP had worked for him before the war and had learned to fly in their off hours, as he provided the airplanes for his employees to learn to fly. Mr. Piper, in fact, sponsored two reunions. He held one again in 1947, this time in Ponca City, Oklahoma. One of the prime functions of the organization, other than social, was to provide a network the women could use to try to find almost nonexistent jobs in aviation.

They met two more times, in 1948 and 1949, and then the organization stalled. "It was getting to be too much trouble trying to find people and keep addresses current," Mary Martin "Marty" Wyall (WASP Class 44-10) said. "Everyone was getting married, having babies, following their servicemen husbands overseas. It became too much."

Marty served unofficially as WASP historian from the early 1960s to the early 1990s, and from that time to the present writing (December 2008) she has held the office officially. In 1964, Marty pulled together a reunion—with Betty Gillies' help—as part of the Ninety-Nines meeting held in Cincinnati. Betty, one of the original WAFS, also was a founding member of the Ninety-Nines and active on its national board. As a former Ninety-Nines president, she had additional clout. And she was eager to help. Eighty-four WASP came. They were able to get Jacqueline Cochran to come and speak and, according to Marty, everyone had a wonderful time.

They decided to meet for a reunion every five years—following the pattern of high school classes. The 1969 meeting was to be in Denver, but before the planning was complete, Jackie Cochran decided she would like to hold it at her ranch in Indio, California. Jackie and her husband, Floyd Odlum, would host a giant barbecue on Saturday night.[2]

What helped spark Nancy Crews's interest in the Indio reunion was that it was practically in her backyard. But also enticing was the fact that Jackie Cochran was organizing a WASP golf tournament. Cochran was a golfer. Nancy was a golfer. Paul knew how important her WASP years had been to her. At his urging, she decided to attend. The event was heralded as the twenty-fifth anniversary of the WASP—dating from their disbanding in December 1944.

Like most of the WASP, by 1969 Nancy had moved far beyond the WWII years. She had been raising her family for twenty years—both boys were grown and Jane was nearing her teen years. And, as would become the fashion among active women in the 1970s and beyond, she had gone back to work. That her work was aviation—her chosen profession made possible by her time as a WASP—was a point of pride. She was ready for reentry into the WASP world.

Paul helped by going one step further. He designed an award to honor the WASP twenty-fifth anniversary celebration and he and Nancy donated it to the WASP. He had designed a similar piece for Nancy to display her wings and Air Transport Command insignia. Paul corresponded with Cochran's secretary at length about this during February and March of 1969.[3]

The WASP award was in walnut and bore an enameled metal likeness of the familiar Army Air Forces' shoulder patch and the WASP wings. The text of the poem "High Flight" was inscribed centered between two Fifinella emblems. A metal plate noted the twenty-fifth anniversary celebration. Paul left it up to the WASP to decide to whom and how the plaque should be presented.

In addition, he got his company, the Norair division of Northrop, to provide a trophy—a walnut stand on which were mounted a 1/40th scale PT-19 and a 1/40th scale T-38 jet trainer to symbolize twenty-five years of progress in the field of aviation training between the WASP's time and the present. Norair also provided Fifinella self-adhesive name tags for the reunion as well as Fifinella decals as souvenirs.

The WASP decided to award the plaque to Marty Wyall, who served as newsletter editor and historian and is credited, to this day, with holding the WASP organization together over the dormant years. (She later served as president of the organization from 1994 to 1996.)

The Indio reunion was a success. Forty-eight, including Nancy Crews and Jackie Cochran, competed in the golf tournament. Of note: Nancy was one of only a few who played in the tournament as a non-handicapped golfer. After giving up amateur competitive golf—following her encounter with her younger son several years earlier—she now limited her golfing to recreation only.

After Indio, Nancy continued her involvement with the WASP organization.

The next reunion was held in June 1972 in Sweetwater. The every-five-year plan had been ditched because 1972 marked the thirtieth year since the founding of the WAFS and WASP. On one of the hottest days of the year, the Texas town held its biggest parade ever. The WASP rode on flatbed trucks and everybody sang. Sweetwater outdid itself to welcome home their returning heroines. Many residents dashed from the curb to hug a WASP they recognized.

At the business meeting, Nancy Batson Crews was elected president of what ceased to be known as the Order of Fifinella and became the WASP WWII. "The Order of Fifinella" didn't sound very businesslike, and, Marty Wyall remembered, they were trying to run things the way an organization should be run.

"I took the WASP president's job because I believe you have to give back. Here was my chance. They thought a lot of the WAFS and asked me to do it," Nancy recalled. "They wanted me to be in charge. And that's what I did, I took charge. I believed in being organized and having a plan. We had a board meeting at Leoti Deaton's in Wichita Falls, Texas,[4] and we rewrote the bylaws for the organization. Mary Jones [Mary Regalbuto Jones, Class 44-9[5]] had been elected secretary-treasurer and we immediately hit it off. She and I set up the procedures—like holding reunions every two years and having a board meeting in the off years for planning. Mary worked with me. She was so capable, and very professional.

"One thing Mary Jones really wanted to see accomplished was WASP militarization, because she hoped to use her two years in the WASP toward her retirement. She worked for the government. She wanted us to contact Hap Arnold's son, Bruce, and see if he would help us. So I got in touch with him. That was the beginning of the move toward militarization."

Planning began for the 1974 reunion, but the oil crisis interfered. Because of the shortages, no one could drive or fly in. So they postponed the reunion until 1975. Nancy served an additional year as president because no election was held.

Reno was the site of the 1975 reunion and it turned out to be a big one as well. Historian Marty Wyall planned to present a history of the WAFS at the banquet because so many of the WASP really didn't know the story of the Originals. Also, most of the WAFS had never considered the organization to be "for them." Marty wrote to all the WAFS she had addresses for and sent them a questionnaire asking about their early flying and how they learned about and got into the Women's Auxiliary Ferrying Squadron. She also urged them to come to Reno.

Nancy also did some recruiting. Between them, Nancy and Marty succeeded in getting seven other WAFS to come—most for the first time. Attending were Delphine Bohn, Teresa James, Betty Gillies, Del Scharr, Gertrude Meserve Tubbs, B. J. Erickson London, and Florene Miller Watson. Counting Nancy, eight WAFS attended.

"I got Delphine and Teresa to come room with me. The Reno-area gals, led by Adele Beyer [Class 44-1], worked really hard to organize the reunion.

Eight original WAFS at the WASP Reno reunion, 1975: Del Scharr, Delphine Bohn, Barbara Erickson London (behind Bohn), Gertrude Meserve Tubbs, Teresa James, Nancy Batson Crews (behind Teresa), Florene Miller Watson, and Betty Gillies. Photo courtesy the Crews family.

Bill and Moira Lear [Lear Jet] invited us out to their ranch to see the new prototype. And Win Wood [Class 43-7] asked me to run for president again. Wasn't that sweet of her. You know she was the first student I soloed down at Embry-Riddle in Miami.

"We had the big banquet in the evening and I sat at the table with the other WAFS instead of up at the head table. It was a WAFS night," Nancy remembered. "Marty Wyall talked about the WAFS and Nancy Love. It was grand!"

Jackie Cochran had been ill, but she and Floyd managed to drive up in their RV. "I had no idea Miss Cochran was coming," Marty remembered. "I was embarrassed because there I was sitting next to her and giving this talk about the WAFS and how wonderful Nancy Love was. Miss Cochran was quite cool toward me. I tried to get Dedie [Leoti Deaton], who was sitting at the other end of the table, to get up and say something about Miss Cochran, but she wouldn't. She said, simply, 'this evening is for the WAFS.'" And, of course, Marty had put her heart and soul into making it just that.[6]

"Cochran was sitting up on the dais by herself," Nancy recalled. Since Nancy had opted to sit with the other WAFS, she was not seated at the head table, as she normally would have been as outgoing president—probably on Jackie Cochran's left. To Nancy, it was—she readily admitted years later in an interview—a small piece of payback, of retribution. Nancy was one of the most adamant of the WAFS that Cochran had messed up Nancy Love's program and ultimately cost them their wartime jobs.

Bee Falk Haydu (Class 44-7) was elected to succeed Nancy as WASP president.[7] It was she who, subsequently, took on the push for recognition of veteran status for the WASP and led the way to that victory.

Trying to get the reunion schedule back on an every-two-year cycle in the even years, the next reunion was held in Hot Springs, Arkansas, in October 1976. This meeting was truly the watershed—the transition from the old to the new organization. Three very big things happened. First, the weather was so bad, they had to stay inside the hotel, so everyone got to know each other quite well as they partied and talked, got reacquainted, and had a good time. The women were into or approaching their sixties, had raised their families, and had the time and the inclination to take on new challenges and new interests.

The second thing turned out to be very sad news. Following Marty Wyall's 1975 presentation—the history of Nancy Love and the WAFS as the first twenty-eight WASP—the WASP had decided to honor Nancy Love as their "Woman of the Year" and hoped to present the award to her in person. But Nancy, they soon learned, lay terminally ill with cancer.[8]

Bee Haydu called Nancy Love on October 1 to find out whether she planned to attend the reunion in Hot Springs, October 21–23. Bee was shocked to learn that Nancy might not live that long. Bee contacted Ann Atkeison (Class 44-10), chairman of the awards committee. Ann immediately had the award engraved and sent to Nancy at her home in Sarasota.

Love's daughter, Margaret, wrote to the WASP: "The Award arrived last Thursday (7th) and Mum has asked me to convey her thanks and appreciation."

Nancy died at 6:30 in the morning, October 22, 1976—as the WASP were gathering to honor her. The December 1976 WASP Newsletter Special Edition carried the following tribute to Nancy Love: "We have lost a fine person who led well in time of great need."[9]

The third and key event to come out of the Hot Springs reunion was the push for militarization. A month earlier—in September 1976—ten women began flight training for the U.S. Air Force. A Pentagon press release heralded them as "the first women military pilots." The WASP were incensed! "We were the first!" they proclaimed loudly. Six weeks before the Hot Springs reunion, the Senate, led by Barry Goldwater, voted on an amendment to make the WASP official WWII veterans. Four days later, the House rejected the amendment. With that, the quest for recognition was on. Bruce Arnold attended the 1976 reunion in Hot Springs—Nancy's initial contact had paid off—and the WASP began to organize the campaign for militarization.

The WASP set up headquarters in Washington, D.C., and began lobbying their congressmen and senators. Bruce Arnold worked with them. The WASP say he made it all possible. "He paid for everything," said Marty Wyall. They also had other help from high places. In addition to Senator Goldwater—Nancy Batson's wartime instrument instructor, who knew many of the Wilmington-based WASP—they had the unanimous support of the women of Congress: Rep. Margaret Heckler, Rep. Lindy Boggs, Rep. Elizabeth Holtzman, and Senator Margaret Chase Smith.

Assistant Secretary of the Air Force Antonia Handler Chayes also supported the WASP. The U.S. military was now an all-volunteer force and the Defense Department was spending a lot of public-relations money trying to convince women that the "new" military offered them an equal shot at a career and the attendant benefits. "'Be all you can be,' the Army promised. What would a public defeat for the WASP do for recruiting?" WASP author Marianne Verges wrote.[10]

Nancy's old pal Teresa James had been lobbying, tirelessly and enthusiastically, for years to get the WASP militarized. She signed on and went to work. Nancy and Teresa, along with Velta Haney Benn (Class 44-7) and Margaret Kerr Boylan (Class 43-2), later were featured in a circa 1980 documentary film about the WASP entitled *Silver Wings and Santiago Blue.* Washington, D.C.-based WASP like Lucile Wise, Dorothy Deane Ferguson, Elaine Harmon, Benn, and Boylan were critical to the effort, "womaning" the office and being the eyes and ears in Washington. President Bee Haydu spent most of 1976 and 1977 there as well.

Now retired General Tunner appeared as a witness before Congress, saying, "Certainly someone today can partially correct the unfairness we showed by making veterans of these women who served so faithfully and well, and with little complaint."[11] His wife, Margaret Ann Hamilton Tunner (Class 43-2)—a WASP who had married the widowed Ferrying Division commander several years after the war—also spoke with quiet dignity at the Congressional hearing on behalf of WASP militarization: "I feel that those few of us still alive should be here in Washington to receive national recognition, instead of this humble plea for positive identification as a veteran."[12]

Countless WASP took an active part. It was an uphill fight that appeared unwinable. Congress, lobbied by the veterans' organizations, resisted. The story is that a high-ranking member of the Veteran's Committee saw, in the material presented to back up the WASP's claim, a copy of a WASP's service discharge. When he read it, he found it was identical to his. With that, he changed his mind and his vote and took others with him in the process. The House passed the necessary legislation.[13]

On November 23, 1977, President Jimmy Carter signed the bill that gave the WASP of World War II veteran status.[14]

Nancy Crews, it turned out, was not in Hot Springs nor was she in Washington for that final victory. Circumstances beyond her control forced her to leave the fight to others. By fall 1976, Paul's health was rapidly declining.

13

Passing the Torch

Radford Learns to Fly

Nineteen seventy-five was a pivotal year for Nancy Batson Crews. She attended the WASP reunion in Reno and handed over the presidential duties to Bee Haydu. She also took part in her third and, as it turned out, final Powder Puff Derby. Once again, she flew the Super Cub solo. Takeoff was from Riverside, California, and the route took her to Phoenix, El Paso, Plainview, Batesville, Nashville, and Knoxville, en route to the Tri Cities airport in North Carolina.

On the flight home, as always, she stopped in Birmingham—this time for a week, July 12–18. This visit was for family business purposes. Nancy was beginning her work with the family real estate holdings in Alabama. Muddy, eighty-four and suffering from debilitating Parkinson's disease, had died April 5, 1975. By then, she had lived with Amy and her family for several years.

On April 1, Nancy had been to Lock Haven, Pennsylvania, to the Piper factory to pick up her newest Super Cub, N7464L. From there she flew to Atlanta where Amy, her husband Luther, and Muddy were now living. Muddy was not doing well. The morning of April 5, Nancy flew over to Birmingham. Muddy died later that day and Nancy, immediately, flew back to Atlanta. The family buried its matriarch next to her husband in the Batson plot in Elmwood Cemetery. The last of the older generation, Ruth Philips Batson had buried two of her children, but two still survived, along with eight grandchildren.

"At Daddy's death, everything went to my mother. Then when Muddy died, all the property came to their four children. Amy got one-fourth and I got one-fourth. One-fourth went to Radford's son and one-fourth to Elinor's two children. I couldn't let that land drift away." Nancy knew she had to take charge.

When her father died November 22, 1961, he left the farm at Rocky Ridge

Nancy and Super Cub N7464L, new in 1975. Photo courtesy the Crews family.

as well as a thirty-acre hog farm across the road, plus another eighty acres of woods inside two subdivisions. "Daddy had dreams of developing that eighty acres and he and I had talked about it. Now, I hoped to make his dream come true. So I got a lawyer to draw up a paper for all of us to hold the land as tenants in common and I would be the manager. Everybody signed the papers. After that, I had to make several trips to Alabama to deal with the family real estate."

When Nancy got home to California July 20 and resumed her glider towing and flight instructing, a new student awaited her. Radford, back from Vietnam and enrolled in college on the GI Bill, had decided to take up flying again, this time with the intention of getting his commercial rating. He wanted to fly professionally. He asked his mother to be his primary flight instructor. On August 7, 1975, he went up for his first lesson.

"From an early age, I had a real affinity for airplanes. My mother fostered that. When I was in second and third grade, I took my mother's old cloth flying helmet and goggles to school for show-and-tell. When we used to fly back to Alabama from California for family visits, I saved those little pilot's wings they gave us and remember looking out at the clouds and loving being up in the sky. We flew in prop planes, probably a DC-4. Seeing the fire coming from the engine exhaust on the back of the wing excited me.

"I watched old World War II movies and built model airplanes that I hung with thread from the ceiling in the bedroom. Paul and I used to play war and shoot rubber bands at them. I was particularly enamored of the World War I pilots and their planes. Those planes were handmade works of art. I ate it up and my mother encouraged me.

"When I was fourteen, my mother started teaching me how to fly. You could solo at fifteen and get a private pilot's license at sixteen. But after several lessons, in her judgment, I wasn't ready. She realized I didn't have the maturity and she didn't solo me when I turned fifteen. After that I got interested in cars, and then in girls. I didn't get my private license until I got back from Vietnam."

The GI Bill could be used only for programs leading toward an occupation. The government would not pay for a private pilot's license. Once a student earned that on his own, he could go for his commercial, multiengine, instrument, and ATP (Airline Transport Pilot) ratings and the government would pay for it.

"When I came back, my mother had the Super Cubs. I got my private license with her—forty hours. I still have my shirttail that Nancy cut off when I soloed. She wrote on it: 'first solo, 8-28-75.'

"I took my ground school classes at Rose Aviation there at Hawthorne and I took my check ride with Jean Rose. My mother had worked for her for several years as a flight instructor. Jean had been a WASP [Class 43-7]. Jean, Nancy, and I went to the Reno Air Races one year in Jean's Aero Commander. I thought I had died and gone to heaven."

Radford received his private pilot's license on October 25, 1975—his twenty-fourth birthday.

"Now I was able to have the GI Bill pay for my ratings, so I was taking friends up, doing loops and rolls, whatever I could to get flight time to qualify for the commercial. I was teaching myself, snap rolling, flying that Cub upside down. I've always been a risk-taker—a bit reckless, though I had grown up a lot by then. I got my necessary 250 hours, then used the GI Bill to get my commercial and instrument ratings and later my ATP."

Radford went on to fly for several commercial ventures—including flying hazardous materials for the government—during his early aviation years. Eventually he signed on with the small regional airline Sun Air, which was then bought by Sky West. Rising through the ranks, Radford has become a Sky West Airlines captain with top seniority, flying the thirty-passenger, turbo-prop Brasilia over several western states.

"I must have twenty-five thousand flight hours now [2006], and all of it hands-on, low-altitude flying in the turbo-props—real flying, less reliance on instruments, more looking at the ground, the kind of flying my mother liked. All airplanes have the same equipment but small planes are more maneuverable. They are designed to carry a certain number of people a certain distance—in a smaller package. The Brasilia flies under the same regulations and same performance requirements as a 747, but it has a different mission.

"I have way more flight time than my mother ever dreamed of having and I excel at technical flying, something she never liked. Nancy was a wonderful natural pilot. She had an inborn feel for flying—an instinctive thing. She was better at the freedom of flight. Put her in a glider, cut her loose, and leave her to fly—there was no one better. I'm better at the discipline of flight.

"Had my mother grown up in today's environment, she would have been fine—but in her day she was a VFR [visual flight rules] person who had a great feel for flying. She could sit in an airplane all day long and be happy. So can I. I am the male version of my mother.

"My mother believed pilots were special people. I don't. I believe pilots are highly skilled people who have a lot of desire. Anybody can fly an airplane if they don't give up.

"People don't succeed unless they have self-esteem. My mother had self-esteem and she was very determined. She didn't like to give up. If she got involved with people smarter than she was, she would keep at it and learn. She proved that when she went into the real estate developing business in Alabama. If the quirks of circumstance that got her into the CPT [Civilian Pilot Training] Program at the University of Alabama had not come about, she would have done something else. With that desire comes discipline and a well-developed ego.

"And well-developed egos can rub people the wrong way. My mother had a strong ego and she was known to rub people the wrong way. So do I, on occasion. Desire, determination, self-esteem, a strong ego, and a love of flying, those are the things that she gave me."[1]

In 1975, Nancy also found a new business venture in which she could use her airplane and flying skills—fish spotting. It was legal then. "We lived close to LAX [Los Angeles International], close to the ocean," Jane remembered. "This company hired Mom to fly around and spot swordfish. She flew with the door of the Cub open and would drop a marker when she spotted a fish. Then the boat would come to the marker and try to catch the fish. It didn't last long" (August to November 1975, according to the logbook).[2]

The business was going well enough that a new airplane loomed on the horizon. On May 2, 1976, Nancy went to Lock Haven to pick up another Super Cub–"brand new," she wrote in her logbook. As usual, she flew home via Birmingham, this time stopping to check on real estate dealings before heading west. She flew into Long Beach May 7, got her Certified Flight Instructor (CFI) renewal, and then took the plane to Compton Airport. The next day, she was towing gliders up at Crystalaire.

There had been periodic warning signs that Paul was losing ground to the diabetes. In 1969, when he was readying the WASP trophy for the WASP reunion at Indio, Jackie Cochran had invited Paul and Nancy down for a weekend prior to the April reunion. Jackie offered Nancy an opportunity to play the golf course on the ranch before the WASP tournament. The date for their visit was set for March 25, but Paul suddenly developed a heart problem, was put on sick leave from work, and was told by his doctor to stay home. They cancelled the weekend trip.

"Diabetes is a disease that, when out of control, causes other kinds of systems to break down," Paul Jr. said. "That's what happened to him. The diabetes attacked his circulatory system and his heart and, in general, played havoc with his overall physical condition. Today, they call it a metabolic syndrome."

From the beginning back in 1965, attempts to regulate the disease only worked to a degree. Paul began to have problems with his vision, with high blood pressure, and with his kidneys, as well as the heart problem. Some conditions were regulated by medication, but as the years went by his health continued to deteriorate.

"My father was unable to work full time all the time," Paul Jr. continued. "He would work and then have to be off for awhile. Of course, this was during the time that my mother's aviation career started to really take off. He and my mother did several things to alleviate what they could. The upkeep of the house was too much and there were only three of them living at home now, so they elected to move to the apartment in Hawthorne." The move, which took place in 1972, also allowed Jane to attend a different high school.

The weekend trips in the RV up to the desert when Nancy started towing gliders were right in keeping with the doctor's orders for Paul to get out, exercise, and relax. His doctor got him on a regimen of medications that kept him stable.

Paul Jr. thought that his mother was taken completely unawares by the sudden downturn in Paul Sr.'s health back in 1965: "She had never considered him to be anything but healthy." That was how Nancy thought. Then this came along. Paul Sr.'s illness became an integral part of their life for twelve years—something she frankly had never expected. Nancy was not blessed with a caregiver's personality. She had left their mother's care to Amy. "Nancy didn't like sick, old people," Paul Jr. said. And for Paul Sr., just living day-to-day became an increasingly more difficult task.

"Dad's quality of life was good when I started college in 1974," Radford said, "but it went downhill from there. One of his goals was to make sixty so that Mom and Janey would get his pension. He did that. He made it to sixty-one. The other goal was to see Paul and me graduate from college and Jane from high school. Paul graduated in 1971 before he went in the service and was working on a master's when dad died. He saw Jane graduate from high school in June of 1976.

"I enrolled in Chapman College when I got back from Vietnam and graduated in December 1976 with a degree in government. I got a standing ovation from my friends when I walked across the stage and my dad was there to see it. It was one of his last outings."

When his doctor moved his practice to another state, Paul had to start over with a new doctor and a change in treatment. When his kidneys began to shut down, the doctors recommended he be put on dialysis. In order to do that, he needed a shunt put in his arm—a surgical procedure.

"He didn't survive the surgery," Paul Jr. said.

Paul died March 10, 1977.

Jane has vivid memories of her father's death. She was in class at the art school in downtown Los Angeles, where she received a message that she needed to come to the hospital.

When she arrived at the hospital, she went to the floor where her father's room was located. Her mother wasn't there. Jane looked in and could see her father lying in the bed. "I knew he was dead. I don't know why, but I knew. I turned and walked back to the lobby and just as I got there, I saw my mother and Radford coming through the door. It was awful."

Jane was eighteen. Though she had never known her father when he wasn't ill, his death hit her very hard. The two boys had less trouble dealing with it. They were several years older, Paul had a wife and child, and Radford had Vietnam behind him.

Nancy, stoic almost to a fault, bore up well. She had lived with the knowledge for a long time that Paul would not live to an old age. That she would be a widow. She later told her children that the grief was terrible, but she didn't say much more. It was something she had to deal with alone, and she did. Nancy Batson Crews still did her crying in private.

Flying would be her salvation for several more years, though, eventually, she would find a new direction, a new challenge, the one that would carry her the remainder of her years. But in the interim, Radford, by far the closest person to Nancy during that time, felt she had lost her stabilizing influence—her husband. "He's the only one I know of that she ever listened to. If she started to lose her temper and go off the deep end—which she could do and did—he could stop her cold with 'That's enough, Nancy!' He was her support, her anchor, and he was gone."

Now, Radford found himself thrust into that position.

"Many times she asked me to accompany her somewhere, particularly if she had something unpleasant to do, like one time she had to personally repossess an airplane that she had sold. The man had not kept up his payments to her. She and I flew down and landed at this guy's airport. She told him she was taking the airplane because he had missed several payments. She got in it and took off. I got back in my airplane, took off, and followed her.

"I took the role of enforcer. I'm big and I can look mean. I glowered a lot and never said a word. The first four years after my dad died, I was pretty heavily involved in my mother's life. During that time she and I had a lot of fun together, flying."

14

California City

With Paul's death, Nancy's life changed drastically. She had lived in a holding pattern as his condition worsened. Now she had to make the best of her situation. Paul left a pension and Nancy had her own business as well as land holdings in Alabama. All this figured in making her financially independent, but far from well off. The transition to widowhood was not easy.

After considering her resources, Nancy asked herself the question, "where do I go from here?" Two factors influenced her decision.

One: she wanted to move to the high desert country where she could pursue gliding. She enjoyed the gliding itself, and she loved the business end— towing gliders and instructing. The owner of a glider operation up in California City asked her to come there and work with him. "They needed an operator up there to do towing."

Two: Janey was nineteen and attending art school in the Los Angeles area. She was not interested in moving to the desert. When Janey and her best friend decided to go to San Diego and attend college there, that left her mother free to follow her own dream. Nancy, after putting Paul's affairs in order, moved to California City in the fall of 1977. Her business, Supercub Services, went with her. She not only towed gliders, she towed banners for advertising, flew aerial photographers and surveyors, flew Bureau of Land Management (BLM) officials around, offered her airplane for a variety of things, and also flight instructed. In addition, she operated Soaring Unlimited, offering glider rides and glider flight instruction.

Nancy held multiple ratings—an Airline Transport Pilot (ATP) certificate, earned in the summer of 1972; a commercial pilot's license for single-engine land planes; an instrument rating; a glider license; and a flight instructor's license for airplane, instrument, and glider all three. She also had a California teaching credential. And she did attend one more WASP reunion, flying Super Cub 83335 to the one held in Colorado Springs, September 28 to October 2, 1978.[1]

She moved to Cal City and settled in an apartment that Radford described as "a motel look-alike—very austere. Her door opened directly out onto the narrow second-floor corridor with balcony. She was cooking off a hot plate." This may have been the first time Nancy lived off of a hotplate and out of a microwave, but it was not the last. She was to repeat this lifestyle a few years later in Alabama.

Radford, now out of school, working odd jobs, and looking for a job in aviation, spent time up in the desert with her. He convinced her to buy a house. "You can afford it," he told her. "You don't have to live like this." She found a small house located in a large subdivision that never really took off and she got it for a bargain price. Nancy had lived through the Great Depression and now—as a relatively young widow of fifty-eight—she was looking at the possibility of living many years on her own. Always frugal, she knew how to pinch pennies.

"I helped her move the Cubs up there," Radford recalled. "I took my buddies up and we fixed up the house for her and painted it. We fixed up the swimming pool and trimmed the trees. She had stored a lot of her and Dad's stuff in her hangar in Compton. I helped her move that into the house, put her TV antenna up for her. I was heavily involved with my mother at that time. She was kind of a loner up there in the desert."

Nancy tended to be a loner wherever she went. She wasn't one to get particularly close to people. "She became a very solitary person," said Radford.

"While I was up there, we heard about this company that wanted somebody to haul hazardous material in Beech 18s—a twin-rudder, taildragger airplane, a real dragon to fly. By then I had 350 hours and, as of January 23, 1978, a brand-new commercial ticket. They were hiring copilots with hardly any qualifications. My mom went up with me to talk to them. They hired me and I worked for them for a year until I decided to use the last of my GI Bill benefits to get my ATP."

Nancy went to work towing gliders at the California City airport. True to form, she got involved in airport politics and soon was a member of the California City Airport Advisory committee. In the fall of 1979, that led to her election to the East Kern County Airport District board of directors. "The people of California City said that they wanted representation on the county board," Nancy said.

Later, Nancy told a reporter that while campaigning for the airport district board job, she "started hearing murmurings that people wanted a change in California City and even before I was elected [to the airport position] people were talking to me about running for mayor."

As she sank her roots into that sandy high desert soil, Nancy felt a mounting interest in the small but growing community. Having lived there for just over two years, in the spring of 1980 she toe-tested politics a second time and put her hat in the mayoral race. "I got the crusade in me. My parents had taught me that you give back, and I liked politics."

Possibly to everyone's surprise but her own, she won.

In a newspaper interview with Judy Barras (*The Bakersfield Californian,* May 2, 1980) following her election, Nancy said: "People had a feeling of apathy, they wanted more industry and opportunities for youth. And there were some people who felt they didn't have enough of a say in city government. . . . Different citizens from different areas in town talked to me after the election last fall and it was enough for me to campaign." The mayor's seat was only a two-year term. "I want things to be peaceful, calm, smooth and now I want to get on with the business of helping Cal City grow."[2]

Though she was never involved in the women's movement, Nancy was tagged with feministic aspirations. She admitted that some people wanted her to "run because I am a woman, but I campaigned as a person. I also campaigned with my own ideas, my own money. I don't owe anybody anything. I only owe the whole city."

Nancy immediately scheduled a series of Town Hall meetings to discuss her platform promises: bringing industry to California City, new sources of energy, and youth programs. She asked Radford and Jane to come for the kickoff meeting.

Unfortunately, Nancy stepped into a pile of strife and bad feelings that were not of her own making. But—given her head-on, black-and-white, you-have-to-do-what's-right, typical Nancy Crews attitude—she added fuel to the fire. She ruffled feathers.

"I had the damn crusading spirit in me. I'm a leader and I got elected. So I'm gonna lead."

All too quickly, past problems, past hurts and slights, petty jealousies—human nature—surfaced and Nancy's hopes for a smooth transition into the office of mayor and for peace and progress dissolved. California City, it turned out, was no different from any other small American city with unsolved problems in conflict with thwarted hopes for improvement. The city budget ran into approval problems that went unresolved for months. Nancy, quoting credit-card records, claimed that the city employees were undisciplined and undirected. That story made the front page. She was immediately called on the carpet by a city employee in the form of a letter to the editor. Another controversy erupted over where the mayor's office would be located. The bickering went back and forth.[3]

"She thought she could tell people what to do," Radford said. "To her it was right or wrong and if you were wrong, you ought to straighten up and do it right. And right meant her way."

Radford thought that his mother, striking out on her own without his father's steadying influence, went "over the top" on several occasions—the mayor's job being by far the most disastrous. It was not that Paul would have said "no," or "that's enough, Nancy," rather that he would have pointed out the downside, the potential mistakes, and asked her to rethink things before they were faits accomplis. He would have provided the ballast Nancy was used to having. Nancy was a risk taker and she was proud of that, but until now she had always had Paul's good judgment and sage advice to fall back on as a leveling influence.

"She went into politics naïve and she got burned."

Two bright spots illuminated Nancy's summer in 1980. In June, she attended Jane's graduation from San Diego Mesa College with an associate in arts degree. Then on July 24, Nancy hosted a bridal shower for Jane in Cal City's Central Park.

Two weeks later, Nancy's world fell apart.

"Police officers are investigating an apparent sabotage attempt on an airplane which California City mayor Nancy Crews owns and flies," said the lead paragraph of a front-page story in the *Mojave Desert News*, dated August 7, 1980.[4]

"When I got done flying Sunday night, instead of putting the Super Cub in the hangar, I tied it down outside. I was going to be going out again very early Monday morning [August 4]. I was flying down to Bakersfield to pick up a BLM official and take him up to monitor signals from radio transmitters tagged on kit foxes for observation purposes. Early Monday morning, I picked up a lady who was going to fly down to Bakersfield with me.

"We got to the airport and I started my walk around the airplane. I found a screw loose on the air filter. It didn't fit. Wasn't the right screw. I took it out and removed the air filter and there was a white powdery substance inside the cylinder. I called the police. [The newspaper article says she called at 5:30 a.m.] I told them they also needed to call the FBI because tampering with an airplane is a federal offense. I thought somebody had sabotaged my airplane."

The police never found out who did it—or if they did, they never told Nancy and no one was ever prosecuted. She, on the other hand, was subjected to nasty rumors that she had sabotaged her own plane to get sympathy. "Sympathy for what? I was doing my job. I was the mayor, trying to act like one and lead." An article dated September 25, 1980, from the *Mojave Desert News*, datelined California City, said that the police there were continuing their investigation and they were eliminating suspects.[5]

Later the police chief had her take a lie-detector test, the process of which frightened her half out of her wits. She admits she should have thought to take someone into the police station with her, but she didn't. Radford was angry when he found out, but by then there was nothing he could do. What was done was done. But the ordeal had a profound effect on Nancy. Never before had her veracity, her integrity, been questioned.

"It was a traumatic experience for someone as idealistic as me. I went home and had hysterics," Nancy admitted in an interview twenty years later.

The miracle is, she stuck with the mayoral job for nearly a year after the incident. The town's, and Nancy's, and the city council's problems continued.

In July 1981, the city's budget was on the radar screen again and the residents once more were complaining about overspending, budget deficits, and assessments. At the July 7 meeting of the California City council, as the session was drawing to a close, Mayor Crews announced that she was stepping down from the office mid-term. She gave her resignation date as effective August 1. Just prior to the council meeting, she had also resigned from the East Kern County Airport District board.[6]

"I am leaving for Alabama to begin again to take care of personal family business," she said at a press conference July 31. "I'm not a quitter," she said, but added that she had become frustrated with not being able to accomplish any of her goals. She blamed this on the "lack of cooperation" shown her by the rest of the council and the city staff. "I have resigned . . . as a form of protest toward what I consider frustrating inadequacies in local government and City management. Too little consideration has been given the taxpayers of California City . . . too much has been given as examples or excuses for continued wasting of taxpayers funds."[7]

Reminiscing again, she said, "I've been hit on the ground by another airplane. I've almost been hit in the air by another airplane. I've been lost. I've had an engine quit on takeoff and I've had one quit on landing. The one thing I haven't done is run out of gas. But if we had taken off that morning, that stuff would have gummed up my cylinders and we sure enough would have crashed on takeoff.

"I did, finally, find out what the powdery substance was—Bon Ami." The steel-nerved pursuit pilot who had forced a balky P-38 nosewheel into position and who had flown many a dangerous, shot-up, war-weary airplane to the boneyard in the fall of 1944 had dodged another bullet.

She was still flying, but her life, once again, was changing. She kept her ratings current, but after leaving California City, her flying career took a decided downturn. She flew occasionally in Alabama, but nothing like she was doing in California. In Alabama, other concerns occupied her time. She may have had a close call in her airplane, but worse, she had had one close call too many in interpersonal relationships. "They were out to crucify me and I wasn't going to let them do it. I was through with politics. I resigned and came back to Alabama."

15

Lake Country Estates

"There I was in California and we had this big hunk of property back in Alabama. The other family members wanted to realize their money from this land we held. Until Jane got married later in 1980, I had to keep things going from California City. So, I got this big real estate firm to help me decide what to do with it. But when it came to a decision, I had to use my own judgment. I didn't do anything until I left California City and came back here to Alabama in 1981."

For Nancy, the move meant starting over. She was sixty-one years old and had been gone from home—from the South—for thirty-two years. Nothing was the same. Family members and old family friends had passed on. The remaining kin were the next generation. The Alabama that she returned to was nothing like the Alabama she had left in 1950. Nancy began to rebuild her life.

Because she planned to live in it, Nancy drove the RV—crammed with the possessions she wanted to keep—from California to Alabama.

At that point, the Rocky Ridge Farm—where Nancy and Paul had lived as newlyweds in the late 1940s—was rented out, but the house was still there, and unoccupied. Nancy planned to use the farmhouse for storage and to live in the RV, which she parked next to the house. She had sold one Super Cub and Radford flew the remaining one back to Alabama when he came for his cousin Luther's wedding.

Nancy also owned a 1949 Mooney Mite that she had been restoring while living in California City. "Mite" aptly describes this pint-sized, single-seater wooden aircraft, built when the aviation world still thought that someday there would be a small airplane in every garage parked next to the family car. A man she knew from the Birmingham Aero Club offered her hangar space for it at the Talladega Airport. She flew it cross-country, east, to Talladega.

"So there I was in the country, living in the RV and trying to decide what to do with all this land. I got a job with a local firm in order to get my real estate license and I started making contacts with people."

Nancy set out to learn the real estate and building businesses literally from the ground up.

The farm at Rocky Ridge was a favorite of Paul Jr. and remains a place he will not forget. Not only did he live there the first years of his life, he returned often as a young child and walked the pastures with his grandfather when Radford Sr. checked on the beef cattle he was raising. "I remember, after my grandfather died, going to a cattle auction with my grandmother and my mom," Paul said. "Some of their cattle were being auctioned. I was in junior high by then and, living in suburban California, that was a unique experience for me. This farm was in St. Clair County, quite near where my grandmother grew up. Both my Batson grandparents came from an Alabama country background.

"In fact, my grandmother kept bees. It wasn't a big thing, but she would go out to the farm every day and harvest honey. She kept a jar with a honeycomb in it and when we visited their house, we would eat the raw honey."

Before he died, Rad Sr. had turned Rocky Ridge into a chicken farm. Paul remembered the chicken coops. "They were long red brick houses. Our grandfather had a contract with the Purina Feed Company. They brought little chicks out to be raised to a certain age. Then the Purina people came and got them and paid first my grandfather and, after he died, my grandmother so much per chicken. That's where some of the money my grandmother lived on came from. After my grandfather died and until she became too ill, Muddy drove out every day to check on the bees, the chickens, and the farm. Tenant farmers lived there and took care of the farm—local folks. When Muddy became ill, they stopped the chicken operation and the farm lay fallow for a while."

When Nancy went back to Alabama in the fall of 1981, she needed to feel safe. Her roots were deep in that St. Clair County soil and she felt comfortable there. Before her father died, when she would go home for a visit, they would walk the eighty acres he had bought after the war and he talked to her about what they could do with it. And she listened.

"'Sis,' he said to me, 'you can do anything you make up your mind to.' And if my daddy said it, it was true." Together, they made plans for the land and for the future. By developing that land, Nancy felt she was fulfilling a contract with her father. Paul related that in those early years back in Alabama, she would go out to Elmwood Cemetery and talk to her father and mother—tell them what she was doing.

What Nancy had learned from her father was that the Rocky Ridge farmland was not suitable for development. The land was full of limestone caves and subject to sinkholes. Nancy wanted to build houses, but she was afraid if she built there that the foundations could collapse if a sinkhole appeared.

As manager of the family's holdings, first she sold the thirty-acre hog farm—across the road from the chicken farm—to a man who built a home and his own landing strip. She liked that, in fact she hoped, eventually, to do the same thing herself. Then a group of developers bought the chicken farm. Nancy had decided to concentrate on the eighty acres.

Nancy owned twenty of the eighty acres and four other family members (her sister, two nephews, and a niece) owned the remaining sixty. They weren't interested in developing the land or building houses. The land was worth approximately nine hundred dollars an acre. So Nancy dug deep in her pockets to determine whether she could afford to take the plunge, financially. She also looked deep into her soul to see if she dared take the risk. Her decision made, she told the other heirs that she would buy out their sixty acres and offered to pay them one thousand dollars an acre. They agreed.

"Sixty thousand dollars—I had to come up with sixty thousand dollars.

"I decided then I'd better sell my airplane. I pinched pennies to pay them off. It took awhile, but I did it, and I owned the eighty acres outright. I started driving around, trying to figure out what I had in those eighty acres."

That was how she happened to find the building that became her home for her remaining years. The one-story structure with cement floors may have been intended as an automobile garage. Another source said it was to be a post office. It most certainly didn't look like a house then. It sat on two lots that were part of another development, but the land was right next door to her eighty acres. The bank had foreclosed on the owner. Nancy bought the property, brought the RV over, and parked it out front.

That eighty-acre plot was destined to become Nancy Batson Crews's final and greatest achievement—Lake Country Estates. But she started small and she started with considerable caution. First, as her father had suggested, she cut the timber and sold it.

"As for the house, I wasn't worried about looking good, but I began fixing it up. It was to be my home." She added a log porch to two sides of the house so she could sit outside and watch the world go by as her investment grew. Eventually she got the house ready for occupancy and moved in. But once again, she opted for cooking on a hot plate and in a microwave. Nancy was a woman of simple tastes in food, in clothing, in her surroundings. She sold the RV and with it went a lot of memories—good ones, bad ones, sad ones. Now, she was truly back in Alabama to stay. California and all its heartaches were history.

About the time she moved back to Alabama, Nancy discovered a book that became her bible for her final twenty years: *Think and Grow Rich*, by Napoleon Hill. The book was written in 1937 when the Depression had taken its toll and was heavy on people's minds. Nancy's dog-eared paperback copy bore a 1979 reprint date.

Steel magnate/philanthropist Andrew Carnegie inspired Hill's book, which is still in print and, decades later, still a big seller. The philosophy behind the book, as per its title, is to help individuals "think and grow rich" in a monetary sense. But it takes the premise that "the riches within your grasp are not always measurable by money or financial gain." Hill lists twelve requirements for gaining wealth—both financial riches and the riches of the spirit. Among them are a positive mental attitude, freedom from fear, the capacity for an applied faith, engaging in a labor of love, and having both an open mind and self discipline.[1]

Nancy believed absolutely in the tenets of this philosophy and she followed them from the day she discovered the book until she died. She preached its gospel to others.

"My mother had two aims," Paul Jr. recalled in a 2004 interview. "She wanted to die in her sleep and be worth a million dollars. She used the property she owned as a device to build wealth based on *Think and Grow Rich*. By the time she died—in her own bed—she was worth more than a million when you figure the land value. And Lake Country Estates continues to grow today, so her vision turned into quite a legacy."

"Master Minding"—as espoused by Napoleon Hill—was Nancy's personal path to the wealth and security she desired.[2] "You gather people around you who are smart, who have the knowledge and the skills you don't have. When I moved here, I didn't know anything, but I built a mastermind group. You can't do it all by yourself. You have to get other people's brains working with and for you. These people I gathered around me, they liked me and they trusted me. They're in the business and that's what it's all about. We discussed how we were gonna do things, determined what it would cost. They did the work. I paid them.

"You get a group to work with. That's what I learned from that little paper-back.

"For instance, somebody told me about a surveyor up in northern Alabama—an old WWII codger who had been with Patton's army. I went to see him. 'Now Miz Crews,' he said, 'you don't try to develop forty acres at one time. You do a little piece at a time and then go on to the next piece.' Then his son helped me. He put up with me. We've been together for twenty years.

"I was lucky. I worked with people who took me under their wing. They told me what to do. One man and his wife wanted to buy one of my lots. They built the first house in my subdivision. They got me started. He bought some more lots and showed me how to build a house. He would help me when I'd get ready. He'd come give me advice.

"Those two elderly men were kind and generous and helped me out. They showed me what to do. In fact, later on, one big real estate developer down here told me, 'you done good, girl!' I hung in there.

"That's how I got started. I had the good fortune to have Southern gentlemen helping me and I didn't go out on a limb as far as money was concerned. Now I'm a businesswoman. My business took on a life of its own."

When she built, she used local carpenters, bricklayers, cement workers, plumbers, laborers. As she built, she met new people and her mastermind contingent grew. Other contractors wanted to buy land from her and build homes. Men would work on one of her houses and decide to build their own home in Lake Country Estates. That was the model Nancy used—employing local craftsmen to work on the houses and building from within.

"I walked down the property with her when she surveyed it in 1989," Paul recalled. "She cleared the land in small sections, one piece at a time, as she had the money. That was her modus operandi. At that time, up the ridge and around the lake was undeveloped. In fact, the lake didn't exist then. It was just raw land. But she had a plan.

"She felt she gave people an opportunity to have homes who might not have been able to afford them otherwise. She was very proud of that. They did it by living on the land—something she had learned from the way my grandfather worked with his tenant farmers. He was always her role model."

Paul Jr. and his mother had been estranged since 1971. He came to his father's funeral in 1977, but he and his mother did not speak. He also attended Jane's wedding in 1980. Nor was a true reconciliation in the cards in 1989, but at least they began speaking again. Lake Country Estates is what drew them together, but the big event that led to a resumption of speaking terms was Nancy's induction into the Alabama Aviation Hall of Fame.

After moving back to Alabama, Nancy did get involved in Birmingham area aviation. She was doing some gliding with the Soaring Society and she had joined the Birmingham Aero Club.[3] She also, until she sold the Super Cub, did some banner towing and performed other professional aviation services. And she had the Mooney Mite parked out in Talladega. She wanted to either fly it or sell it, but she ran into a problem with the Federal Aviation Administration (FAA).

"The FAA said I had to have the spar on that airplane inspected. Now I knew that airplane was perfect because we had just put it together. I did *not* want to tear it up again just so they could tell me it was OK. I couldn't fly it and I couldn't sell it, so I donated it to the Southern Museum of Flight."

The board of governors of the Birmingham Aero Club established the Birmingham Air and Space Museum in 1965. The first public aviation exhibits were in the library of nearby Samford University. Then, in 1967, the collection was moved to the original Birmingham airport terminal. In 1969, the museum was renamed the Southern Museum of Flight. In 1978, building of a permanent home for the museum was begun on land two blocks east of the airport. Two wings were opened in 1983. Since then, two more wings have been added and the museum is now an X-shaped structure with an atrium in the center.[4]

Nancy thought this new museum would be the perfect home for her little airplane. On November 6, 1988, she turned it over to them. "I flew it from Talladega to the Birmingham Airport—not quite an hour's flight—and taxied it to the far end of the runway to the fence. I got out. There, a bunch of guys lifted the airplane over the fence. Then I got back in and taxied it down the road to the museum. And that's where it is today."

The Alabama legislature established the Alabama Aviation Hall of Fame in 1975. The nonprofit, financially self-supporting organization receives no government funding. The governor of Alabama appoints two members to the seven-member board of directors; the mayors of Huntsville, Birmingham, Montgomery, and Mobile appoint one each; and the Southern Museum of Flight appoints one. The museum is the home of the Hall of Fame. Nominations come from the interested public. The first inductees were elected in 1981.[5] As of 1988, no woman had been enshrined in the Alabama Aviation Hall of Fame.

By then, Nancy once again was well known in aviation circles around Birmingham as well as in real estate circles and in social circles due to her family's long-time standing in the community. It was only fitting that the Alabama native who was in the historic first Civilian Pilot Training (CPT) class at the University of Alabama in 1939, who was one of only 134 women to fly pursuit airplanes for the Air Transport Command in World War II (and the only one from Alabama), and who was about to enter her sixth decade as a qualified, active pilot was the obvious selection for the first woman inductee into that prestigious assembly.

The date was October 13, 1989. It would have been Paul Crews Sr.'s seventy-fourth birthday. He would have been very proud. Nancy wanted her children there and issued the invitation to all three. Radford told Paul how important this was to their mother and Paul opted to come.

That evening, two other individuals were inducted as well. One was Ed Long, an Alabamian with an incredible flight record of nearly fifty thousand hours. And he was still flying in 1989, adding to that record. The other—so fitting that he and Nancy were inducted at the same time—was U.S. Air Force General Daniel "Chappie" James Jr., one of the Tuskegee Airmen in World War II.[6]

Chappie James learned to fly while attending the Tuskegee Institute and after graduation in 1942 continued civilian flight training until he received appointment as a cadet in the Army Air Forces in January 1943. He was commissioned in July 1943 and throughout the remainder of World War II he trained pilots for the all-black 99th Pursuit Squadron.[7] His men flew—in combat in Europe and North Africa—the same airplanes Nancy was ferrying back in the states.

Though the WASP and the Tuskegee Airmen fought different battles for acceptance and recognition during and after World War II, their struggles have similarities rooted in the discrimination of the times. As the remaining veterans of both groups have aged and the surviving individuals have taken their rightful places alongside the much more numerous white male veterans of the U.S. Armed Forces from World War II, the two groups—elderly black men and elderly white women—over the past ten to fifteen years have formed a bond. One group fought racism, the other sexism back in an era—the 1940s—when the world looked and thought and acted quite differently than it does today. Each group appreciates the other's journey and today they can be seen hanging out together, chatting enthusiastically—hangar flying—at aviation events around the country.

Chappie James went on to become the first black four-star general in the

U.S. military. Sadly, he had been deceased for ten years when his induction into the Hall of Fame came about. His wife, Dorothy Watkins James, accepted the silver bowl in his stead. He was a native of Florida, not Alabama, but when he set foot on the Tuskegee campus back in the late 1930s, he made his date with destiny—just as Nancy did when she tore across the University of Alabama campus that fall day in 1939 to sign up for CPT.

16

Enhancing the Legacy

In 1979, Sally Van Wagenen Keil, the niece of one of the seventeen women pilots Jackie Cochran sent to Lockbourne Army Airfield for B-17 transition in the fall of 1943, published the first popular history of the WASP, *Those Wonderful Women in Their Flying Machines.* Well written and full of personal stories told by WASP, the book is the benchmark when it comes to telling the WASP story. A second edition with updated material was released in 1990.

In her author's note, Keil tells of her fascination with her five-foot-eleven-inch-tall aunt, Mary Parker Audain (Class 43-5). Cochran sent her tallest, biggest, and best recent Sweetwater graduates to learn to fly the Flying Fortress. Audain had gone on to live a life that enthralled all of her nieces and they all, Keil wrote, wanted to be like her. But it was the fact that she flew the B-17 that thrilled them the most. When Audain died in 1973, Keil and her sisters discovered that the only memorabilia their fifty-five-year-old aunt had saved were photographs from her flying years, her graduation certificate from Avenger Field, and a WASP roster. They also realized they knew little about her WASP experiences because she rarely talked about them. To learn the story and ultimately share it with others, Keil spent five years researching and interviewing many WASP in order to write that book. Nancy Batson Crews was one of the women she talked to.[1]

Beginning in 1978, the reunions began to happen every two years like clockwork. Getting together regularly, the WASP began to recall and to share their memories of that cherished time long ago. The reunions and Keil's book opened up the floodgates, after which many WASP books began to appear. In the 1980s, WASP began to write their memoirs. In the 1990s, journalists and scholars began to write about the WASP. The public began, ever so slowly, to learn about them.

The fiftieth anniversary of the founding of both the WAFS and the WASP fell in 1992. The aviation and military worlds woke up to the realization not only that this small group of female World War II veterans existed, but also that more than half of them were still alive and, just like their male veteran counterparts, they were reaching their seventies and eighties. Also came the realization that the inevitable passage of time was depleting their ranks at the same rate as the men. Now organizations scrambled to recognize these women in their midst.

San Antonio, the home of three Air Force bases and within reasonable proximity of the training field at Sweetwater as well as the WASP's first home, Houston, was the site of the big fiftieth WASP reunion. Yvonne "Pat" Pateman (Class 43-5) was the president. Pat was, by then, a retired Air Force lieutenant colonel who had served more than twenty years on active duty, including service in Korea and Vietnam. Another 156 WASP, like Pateman, took Reserve commissions when the newly designated U.S. Air Force offered them beginning in 1949 and during the Korean War. Eleven of the WAFS were among that number. Nancy Batson Crews did not opt for a commission, but her friends Teresa James, Barbara London, Helen Mary Clark, and Betty Gillies were among those who did.

In January 1992, the International Women's Air and Space Museum (IWASM), located at that time in Centerville, Ohio, decided to bring in a panel of WASP to do a program at the local cable television station. Seven WASP made up the bulk of the panel. Moderator Nadine Nagle (Class 44-9) was joined by Caro Bayley Bosca and Katherine (Kaddy) Landry Steele (Class 43-7 classmates), Emma Coulter Ware (Class 43-3), Margaret Ray Ringenberg (Class 43-5), Ann Criswell Madden (Class 43-6), and Marty Martin Wyall (Class 44-10). The representative WAFS on the panel was Nancy Batson Crews. Of note: that panel of eight included a past WASP president, Nancy Crews (1972–1975), and two future presidents, Marty Wyall (1994–1996) and Caro Bosca (2004–2007). Kaddy Steele chaired the WASP Future committee.

These programs put on jointly by IWASM and the Miami Valley Cable Council (now known as Miami Valley Communications Council) were done live before a studio audience and still are broadcast today. In the process, these women, their voices, and their stories—oral history—were recorded for posterity.

Eight WASP, it turned out, were far too many for such a rich discussion. Each of the women could easily have been a program unto herself. Nevertheless, the women enthralled the live audience with their reminiscences. When the hour was up, the director kept the cameras rolling as the women continued to talk. The result was an additional forty-five minutes of stories and exchanges that further delighted the studio audience. The WASP were a hit in the Dayton, Ohio, south suburbs.

In 1992, Lake Country Estates was a thriving enterprise. Nancy was in the midst of making her dream come true. And though she wasn't flying much, she was involved with the aviation crowd and culture through the Birmingham Aero Club. She also had reconnected with the Birmingham chapter of the Ninety-Nines. In the mid-1990s, she served on the St. Clair County Airport Authority. And she continued to strengthen her friendships with old aviation friends, like Joe Shannon from her prewar days at the Birmingham Airport, and to make new aviation friends, like Dr. James A. Pittman, dean of the medical school at the University of Alabama Birmingham.

Shannon was the one who had helped her get the brakes on her A-20 fixed in Meridian, Mississippi, in 1944. Whenever the two were at an aviation gathering, one of them would be called on to relate the "how long do you want to keep her here?" story. Joe spent much of the war in North Africa, shot down three-plus enemy planes, and later flew critical missions with the Alabama Air National Guard during the Bay of Pigs encounter. He was still flying his Cessna 140 in 2008.

Pittman, who was too young to serve in World War II, became enamored of the sleek warbirds as a teenager during the war. His father had flown for the Navy in World War I. Pittman learned to fly J-3 Cubs immediately after the war and bought a Stearman for $275 in 1947 while he was in college. "That's when I really learned to fly," he said. In 2008, Dr. Pittman and his son still owned a yellow and blue Stearman PT-17—like the one Nancy flew on the Great Falls, Montana, to Jackson, Tennessee, ferrying trip in December 1942.

In the early 1990s, Nancy received a call from Diane Ruth Armour Bartels. A Nebraska elementary school teacher and a private pilot, Bartels had received a National Endowment for the Humanities/Reader's Digest Teacher–Scholar Award to research and write the life story of WAFS Evelyn Sharp—the all-American-girl war heroine from Ord, Nebraska. Diane was conducting interviews with the living WAFS as part of her research into this young woman who had become the idol of a small town and of many a Nebraska schoolgirl. Nancy told Diane everything she could about Evelyn, including the story of escorting her body home to Ord for the funeral in April 1944.

Diane shared with Nancy—and later wrote in her introduction to the Sharp biography—how she came to write Evelyn's story.

Diane had met Evelyn's friend and mentor, Dr. Glen D. Auble, at the 1973 Nebraska State Air Show in Ord. Dr. Auble had told her about Evelyn and that it was his mission to make sure that she was not forgotten. "I have often wondered if he saw me as just one more person to tell, or if he sensed I would fulfill his dream to have her life story written," Diane wrote.

Diane pursued her own life and her teaching but, over the next eighteen years, she collected memorabilia and information on Evelyn. She corresponded with Dr. Auble until his death in 1986 and continued his and her own efforts to keep Sharpie's name and story out in front of the Nebraska public. In the summer of 1988, she participated in the National Endowment for the Humanities institute, "The Struggle for Freedom and Equality: Life Stories of Great Americans." She wrote about Evelyn. Her presentation brought tears to the eyes of many of her colleagues and they encouraged her to continue her research and finish her manuscript. Three years later, the teacher–scholar grant allowed her to take a year off from teaching to finish her research and write her book.

Sharpie: The Life Story of Evelyn Sharp–Nebraska's Aviatrix was published in 1996.[2]

Soon after Evelyn's death, the airport at Ord was renamed for her. The sign reads: "Sharp Field, Ord Municipal Airport, Elevation 2042." A three-blade aluminum, red-tipped propeller from a P-38 is mounted there and the official dedication was held September 12, 1948. On June 24, 1973, through the efforts of project coordinator Dr. Glen D. Auble, a Nebraska State Historical Society highway marker telling the story of Evelyn and the WASP was placed at the entrance to Sharp Field.[3]

The year *Sharpie* was published, 1996, the first annual Evelyn Sharp Day was held in Ord in June. A granite monument was to be dedicated. Diane Bartels contacted Nancy Crews again. Diane was hoping some of the WAFS would come to that dedication. She particularly wanted Nancy since Nancy had brought Evelyn home in 1944 and a few people surely would remember her. Nancy went. She wouldn't have missed it for the world!

"She got in her pickup truck and drove all the way up here from Alabama," Diane said, with admiration in her voice. "What a woman!"

When one stops to consider it, Nancy was simply doing what she spent more than two years of her life doing–crisscrossing the United States sitting alone in the cockpit of an airplane–only this time she was driving a pickup truck. She probably RONed (remained overnight) somewhere in Missouri en route.

The fact is, Nancy had rather quietly begun a quest similar to that of

Dr. Auble and Diane. Her desire was to get the story of the WAFS out and to have Nancy Love's role given the full recognition she felt it deserved.

A year later, June 1997, Nancy climbed into her pickup truck and drove north again—this time to Atchison, Kansas, the birthplace of Amelia Earhart and the home of the International Forest of Friendship. The Forest honors those who have contributed, or still are contributing, to all facets of aviation and aerospace. Betty Gillies—to honor her friend and fellow women's squadron member, 2nd Ferrying Group, New Castle Army Air Base, Wilmington, Delaware—had sponsored Nancy for induction into the Forest that year.

Some of the other women flyers inducted that year included Diane Bartels, Ninety-Nines and an aviation author; Joan Hrubec, IWASM and the Ninety-Nines; two of the earliest women military aviators, Capt. Lucy Young (U.S. Navy Reserve, retired) and Col. Kelly Hamilton (U.S. Air Force, retired); WASP Jean Pearson (Class 43-3); and two of the Mercury 13 (women pilots who passed the astronaut physical testing in 1960–1961), Irene Leverton and Sarah Ratley.

The Forest, begun in 1976, was a bicentennial gift to the United States from the city of Atchison and the Ninety-Nines, the international organization of women pilots of which Earhart was a founder. Trees have been planted representing all fifty states and the thirty-five countries where honorees reside. Each tree has its own flag, and on special occasions, "the Forest is ablaze with the brilliance of colors of more than 100 flags blowing in the breeze."[4] Honorees may be living or deceased and represent the following areas related to aviation:

- Women and men who have given dedicated service, leadership, friendship, and supportive effort to help others achieve aviation goals.
- Women and men who have been supportive and contributed to the furtherment of aviation. The honorees need not be pilots.
- Pioneers in aviation and aerospace.
- Aviation writers and educators who spend their lives encouraging others to fly.
- Women and men who have made significant contributions to the development of aviation, and those who have established recognition for setting world aviation records.

The Forest of Friendship was founded and led by Fay Gillis Wells and Joe Carrigan. Wells, like Earhart, was one of the charter members of the Ninety-

Nines and has been honored for her great interest and support of aviation and as an outstanding journalist. Carrigan resided in Atchison and was responsible for the daily decisions needed to run the Forest. Both are now deceased and their sons are carrying on for them.

The Forest—truly a national treasure—is nestled on a gentle slope overlooking Lake Warnock, on the outskirts of Atchison. Memory Lane, a five-foot-wide, wheelchair friendly, concrete walkway, winds through the forest. Embedded in the walkway are granite plaques honoring more than twelve hundred individuals (as of 2009) who have contributed to the advancement of aviation and the exploration of space. The grounds also contain a statue of Amelia Earhart and a NASA astronaut memorial.[5]

Nancy Batson Crews's plaque lies along the western loop of Memory Lane near the white pine representing the state of Alabama.[6]

After Nancy donated her Mooney Mite to the Southern Museum of Flight, and after she was enshrined in the Alabama Aviation Hall of Fame there, she also donated her WAFS uniform, her silver wings, her first logbook, and other memorabilia including several photographs. Her materials occupy a case near the main floor entrance to the museum right next to the gift shop.

Nancy no longer owned an airplane. All of her money was going into Lake Country Estates. Then, by chance, in 1991, she heard of a J-3 Cub that was, in her words, "a basket case." But it had restoration potential.

"It was a 1940, the year I soloed and got my private pilot's license. It had a seventy-five-horsepower engine. The one I learned on at the University of Alabama was only fifty. The ones we flew in the Ferry Command in the fall of '42 were sixty-five horsepower. It cost me seventy-five hundred dollars, but finally, I had my heart's desire—a yellow J-3 Cub. They told us in Civilian Pilot Training that if you could fly a J-3 Cub, you could fly anything." Nancy's Cub, at that point, however, was anything but flyable.

First, she loaned the Cub to a community college in northern Alabama, where they used such planes to teach students to be airplane mechanics. "Later, I even tried to learn to be a mechanic. I took the class myself and took the engine apart. I figured I could do it. What the heck! But then the school closed. So I brought the Cub home and stored it in my garage. In the meantime, I had heard about this fellow up in Delaware who worked on Cubs. I called him and he said, 'sure, bring it up.' I loaded it on a trailer and drove it up there. He had it for three years."

Writers, journalists, historians, and scholars periodically contacted Nancy for information on the WAFS or for her personal stories. She was well known to WASP followers and she was accessible. Sally Keil had interviewed her, as had Diane Bartels and Marianne Verges (*On Silver Wings*, 1991). Now Rob Simbeck also sought her out for insight into his subject, Cornelia Fort (*Daughter of the Air*, 1999). Air Force historian H. O. Malone checked in with her when he was looking for material to nominate Nancy Love for the National Aviation Hall of Fame. Dawn Letson, director of the Woman's Collection at the Texas Woman's University library, taped Nancy's oral history for the WASP Collection.

Nancy gave talks about the WAFS in Alabama and elsewhere when asked. She was always happy to spread the word about the WAFS and Nancy Love.

On March 24, 1983, eight men who had served as ferry pilots with the 2nd Ferrying Group at New Castle Army Air Base (NCAAB) in Wilmington got together to hangar fly and tell war stories. During lunch at the Fort Myer Officers' Club near Washington, D.C., they discussed forming an organization. They became known as the founding eight. Others were invited to a second meeting, held in September 1983 in Denver. There, plans were laid for the first official reunion of the group that would be known as the Wilmington Warriors Association (WWA). That reunion was held October 20, 1983, at the Presidio in San Francisco.

The potential membership was vast. Ferry pilots from the 2nd had flown all over the globe in WWII as the Air Transport Command and the Ferrying Division pioneered new routes to the far corners of civilization—all in the interest of winning the war. Flights across the North and South Atlantic and, later in the war, flights via the Crescent route to Africa and India and on over The Hump originated at NCAAB. In addition to the thousands of male ferry pilots, there were the sixty or so women who also had been ferry pilots with the 2nd.

When the group met for their second reunion in 1984 in Colorado Springs, a WASP liaison had been added to the list of officers in the person of Betty Gillies, the commander of the 2nd's women's squadron from January 1, 1943, to December 20, 1944. Barbara London soon joined her. Beginning in 1988, B.J.'s name appeared as the WAFS/WASP liaison. Nancy Crews and Teresa James had joined the group as well.

The tenth reunion, held in 1992, was actually the Big Five O as the Warriors, like the WASP, marked fifty years since the group's inception. Wilmington—where it all began—was chosen as the site. Seven women ferry pilots who had served as part of the 2nd Ferrying Group attended. Joining Nancy, Betty, B.J., and Teresa were Del Scharr, Florene Miller Watson, and

Jane Straughn, who was a graduate of the first WASP Class, 43-1. She was one of the "guinea pigs" who trained in Houston before the operation was moved to Sweetwater. Upon graduation, she was sent to Wilmington.

Following the 1992 reunion, Onas P. Matz (Colonel, U.S. Air Force Reserve, retired), who served 1942–1944 as operations and training officer at Wilmington, wrote and published *The History of the 2nd Ferrying Group.* Parts one and two deal with the actual history—including the WASP's contribution—and part three tells about the reunions between 1983 and 1992.[7]

Nancy continued to attend the reunions throughout the 1990s. The 1999 Wilmington Warriors reunion was to be held at the U.S. Air Force Museum in Dayton, Ohio.

17

Nancy and the Planes She Ferried

Early in May of 1999, Nancy called yours truly. She was coming to Dayton for the reunion, May 24 and 25. Could we get together? Nancy and I had met in 1992 when she came to the International Women's Air and Space Museum (IWASM) for the WASP program.

Nancy was planning to visit the U.S. Air Force Museum. Would she agree to have a videographer follow her around the museum and videotape her looking at and talking about the various airplanes she flew?[1]

She was amenable.

A call to Judith Wehn, education specialist at the museum, verified that such an undertaking was permissible.

John Moraites, who volunteered his time and talents at Miami Valley Cable Council, where we had, in the early 1990s, taped IWASM's "Women in Aviation" programs, would do the videography.

John, his wife and production assistant Barb, and I met Nancy at the Air Force Museum the morning after her arrival in Dayton. Judith met us as well and told us that we were invited to have lunch with Gen. Charles Metcalf, the museum director. Judith also had met Nancy at the IWASM WASP panel in 1992 and she had told the general about her. He wanted to meet the Golden Girl of the Ferry Command.

As we toured the museum, Nancy stopped in front of all of "her" airplanes and talked about her experiences flying them. "Now look here . . ." We were standing by the A-20, her favorite airplane—a big, powerful-looking, camouflage-green, twin-engine attack bomber. "This is how we got up and into the cockpit," she said, pointing out two covered footholds on the fuselage behind the wing.

"Here's the nosewheel that wouldn't lock in place," she said when we stopped at the P-38. She related the story of her November 4, 1944, flight over Pittsburgh and acted out for us the arm, hand, and body gyrations she went through in the cockpit to blow the CO2 cartridge and lock that errant nosewheel down.

"I wore a flight jacket just like that," she said, pointing to a case containing the famous brown leather bomber jacket with the Air Transport Command emblem on the left breast.

"Now this is the Link trainer—a flight simulator. We got inside and pulled the top down and we were completely enclosed. All we could see was the instrument panel. See the operator, sitting over there at the desk," and she pointed to the mannequin dressed in a khaki Army uniform sitting at a desk outside the stationary blue and yellow simulator. "He would talk to us and put us through all sorts of problems. That was our first instrument training."

Occasionally a museum visitor would stop and listen to Nancy and then ask her a question or just talk with her. She responded cordially, always with that smile. John, without showing the face of the questioner, managed to get the conversations on the tape—adding more interest to our program.

"This was the first pursuit plane I flew," she said, as we approached the museum's P-47. "I got out of the back seat of an AT-6 and into this. What a jump! A taildragger with that great-big engine. See that big, wide landing gear. Beautiful! Easy to fly!"

When we got to the prominent plaque that displays pilot John Gillespie Magee Jr.'s famous poem "High Flight," John videotaped Nancy reading it.

Judith appeared to escort us upstairs to lunch. Awaiting us was not only General Metcalf, but also some other staff members and a couple of members of the Friends of the Museum—all there to meet Nancy. And Nancy didn't disappoint. She entranced the entire gathering with her Southern accent, her smile, and her stories and came away from lunch with an invitation to come back and speak as part of the museum's lecture series the following season.

After lunch, we went over to the Presidential Hangar. All the airplanes that have served our various presidents are kept in a separate hangar across the field from the museum proper. Nancy wanted to see them. Back then—long before 9-11 and heightened security—the only way to get there was to climb in your vehicle and drive over. The hangar was actually on Wright-Patterson Air Force Base and you needed permission to enter, but permission, in 1999, was not hard to get.

The minute we were in the van, Barb asked what Nancy's mother had thought about her flying and Nancy began to talk about her childhood. John was driving, Barb was in front with him, and Nancy and I were in the back. I motioned to Barb to hand me the camera.

Seated on Nancy's left, I started filming her in profile and kept the camera on her the entire drive over. We stayed in the van long enough to finish the thread of the conversation. The result wasn't video photography at its best, but it certainly was better than missing the whole thing. Talk about oral history—I had just recorded a significant piece of the young Nancy Batson's life, including when she told her father about the Civilian Pilot Training course at the University of Alabama. The text in chapter 3, "Flight!," repeats her words spoken in the van that afternoon.

When we finished for the day, we had the makings of a really good video.[2] We had the Who (Nancy), the Where (the Air Force Museum), and the What (the planes she flew), but we lacked the When and Why. Our video footage, at that point, existed in a vacuum. We still had to shoot an intro and tell why she was in Dayton.

It was late and Nancy was due to go to dinner with her Wilmington Warrior friends. She had invited me to join her. John, Barb, and I arranged to meet her the following day at the Hope Hotel next to the base for lunch and to tape the intro there. She and I were to wear the same clothes for the sake of continuity.

At dinner, I broached the subject of writing her biography. She looked at me, those gray aviator's eyes seemingly searching my very soul. "You need to tell the story of Nancy Love and the WAFS."

I explained the difficulty. The nine still alive lived in different corners of the country. Interviewing them would be an almost impossible chore given that they did not know me, and all valued their privacy. Not to mention that that kind of travel was an expensive proposition.

"Well," she said, "how about I invite them all to Birmingham for a reunion. Then you can meet them and interview them there. We'll have it at the Southern Museum of Flight. We'll have a press conference and I'll host a reception there for the aviation community to meet them all."

There it was, as simple as that. "When?" I asked.

"When can you do it?"

The fourth week in June would work best. But that was only four weeks away.

We went back to Nancy's hotel room. She called B. J. London in California. It was nearly 10 p.m. in Ohio, but in Long Beach it was only 7. Nancy and B.J. talked a few minutes, Nancy told her our idea, and B.J. agreed to come. When she hung up, Nancy let out a whoop. "I'll call the others in the morning before we meet for lunch and the rest of our taping."

Her delight was written on her face. Seventy-nine-year-old Nancy laid back on her bed, kicked her feet in the air like a teenager, and hollered, "Whoo-eee, we're gonna have a WAFS' reunion."

It was like I had a glimpse of the twenty-three-year-old Nancy Batson when she heard about the spring 1943 trip to Alberta, Canada.

When John, Barb, and I arrived the following noon, Nancy greeted me with a big smile. Teresa, Florene, Gertrude, and Barbara Poole had also said yes. Barbara Donahue was a probable no and Phyllis Burchfield a definite no. Nancy had not been able to reach Bernice Batten, but she would write to her. The word BIRMINGHAM went into my calendar for the dates June 21–25, 1999.

We finished our taping. We had shot our program in reverse, but it would hang together. When John finished editing it, we had an hour of Nancy Batson Crews on center stage. We had Nancy and her oral history through her WASP years forever documented on videotape.

Nancy returned to Birmingham the following day and began planning the WAFS reunion.

18

The Reunion

"Lake Country Estates," the sign read. A pickup with the Stars and Bars emblazoned on the side went by going toward town. I turned onto Stuart Drive.

The house, as Nancy had described it, sat at a ninety-degree turn in the road. As I rounded the corner and pulled into the drive, two women sitting on the front porch rose from their wicker chairs, waving. One of them was Nancy. The other, I knew the minute I got a good look at her, was Teresa James.

The Reunion had begun.

Nancy enlisted the help of a lot of people to bring off this gathering of eagles. She convinced Birmingham's newest Marriott to give her complimentary rooms for the visiting WAFS. The current owners of the Irondale Café (the McMichaels family) and Fannie Flagg, the Alabama author/humorist who immortalized the café in *Fried Green Tomatoes at the Whistle Stop Café*,[1] treated the WAFS to Southern fried chicken and some of those legendary fried green tomatoes. The Southern Museum of Flight hosted the press conference to introduce the WAFS to Birmingham and Nancy, true to her word, put on a reception in honor of the WAFS and invited the aviation community as well as her family and her friends.

I wasn't the only interviewer who would be there. Aviation historian H.O. Malone drove down from Newport, Virginia, to meet and interview the WAFS. Sammy Yakovetic, a documentary filmmaker and a friend of B. J. London, drove all the way from Long Beach, California, with her cameraman.

Teresa had come up from Florida early to spend time with Nancy. They had gone out to the St. Clair County airport in Pell City Saturday and Nancy's friend Dr. Pittman had taken Teresa up for a flight in his Stearman. The other four WAFS arrived the following day, June 21.

Monday evening, after two trips to the airport to meet arriving flights, we all congregated in the hotel lounge. The six WAFS totally captivated the serving staff, and the young men and women—new employees because the hotel was newly opened—fought for the opportunity to bring them drinks and food and then hung around for conversation.

The WAFS are nothing if not gregarious, entertaining, and fun to be around. For me, it was reminiscent of the Sunday night in Centerville, Ohio, before the International Women's Air and Space Museum (IWASM) taping seven years earlier. On that night, the eight WASP kicked off their shoes, sat around, and told war stories. The only difference that night in the Marriott lounge was they kept their shoes on, literally if not figuratively.

With the other five situated at the Marriott, Nancy and I called it a night and drove back to her place—tired but happy. We were on our way. Nancy was beaming.

Tuesday morning, H.O. arrived at Nancy's. The day was off and running. We were to gather at the Southern Museum of Flight at eleven, tour the museum, and get ready for the afternoon press conference. Dr. Don Dodd, curator of the museum, brought his van in which to haul the WAFS from the hotel to the museum.

We set up in the program room on the second floor. The WAFS sat behind an L-shaped table with their service portraits in front of each of them. Museum director Dr. J. Dudley Pewitt (Colonel, U.S. Air Force, retired) welcomed the six WAFS to the museum and opened the presentation. Then Nancy introduced them individually and each gave an opening biographical statement.

Reporters and press photographers were there and Sammy's photographer was filming. The museum had hired a videographer to tape the entire press conference. The WAFS patiently told their stories and answered questions from the press and the general audience there to listen. Nancy was beaming.

That night, Nancy had planned a special treat for Teresa, a devout Catholic. For years, Teresa had been watching the TV nun Mother Angelica on cable television. Mother Angelica's show was broadcast daily from Birmingham on EWTN (the Eternal Word Television Network) founded by Mother Angelica and located on the grounds of Our Lady of the Angels Monastery. Nancy had gotten four tickets to the Tuesday night taping.[2]

"Teresa and I are going," Nancy announced. "We have two more tickets. Who else would like to go?" Gertrude and I had never heard of Mother Angelica or the TV show so we opted to go along and see what it was all

The six original WAFS who gathered in Birmingham, June 1999: Barbara Erickson London, Barbara Poole Shoemaker, Teresa James, Florene Miller Watson, Gertrude Meserve Tubbs LeValley, and Nancy Batson Crews. Photo by Sarah Byrn Rickman.

about. Don Dodd took us, dropped us at the monastery, and promised to pick us up when it was over.

The monastery staff had told Mother Angelica about the WAFS and that our group was coming. After we were seated in the spacious and crowded studio, a young brown-robed monk came to us and asked us to follow him. We did. We retraced our steps in front of the entire studio audience, all of whom watched our exit—"Who *are* those women?" He led us down a corridor into a waiting room. A few moments later, the little nun in her black habit with white collar and headpiece entered, talked to us all, shook our hands, blessed us, and thanked us for our service during the war. I felt a little like a fraud, since I was in kindergarten when the other three were flying for our country in World War II. But I accepted the blessing in the spirit it was intended.

The young monk then escorted us back through the audience, across in front of the stage to our seats. Again necks craned. Eyes followed us. Then all quieted down as the program was about to begin.

Needless to say, Teresa was thrilled. When it was over, Mother Angelica wanted her picture taken with the three WAFS and several staff members obliged.

Don Dodd, there to pick us up and take us back to the hotel, came in just as Nancy knelt down at the coffee table in front of Mother Angelica—to write her address and phone number for the nun. Don looked at me, eyes twinkling, and in a very audible stage whisper said, "Oh my God, she's signing over the deed to Cool Springs." (Cool Springs was a prime piece of property Nancy owned and hoped, someday, to build a home on.)

We both laughed and told the story several times again that evening—back at the lounge with the rest of the crowd. Nancy laughed the hardest.

A color photo I took that night of Nancy, Mother Angelica, Teresa, and Gertrude—to this day—sits atop my computer desk bookcase as I write, a reminder of a wonderful week.

Wednesday, H.O. and I began interviewing. To keep the WAFS from having to be interviewed three times—an exhausting proposition—H.O. and I combined forces. He used an audiotape recorder and I captured them on videotape. Again, it wasn't prize footage, but it was a once-in-a-lifetime opportunity. We interviewed Barbara London and Gertrude Wednesday morning and Barbara Poole and Teresa Thursday morning in the hotel's main-floor business center.

Lunch at the Irondale Café was scheduled for Wednesday at 1 p.m.—after some of the regular lunch crowd had cleared. Dr. Dodd and his van again were pressed into service. While we were having lunch, Fannie Flagg called personally to wish the WAFS well for their reunion. The café, an institution in the little railroad town of Irondale just east of Birmingham on I-20, was owned from 1932 to 1972 by Flagg's great-aunt Bess Fortenberry. When she wrote her novel, Flagg wrote about what she knew—her aunt and the café—and the café became famous. Bess, after suffering a small stroke in 1972, sold the café to Billy McMichaels and his family, who carried on the tradition. When the movie *Fried Green Tomatoes*, based on Flagg's best-known novel, came out in 1992, business really took off and the tourists began to come. The McMichaels family still owned and ran the restaurant when we were there in 1999, but they sold it the following year.[3]

We returned to the museum to get ready for the reception. Nancy's friends, family, and the aviation community turned out in force for a chance to meet and talk to these ladies in person. Nancy, the hostess with the mostess, was elegant in a long, straight white skirt open to the knee and matching top decorated with sparkly things. Not a woman who paid much attention to clothes, when Nancy wanted to look good, she carried it off with aplomb.

I met many people that afternoon, but the most important acquaintance I made was Dr. Pittman. Nancy introduced us. He asked me if I had ever had a ride in a World War II trainer airplane.

"No, I haven't," I answered.

"How would you like a ride in a Stearman?"

"Oh yes," I said.

"Have Nancy bring you out to the airport Saturday."

When the reception was over, the caravan returned to the hotel, again with the assistance of Dr. Dodd and his van. Once again we congregated in the lounge. Once again the young help vied for the opportunity to serve and therefore talk to these personable ladies who were their grandmothers' age.

Thursday morning, H.O. and I were back in the hotel's business center, recording. We had to hurry to finish with Barbara Poole, because she, Gertrude, and B.J. were leaving that afternoon. Florene, Teresa, and I were going to spend the night at Nancy's and Nancy was going to take Florene to the airport Friday morning. Teresa wasn't leaving until Saturday.

A few discrete tears were shed as Don Dodd packed up the three who were flying out Thursday afternoon. They hugged me like I belonged with them and said they hoped we could all do this again. It had been wonderful. They all thanked Nancy repeatedly. She was the reason they had all come together again fifty-seven years after it all began in Wilmington, Delaware. Nancy was beaming!

Sammy and her photographer headed back to California, and H.O. was soon on his way back to Virginia.

The four of us who were left went to Cracker Barrel for dinner and then started driving around looking for a copy of the *Birmingham Post Herald*. Reporter Abiola Sholanke had attended the press conference Tuesday and sent a photographer to the Irondale Café Wednesday to get a photo to run with her story. She had told us it would be in Thursday's paper.

We found several copies in a news box in front of Kroger and bought them all. The story and photo had made the front page of the Metro-State section. I took a picture of Nancy, Florene, and Teresa reading a copy and another of the three of them holding up copies, mugging for the camera.[4]

When we got back to Nancy's, I prevailed on Florene to let me interview her. In our rushed schedule, I had not been able to make time for the fifth interview. Besides, H.O. had already interviewed Florene so he was more interested in getting the others. She agreed.

Nancy and Teresa went to bed and Florene and I sat up until midnight. I asked questions and filmed. The audio portion of the videotape is alive with the sounds of an Alabama country summer night. The windows were open to let the night cool in. To a chorus of cicadas and other insects and the croaking of frogs, Florene talked about her WAFS years.

Nancy was back from the airport before either Teresa or I stirred the next morning.

We spent the day relaxing and talking and went out for a ride in the country. Nancy showed us Lake Country Estates and her property at Cool Springs where she hoped, someday, to build a house on top of the mountain she owned. She showed us where there was room for a grass landing strip across the road.

It was a marvelous day. The pride in her land, her accomplishments with it, and her hope for the future radiated from her descriptions.

Nancy and I talked about Dr. Jim's offer to take me up in the Stearman. "You should do it," she said. Nancy didn't elaborate on such things, but I sensed an importance to her that I do this—for myself, yes, but also for her and for Jim Pittman.

Nancy's next-door neighbors invited her, Teresa, and me over for a steak dinner that Friday night. Saturday morning, Nancy and I took Teresa to the airport, stopped for lunch at one of Nancy's favorite barbecue joints, and headed to Pell City airport. It was trying to rain.

We drove up to Dr. Jim's hangar as a two-seat Aeronca Champ was landing. Moments later, it taxied up to where we were standing. Dr. Jim had just taken a friend up for a spin. They pulled the little plane into the hangar and the other gentleman left. Then Nancy, Dr. Jim, and I went in the other side of the hangar to look at the blue and yellow, bi-wing Stearman. I climbed up on the lower wing and into the front seat and checked out the cockpit.

Dr. Jim and Nancy kept looking at the sky. The clouds were low and looked full of rain. "Let's go check the weather station," he said. The three of us piled into Nancy's car and drove over to the operations building. In a small room sat the radar screen with the ever-changing weather picture. He studied it for a minute, then pointed to a slightly lighter area on the screen. "We've got a half an hour, maybe," he said. "You want to go?"

I nodded.

Back at the airplane, he helped me buckle into a WWII vintage parachute. It was so heavy it almost pulled me over backwards until I set my shoulders against its weight. I'm not sure I could have pulled that ripcord, but I suppose if my life depended on it I would have found the strength and leverage. I climbed back up into the front seat. Dr. Jim handed me earphones

Nancy with Dr. Jim (James A. Pittman, M.D.) and his Stearman PT-17, taken June 1999. Photo by Sarah Byrn Rickman.

and helped me adjust them. "So I can talk to you," he said. Then he helped me fasten and check the safety harness. I was in. I was ready.

We took off into a lowering sky. The ceiling was, maybe, three hundred feet. Bare minimum. He flew out over Logan Martin Lake, a recreation area created by the Tennessee Valley Authority in the 1930s. "We're gonna do a roll," his voice came through my earphones.

The airplane began to turn over to the right, hung upside down for an instant, and came up the other side. Whoa! What a feeling! That was my first roll. We didn't do rolls in the Cessna in which I took my flight lessons. Before I knew it, we were rolling the other way, to the left. Then we were right side up again. I looked down at the boats on the lake and wondered if they could possibly be having as much fun as I was.

"OK, now for a loop," he said, and the airplane started up, up, up, until my feet were over my head and I was hanging upside down in the harness. Then, smooth as silk, it went on over the top and came down and back to level flying. Now that one almost got me. My stomach wasn't quite sure what had happened and didn't believe me when I tried to tell it, "Hey, it's OK."

"We better head in," I heard Dr. Jim saying, and I saw the darkening clouds heading in our direction. A couple of minutes later, the airport was off to the left. "OK, to help us lose altitude and get down quicker, we're going to do a falling leaf," he said, and the airplane began to lose altitude, not in a spin, not in a dive, but in what seemed like a drifting motion—like a falling leaf. He entered the landing pattern on what I knew to be the base leg. The ground was coming up to meet us. He turned onto final and moments later the wheels touched down. Slick as a whistle. As we sped along the runway and took the turnoff, I could feel gentle rain beginning to fall on me.

We had done it, we were down, and the rain had come to stay.

I was elated, if a little woozy from the loop. Nancy was sitting in her car reading a magazine. When she saw me, she said, "how was it?"

"Fantastic," I said. I wondered if I looked a little green around the gills, because she looked closely at me, but then she beamed. She had been doing a lot of that.

I got to meet several people at the airport that afternoon—among them Ed Stringfellow, the FBO (fixed base operator), who owned a lot of vintage airplanes that stood in the big attached hangar. I sat in several of them—an AT-6; a rare two-seat P-51; a J-3 Cub like the one Nancy was having restored.

Nancy and I headed for home. It had been a full week—a phenomenal week—but now it was almost over. After dinner—takeout from Cracker Barrel and a beer from her refrigerator—we sat and rehashed the whole extraordinary experience. It was truly a time neither of us would ever forget. She had made it happen. That was Nancy. She was someone who made things happen.

The next morning, Nancy and I said good-bye. I would begin working on "the book" about Nancy Love and the WAFS—though at that point I hadn't a clue how to go about it. I had recently spent two years of my life sharpening my creative skills in order to write fiction. Now here I was being challenged to go back to my first calling, nonfiction, to train myself to be a historian and to write a history of twenty-eight women, nineteen of whom were dead. I knew nothing about historical research and when I got home, my day job—writing and editing newsletters for two nonprofits—was waiting. But Nancy had given me an assignment.

19

From Cub to King Air

A month after the reunion, Nancy's yellow J-3 Cub came home.

Being Nancy, she planned ahead. Prior to the airplane's arrival, she accompanied her friends Ed Stevenson and Jim Harris, past president of the Birmingham Aero Club, to Sun 'n Fun in Lakeland, Florida, in April 1999. They flew down in Jim's Cessna 182. Nancy went for the fun of aviation's annual spring fling, but she also had some serious-minded intentions for going.

"Nancy was like a kid in a candy store," Jim Harris wrote later in the Aero Club newsletter. She had decided that a GPS (global positioning satellite navigational system) and up-to-date radio equipment were a must for her Cub. She had her eye out for any modern improvements that would aid her when she went flying in the little airplane she hoped to have in her hangar by summertime.

"At one of the booths, this young salesgirl was talking down to Nancy," Ed recalled. "I finally called her aside and told her who Nancy was and the young lady changed her tune.

"Then there were the three guys from New Jersey. We were having lunch and these guys sat down across from us. 'Ma'am, do you have an airplane?' one of them asked her. 'Well, I'm getting one,' she said, 'a J-3 Cub.' He looked at her and said, 'Well, ma'am, have you ever flown one?'

"By this time Jim and I were having a good time watching Nancy handle these guys. And we didn't interfere—kind of let the line out on the reel before pullin' in the fish. But finally, I had to set him straight. 'Before you get too far in, let me explain who this lady is and what all she has done.'

"Well, when I told him, he hollered and stood up and threw his hat on the ground and said, 'Damn it, I sure stuck my foot in my mouth, didn't I.' And we all got a big laugh out of that."

Nancy's friend Ed Stringfellow gave her her biannual flight check in his

J-3 Cub and renewed her license on June 5, 1999. And then she flew Ed's Cub a few times for practice. So when Jim Dayton arrived at St. Clair County Airport, July 29, with her long-awaited Cub, Nancy was ready.

Dayton took her up in the Cub that day and showed her what he had done with it. She was thrilled to be at the controls of her own J-3 and she flew a lot in August and September.

Because she was out at the airport more now that she had her plane hangared there, Nancy began to visit with the other woman who spent a lot of time at the airport, Chris Beal-Kaplan. They hit it off. In a taped interview, November 14, 2000, Chris and Nancy explained just how good friends they became.[1]

"I had just lost my copilot to the airlines," said Chris, who was chief pilot for American Equity Insurance Company. She flew a twin-engine King Air corporate turbo jet owned and operated by a subsidiary of the parent company. The owner decided to base the airplane at St. Clair County Airport outside of Birmingham, instead of in corporate headquarters in Des Moines, Iowa. Chris—a divorcée with grown children and no problem trying new horizons—moved to Alabama with the airplane.

"When we came here from Des Moines, the owner decided he wanted his own maintenance people on the field, so he started Sarco, the maintenance arm of the business. We grew to be pretty busy. We take care of other people's planes as well as the King Air," said Chris.

All of Chris's copilots were young men—a succession of them who, as soon as they got experience and flight time, would move on to a better job. "I don't blame them," she said. "Then one day Nancy walked in and she was talking about flying her Cub. I thought to myself, Nancy's not going anyplace and she knows how to fly.

"'How would you like to fly copilot on the King Air?' I asked her.

"'I don't know anything about the King Air,' Nancy said.

"'You don't have to,' I said. 'You'll learn.'"

This was a turbo jet! *Jet* was a magic word even to someone who had flown the fastest pursuits in World War II. The P-47 and P-51 were, after all, still prop planes.

Nancy was current with all her licenses. That was a requirement before Chris could hire her.

"She had a lot of faith in me," Nancy said.

Chris was on her way to Arizona to take her recheck in the King Air flight simulator. "I called the Simcom Training Center in Scottsdale and told them

I wanted to bring along my new copilot and have her check out in the simulator. I asked him if he'd give me a two-for-the-price-of-one deal. He said he'd work something out.

"'Tell me something about her,' he said.

"I said, 'well, she flew in World War II.'

"He said, 'I beg your pardon.'

"'She flew in World War II,' I repeated.

"'How old is she?' he asked.

"'Almost eighty,' I said.

"There was this long silence at the other end of the phone. Then, finally, he said 'OK.' I think he thought, well money's money."

Nancy was apprehensive. "All I had ever been in was a Link trainer and here I was going in a real simulator. Chris said to me, 'don't worry about it. You probably won't pass, but come on and go.'"

"Actually, what I told her was, she didn't have to pass to be the copilot. You get the experience," said Chris. "Well, that was spurs to the horse. When we got out there, she did fine. She had to fly the left seat in the simulator with me in the right seat so she could check out. But we had a nice instructor.

"'You ladies are having entirely too much fun,' he told us. And we were. We were having a ball. We ate in all these good restaurants. Went shopping in all kinds of stores—bought presents for our grandchildren. Sure we had a good time. I told him, 'we're too old for the airlines. We don't have to prove anything to anybody.'"

"When he told Chris how I had done," Nancy recalled, "she came out and in this incredulous voice said, 'He passed you!' She was so surprised." Nancy could barely contain her delight. She had just done what neither Chris nor the instructor thought she could do. Radford's words rang true. Nancy had an inborn feel for flying.

"She took to it like a duck to water," Chris said.

The date was September 18, 1999.

Nancy called me right after she returned from Scottsdale with the news that she was going to fly copilot for Chris. I will never forget that phone call. She was breathless with excitement—so much so, I sensed from the beginning that she was calling to talk about something important, not simply to relay a piece of information and hang up.

She told me all about Chris, her offer, their trip to Scottsdale, and qualifying in the simulator. Her excitement was that of a teenager getting her

The Flying Grannies: Nancy and Chris Beal-Kaplan, June 2000. Photo by Sarah Byrn Rickman.

driver's license, or a twenty-one-year-old college graduate getting her first and long-anticipated "real" job. Nancy—cool, calm, collected, very businesslike, the mature woman who planned ahead—exhibited, when she felt strongly about something, an unbounded enthusiasm, a passion. She kept this trait beneath the surface, carefully guarded. She let it show only on certain occasions and to certain people. I had become one of those people to whom she was not afraid to show it.

For seven months, Nancy and Chris had the time of their lives—and got paid for it. They spent the fall making several "little trips to places"—a series of shakedown flights, so to speak.

"I had to do some studying to catch up. The Alpha Baker Charlie stuff," Nancy explained, "working with the controllers."

"You have to call back exactly what they say to you. And they aren't always the most patient," Chris added. "Down in Florida she said to one of them, 'I just told you to talk slower.' But he would not slow down at all. He made some snide remark to her like, 'Did you get that?' And she said, 'No!'

"I finally said, 'if you'd talk slower maybe she'd get it.'

"Nancy got better right after that. She didn't want to go through that hassle again."

They went to Des Moines several times, transported passengers to various meetings in various places, and returned them. Chris kept an apartment in Des Moines and Nancy stayed in a hotel.

The fun they could have aside, Chris had a practical reason for wanting Nancy along as copilot. Nancy had experience flying over the western mountains. Not only had she flown in California with its variable terrain including mountains and deserts, she had flown cross-country—that is, across the Rockies—in everything from a Super Cub to a P-38. Chris knew she was going to have several big western trips and the first one was coming up in January.

They left from Des Moines. Chris chose the route that took them to Scottsdale and then across the desert and mountains of Arizona on to San Diego. "I was apprehensive about flying over the Rockies," Chris admitted. "I planned the route to the south—thus Scottsdale—and at an altitude that if we lost an engine we could still get over the mountains."

Her planned minimum altitude was 18,000 feet so that the loss of an engine would only take them down to 15,000—thus over the highest of the Rockies. From Scottsdale, they were to go to San Diego and then up the coast of California, over to Reno, and back to Des Moines. And, as always, they were carrying passengers—corporate bigwigs.

"We were cleared into Scottsdale, but it was solid overcast and I'm nervous as a cat on a hot tin roof. Nancy says, 'oh for heaven sakes, calm down, I've been through here in a Super Cub.'

"The lady controller works us down and I know the mountains are coming up. That's all that's ahead of us are mountains—mountains higher than we were. Then all of a sudden, we're in a deep valley and we had a VFR approach [visual flight rules—as opposed to an instrument approach] the rest of the way into Scottsdale.

"They were so nice to us there. They gave us a car overnight. A big golf tournament was getting ready to start and there were private jets all over the place. We were the smallest one there."

The next day they flew into San Diego. "The weather was terrible there, too. We were coming over the mountains approaching Lindbergh Airport—which sits on the ocean. I told Nancy, 'you call out the names of the towns on the chart as we go over them. Well, she gets to looking for the ground—Nancy likes to do that—and we're going back and forth at each other like we do. David [their boss] asked me later if we were arguing up in the cockpit. I said, 'no, we were discussing.'"

Chris is of a volatile nature, speaks her mind, and then goes back to being quite equable. Nancy, never in the habit of backing off, would respond in kind. But they were friends, they understood each other, and each forgave the other her trespasses.

The stop in San Diego gave Nancy the opportunity to see Janey and her family and Chris the opportunity to meet them. Janey had them over for dinner. The next day they went to Torrance, over to Catalina, and back to Torrance. They were due in Sacramento that evening and it was getting dark. Chris wanted to get out before the charter planes from Las Vegas started coming in. Nancy, of course, was quite familiar with Torrance, having flown out of it many times.

"It was a beautiful clear night," Chris remembered. "But we rang the bell when we took off. We were heading for the mountains and I poured the coals to it. Turns out Torrance has a noise abatement rule and we managed to exceed the decibels limit."

A letter from the airport authority caught up with them several days later at corporate headquarters in Des Moines.

"Our boss couldn't believe it. 'You did WHAT?–IN A KING AIR!'"

"Nothing came of it. Basically, they simply said, 'don't do it again.'"

"Other than that, we had a beautiful flight over the mountains to Sacramento," Nancy added.

Reno was the next stop. Nancy knew how to gamble and enjoyed it. Chris wasn't so sure, but they headed for the gaming tables together. They were a hit with several of the dealers as they were having such a good time and kept making crazy bets. They managed to break even for the night.

"We really had to climb to get out of Reno the next day. Usually we climb at 140 knots, but we climbed out at much lower than that. I pulled that nose up. Nancy, over in the right seat, said, 'I can't even see the sky, all I can see is the nose.'"

They were headed home to Des Moines with fuel stops in Salt Lake City and Grand Island, Nebraska, where it was snowing. "They didn't have radar in Grand Island and we were flying IFR [instrument flight rules]. When we broke out of the soup there, the runway was right in front of us.

"It was gray, cold, and windy, and getting dark. But we had to go on to Des Moines. We had two passengers. After refueling, we took right back off–up into the soup where it was sleeting. Our strobe lights on the sleet looked just like diamonds in the sky. Nancy was not at all appreciative of the beauty."

"All I wanted to do was get home," said Nancy. "It scared the hell out of me."

"Nancy doesn't like sleet and snow. I don't like mountains—a friend of mine was killed flying in the mountains in Germany," said Chris.

Within a couple of days, they were supposed to take off for Minneapolis/ St. Paul. The company heads had a meeting up there. "You couldn't see across the airport it was snowing so badly," said Nancy. "I'm quaking when we get in the plane and start to taxi. I couldn't see the runway."

"The tower called and told us to stop," Chris said. "They had to clear the runway before we could take off. Then they called to tell us that some of the runways in Minneapolis/St. Paul had been closed and we had to wait because landing slots there were limited. When the guys in the back figured out that they were going to be so late they would miss the meeting, they cancelled the trip."

Nancy's response: "Oh thank God!"

Nancy had been invited to Dayton to speak at the U.S. Air Force Museum on January 21, 2000. She and Chris had gotten the company's permission to fly the King Air to Dayton for Nancy's speech. The night before she was scheduled, Dayton was hit by a horrendous ice storm accompanied by snow. It was so bad, the Air Force Museum—that only closes on Thanksgiving, Christmas, and New Year's Day—was shut down. The Dayton Airport was closed. Wright-Patterson Air Force Base was shut down. Nothing moved in the Miami Valley that day. Everything was cancelled. Nancy's talk was rescheduled for April.

Their trip to Florida at the end of January was the most fun of all. They flew to south Florida and then made their way up the east coast. They were due in West Palm Beach, of all days, on Nancy's eightieth birthday— February 1, 2000. "It was preordained that we be there," said Chris. A celebration was called for. When they landed, they called Teresa James, who said, "Hell yes, just tell me where to come."

She took a taxi over to meet them at their hotel for dinner. "We started with champagne, and they toasted everyone they could think of. Then we switched to beer because champagne was too expensive. They kept it up until late into the evening. I couldn't keep up with them," said Chris. "They drank me under the table.

"Laugh! I just listened to those two tell stories. Teresa is a hoot. She kept flirting with the young waiter. 'You with the pretty eyes, come over here.' Teresa gave Nancy two gardenias from her yard and a birthday card. While we were there, Nancy bought herself a birthday present—a tennis bracelet with amethysts. She said she liked it and I said, 'well why don't you buy it.' And she said, 'I think I will.'

"We really had some good times. And Nancy learned fast. Amazing, because she had to go from flying on the beam back in World War II to the GPS. But she decided she was going to do it and she did.

"We called ourselves the flying grannies. Between us, we had ninety years' cockpit experience. She had sixty and I had thirty. We were probably the oldest flight crew in history. We didn't take anything off anybody."

Nancy and Chris had a few more flights after Nancy's birthday party in West Palm Beach, but as it turned out, that stop and the meeting with Teresa proved to be the absolute highlight of their brief flying partnership.

20

Pneumonia, or Something Worse?

The cough rattled deep in her chest. A chilly wave of apprehension washed over the scene, leaving me with a sense of dread. We sat facing each other in a booth in the bar of the Hope Hotel, Wright-Patterson Air Force Base, Dayton, Ohio, nursing glasses of Killian's Red.

Nancy Batson Crews had just given the April 2000 evening lecture at the U.S. Air Force Museum. Her subject, of course, was the Women's Auxiliary Ferrying Squadron and her experiences as one of the Originals. This was the talk that had been rescheduled from January when the ice storm blew into Dayton and prevented her from flying in.

April in southern Ohio brings not snow and ice but weather of a completely different variety. Earlier that evening, as we met a group from the museum for a pre-lecture dinner, we were under a tornado alert. As the sky darkened outside the restaurant, the TV above the bar announced that a funnel cloud had been spotted south of town and that the whole area was now under a tornado warning. Someone wondered aloud to Nancy if her impending arrival in our fair city was the precipitating factor of inclement weather—since it had now happened twice. We all had a good laugh.

We did get a big rainstorm on the way to the museum for her talk and later wondered whether it, along with the local uncertainty over the tornado warning, had kept people away from Carney Auditorium that night. Still, it was a good crowd and they asked good questions.

As usual, Nancy captivated her audience with tales of cross-country flights in swift pursuit airplanes; of catnapping on a hard bench in the Alert Room between "gear-up, gear-down" ferry flights from the Republic factory on Long Island to the nearby docks at Newark, New Jersey; and of flying a bunch of her fellow women ferry pilots back to the Republic factory in a twin-engine C-60 following a series of successful P-47 deliveries. The blonde Golden Girl of the Ferry Command never failed to hold her audience breathless.

Now, suddenly, it was she who was breathless.

The date was April 20, 2000. I hadn't seen her since the reunion the previous June, though we talked frequently on the phone. The cough was new.

In February 2000, I had visited the WASP Collection at Texas Woman's University in Denton to look at the WAFS materials there. In March, I had spent five days in Florida with Teresa James. Teresa's memory of their WAFS days was excellent and she had the September 1942 to February 1943 portion of the journal she had kept during her early days in the ferrying squadron. Her hand-written words had been typed for her on onionskin paper by a succession of hotel stenographers as she moved around the country ferrying airplanes in those early days of the WAFS. The remainder of the journal had been destroyed in a flood in the family home in Pittsburgh.

The two major pieces Teresa had recorded that were of particular interest to me were her version of the Great Falls to Jackson, Tennessee, trip (I had heard Nancy's version already) and her first coast-to-coast trip for the WAFS ferrying an open-cockpit PT-19 from Hagerstown, Maryland, all the way to Hollywood for use in the movie *Ladies Courageous.* Loretta Young starred in that movie, which was based *very* loosely on the WAFS' story.[1]

That night in Dayton, Nancy and I discussed the next step in my quest to get the WAFS' book written. Nancy Love, of course, was the key to the WAFS. I needed to interview her three daughters. I needed to understand Nancy Love and her motivations. I needed to read anything she had written and anything that had been written about her—of which there was precious little. Nancy promised to get addresses and phone numbers for the three girls and get back to me.

On Mothers' Day—three weeks later—Nancy called me. Once again, that excitement—that passion—was evident in her voice. She had just spoken with Nancy Love's middle daughter, Marky, and she would be willing to talk to me. I was to call her that very afternoon.

Marky was a delight to talk to and, yes, she and her sister Allie, who lived next door, would be happy to have me come to northern Virginia, look at their mother's papers, and interview them. Marky told me what a thrill it had been for her to talk with the incomparable Nancy Batson. Not only had her mother thought a lot of Nancy, but her father had greatly admired Nancy Batson as well. Marky was captivated—Nancy's unpretentious and infectious Southern drawl had won her over immediately—and the fact that Nancy vouched for me convinced Marky that talking to me would be the right thing to do.

Nancy had opened yet another door for me.

We began making plans for late June. I told Marky I hoped Nancy would make the trip with me.

I immediately called Nancy back to have her put the dates on her calendar. I would drive to Alabama, pick her up, and we would drive up to northern Virginia. While there, we would pay a visit to Barbara Donahue Ross, who lived thirty miles from the Love girls. Nancy was delighted at the possibility of seeing Donnie again. They had been good friends. I would interview Donnie—who had missed the reunion—while we were there. And, while we were on a roll, we would drive back by way of eastern Ohio to visit and interview Phyllis Burchfield Fulton, who Nancy had not seen in fifty-seven years. She too had missed the reunion.

The thought of sitting in on those two reunions and of meeting Nancy Love's daughters—all the while in the company of Nancy Batson Crews—spurred me on. Talk about a fly on the wall! The only downside to the conversations I had with Nancy that Mothers' Day was that she still had that cough and now was taking antibiotics for it. Probably some kind of bronchial bug, she said. She was concerned about giving it to Chris since they traveled in the close confines of the King Air cockpit.

Later in May, I received another call from Nancy. This time, the bottom of my world dropped away. "Sarah, I'm not going to be up to making that trip to Virginia in June."

A very disheartened Nancy was being treated for what now appeared to be a virulent form of pneumonia. It all began when she made a trip with Chris to New Orleans, even though she didn't feel well. The cough had gotten progressively worse, but Nancy never gave in easily. She collapsed in New Orleans but refused to go to the hospital even though Chris called Dr. Jim Pittman to find her a doctor there. He did. He talked to the chief of medicine at the VA hospital. "He was a pulmonary guy," said Dr. Jim, "and he said 'send her right in, I'll be glad to take care of her. She shouldn't fly. She's not in any shape to fly.'"

But Nancy did fly. Chris was heading back to Pell City and Nancy insisted on returning home with her, saying, "I'm not staying behind in New Orleans." Once home, she did go to the hospital, was promptly grounded, put on an antibiotic drip in her arm, sent home, and told to stay quiet. She felt rotten. And she would have to have more tests.

Nancy and I talked again a few days later. We decided that I should go on down to Birmingham and spend a few days with her before heading to Virginia to interview the Love girls. She felt up to that—in fact, was anxious to move ahead with the book.

By the time I got there in the middle of June, the doctors had decided Nancy didn't have pneumonia. One resident told her, "Mrs. Crews, I think you may have lung cancer," but subsequent tests revealed nothing. She continued the exhausting battery of tests to determine just what was wrong. The major one, to determine her lung capacity, was scheduled right after I left.

Chris had been making sure she got to the hospital for her tests. Nancy consulted with Dr. Pittman. Though his specialty was endocrinology, not pulmonary disease, because of her trust in him and their friendship, he became her consulting physician. Later, he would become her primary physician. In June, I met Chris for the first time and renewed my friendship with Dr. Jim. The four of us saw a good bit of each other while I was there staying with Nancy.

My visit was at almost the exact same time as the reunion the year before, but June 2000 was a dark contrast to June 1999. The shadow of the unknown hung over us. Nancy and I began a series of taped interviews.

The following week I was in Middleburg, Virginia, interviewing Marky and Allie Love. And through Air Force historian H.O. Malone—whom I had met at the reunion—I also met and interviewed Ann Hamilton Tunner, a WASP (Class 43-2) and General Tunner's widow.[2] Ann was a delight and gave me a most helpful interview regarding the original WAFS and how she—as a member of one of the earliest of Jacqueline Cochran's classes—became a ferry pilot under Nancy Love.

Back home for the Fourth of July, I reviewed what I had written that spring and settled down to writing in earnest. I immersed myself in my work. Uneasiness about the unforeseen turn of events spurred me on. Then e-mails from Chris and Dr. Jim informed me that the doctors had found cancer. Nancy was to undergo surgery for removal of a cancerous tumor in her lower left lung. Her son Paul was coming to be with her during and after the operation. The prognosis was that the tumor was confined to the lower lobe and surgery to remove it should be successful. The date of the surgery was July 24, 2000.

The following e-mail from Dr. Jim to me dated July 25 tells the outcome.

Re: Nancy—News Not Good

The news is not good. She was operated on to remove the cancer in her left lower lobe (lung). It is a bronchoalveolar carcinoma, and they are not usually very responsive to X-ray, Rx, or chemotherapy. So the hope is to be able to get the whole thing out surgically and leave the patient cancer free. A very complete pre-op workup, including a

PET scan and a surgical exploration with biopsies of the mediastinum (middle part of the chest), revealed no cancer outside that left lower lobe. So the surgeon went in yesterday expecting to get it all.

However, when he actually got into the left side of the chest, he found that it had spread to the upper parts of the left lung and it had spread by metastases (i.e. by blood-borne cells—to other parts of the body) not by direct extension, which would have been more favorable and have made a more aggressive surgical attempt worth while. That is, she probably has small deposits of cancer in such places as the liver, spine, brain, etc—a lousy situation[.]

At this point, Dr. Jim lapsed into a language he knew I understood.

"10 Me-109s plus a couple of FW-190s on your tail when you're out of fuel and out of ammunition with your plane already shot to pieces and over Berlin."

Then he continued with his medical report.

The surgeon actually telephoned the medical pulmonary oncologist from the OR and asked whether he thought it might help—at least psychologically if nothing else—to go ahead and remove that LLL (lower left lobe), but he said no, she had some normal lung there and this would just make her short of breath and probably hasten the end. So the surgeon just closed her up, removed nothing except the confirmatory biopsies.

Paul told her yesterday afternoon, and she took it very stoically. Outlook is for a downhill course, amount of misery and duration unknown. I think she'll probably remain here in Alabama with the kids coming on a rotating schedule from California.

His closing note to me:

THE BEST THING FOR YOU TO DO IS GET THAT WAFS BOOK FINISHED BEFORE SHE LEAVES US.

Time was no longer on our side. I contacted my agent, Liz Trupin, who had been following my progress reports. "Put together what you've got along with a proposal and send it to me," she said. "Let's see what kind of interest we can generate." I made the revisions she suggested and sent her seven copies of the finished proposal to circulate to several New York publishers.

Early in August, I was back in Alabama. Nancy and I had planned to get together then and in spite of the surgery and the devastating news she had received, she wanted to go ahead with the book. In fact, she was even more determined that we would get it done and get it published. We sat in her living room, she in a recliner, and I in the easy chair across from her. On the piano bench sat my tape recorder whirring away as we began several days of soul searching.

This time, the story I heard from her was one filled with frustration, anger, and despair—it was about a mistaken diagnosis of pneumonia, about a positive diagnosis of lung cancer, and of surgery that did not alleviate the illness.

Already her fit, wiry body and her iron will were warring with an unrelenting opponent. Her stamina, along with her breath, was gone. Her face was drawn. The lines I hadn't noticed before—in spite of her eighty years—had become prominent creases. Her once clear gray eyes—with that eagle's gaze, searching the distant sky for encroaching aircraft—were awash with the mist of memory and time. The dry skin on her arms and legs left scaly white flakes on the recliner's gray velour upholstery.

In the early mornings, we sat out on the porch in the rising heat of summer in Alabama and watched her world go by. Her house sits at the entranceway to the subdivision that she has created. Trucks of workmen who are building on her current project go by, slowing to make the ninety-degree turn at the corner of her property. Most wave as they pass. They all know "Miz Crews." Also waving are neighbors, most of them living in houses she has built. Occasionally, someone stops to talk, but rarely. They seem shy about coming over because "the writer from up north" is there. I am an exotic creature. An interloper in their lives. They call on the phone and inquire as to her state of health. They will check on her when I am gone.

Every morning, when we open the front door, a plastic bag of fresh home-grown veggies is hanging on the knob or sitting on the table between the wicker chairs.

That Sunday morning—August 13—we were once again seated on the porch. It was then that Nancy told me about Camp Winnataska and about her take on religion and her personal belief in God. She told me things she had never told another soul. Nancy didn't share her feelings easily. In fact, she had few close women friends. Nancy always was more at home in the company of men.

"I'm telling you what is in my soul, Sarah," she said as we talked about what it all means—life, and why what happens does happen. She was, by this time, terminally ill and knew it, though she didn't fully admit it. She was in tears. I was profoundly moved. There we sat on her porch in the shimmering heat of summertime in Alabama, doing self-examination of the deepest, most painful kind.

Chris said that Nancy told her she was a church dropout and didn't want anyone to try to make her into anything. Nancy had put together a lifetime of values and beliefs—starting back at Camp Winnataska, which had had such a profound influence on her—and she had built her own Christian-based spirituality.

But, as was Nancy's style, she did it her way.

She appreciated prayers sent by others—and there were many. Teresa notified Mother Angelica and the entire monastery prayed for Nancy. Joe Shannon and his wife, Helen, brought her audiotapes on spirituality. They carefully reviewed them before passing them on. They knew Nancy and truly wanted to help her—not convert her.

I stayed a week. Chris came by frequently and provided several caretaking chores in her brusque but competent, caring manner. She had been a nurse before she became a corporate pilot. I was good for grocery shopping, fixing breakfast coffee, making tuna salad for lunch, and going to Cracker Barrel and bringing home dinner.

We talked for hours. I learned of Nancy's dreams, disappointments, demons, and delights.

When I look back now—through the memory haze of eight years—it is the August visit that I remember most vividly. We both were emotionally raw. She was dealing with her relentless realities that had, it appeared, only one outcome. I was dealing with the impending loss of a friend. A friend I was just truly beginning to know—nevertheless, a friend who had come to mean so very much to me. And I was dealing with the impending loss of a mentor I could never replace.

I had a book to finish, the Grim Reaper was pursuing my heroine, and I couldn't get her untied and off the railroad track.

Early in the fall, my agent, Liz, began to hear back from New York. "Great story, but we can't sell it in today's market." "Fascinating women, but won't reach a large enough market." "Thanks for letting us look but no thanks." "Not for us, but good luck." Periodically, I had to report to Nancy that we were not getting anywhere.

The news from Chris and Dr. Jim regarding Nancy's condition got worse. The possibilities of two different treatments arose but were ruled out—one because she already was on oxygen.

Toward late October I had to tell Nancy that my agent had heard from the last of the big publishers to whom she had sent *The Originals*. No one was buying. The next step was to begin the process all over again with the mid-sized and specialty presses. That would take months—months we didn't have.

"What if I put money into it?" Nancy asked.

"Let me ask Liz," I said.

Liz and her husband and partner Gregory Vincent Pulli had been experimenting with publishing POD (Print on Demand) books and E-Books (electronic books) under the name Disc-Us Books, Inc. With Nancy financing the printing costs, they took on the design, formatting, and publishing chores.

By early November, I had a publisher and a book contract. Because Nancy wanted what she considered "a real book"—a hardcover edition—POD was out of the question. So we all took a deep breath and decided to do a print run of four thousand: one thousand hardcover and three thousand softcover—identical to the hardcover but without the dust jacket. Nancy—actually, Lake Country Estates—would pay the printing bill.

I prepared to make yet another trip to Alabama.

21

Terminal

Nancy's condition had worsened dramatically in the three months I had been away.

Treatment was out of the question. Her illness was terminal and she had accepted that. She was permanently on oxygen and several auxiliary tanks lay on the floor next to the dining room table. A deliveryman appeared twice a week to remove the used tanks and bring fresh ones.

Plans to care for her were in place. Nancy was to remain at home with regular visits from Hospice. Paul was coming the day after Thanksgiving and would remain indefinitely. Before Paul's arrival, and immediately following my stay, Radford was coming to visit.

Nancy could get around, but she spent most of her time in bed. The big concern was her falling if she had a dizzy spell. When she did come out to the living room and tried to sit in the recliner, she tired quickly. A neighbor had been coming in to fix her lunch and dinner.

I needed for Nancy to begin reading the manuscript, which she did, while I worked on my laptop computer at the dining room table, fine-tuning the prose. And we talked. Nancy reminisced a lot and my tape recorder and I were a willing and attentive audience.

She talked about her father and her dream of following in his footsteps— of doing with the land the things they had planned, together, to do. And she talked about all the things she had done. "I had a voracious appetite to sample everything life had to offer. At least I wanted to try it. I was a cheerleader in high school—just to see if I could do it. I didn't miss a damn thing, though some things were harder than others."

One night, after dinner—brought in by Chris—Nancy and Chris talked to me about their seven months of flying together in the King Air. That story is retold in chapter 19 from a tape of that evening's conversation. Give and take defined their relationship, a dynamic example of a later-in-life friendship. Those two very different women from very different backgrounds complemented each other. They worked well together and they genuinely liked each other.

Chris was a modern-day instrument pilot, imbued with the technologies of aviation today. Nancy was a 1940s J-3 Cub pilot who loved nothing better than to fly on what pilots call a "severe clear" day and–like a soaring eagle– look down at the ground and all its wonders. Flying to Chris was practical–a job–not to say she didn't enjoy it. Flying to Nancy was the magical world she could see from the air. That is why she loved gliding above all other aviation experiences–with the possible exception of flying that A-20. In her youth she flew the mighty power planes. In her mature years she soared, powerless and silent, above the earth, riding capricious thermals with grace and finesse.

Nancy loved to talk to Chris about the old days. "I told her what it was like to fly without a compass. It is amazing to me what you can do when you look down at the ground, at the section lines. And I had my trusty old charts. I flew by the seat of my pants and you get pretty damn good at it when you do it all day, like we did ferrying across country in World War II. When we were flying those beat-up war wearies, sometimes the radio and navigation equipment didn't work. Flying them became a matter of life and death and I got real good at it."

The book *Think and Grow Rich* remained in close proximity to Nancy's sickbed. During this time she introduced me to it and began to talk to me about the concept of masterminding.

"I want you to look at that book, Sarah. Chapter 10–'The Power of the Master Mind–The Driving Force.' It's about gaining power through the Master Mind. You don't have to be smart. You gather people around you who are smart. You build a mastermind group.

"This book that you are writing is our goal. We're getting up a mastermind group for that book–you and me and Liz and her associates in the publishing business. I understand how it works. I want you to understand how it works as well. If I can give you one thing, that's it–how to gain power through the Master Mind.

"I've got power. Masterminding built Lake Country Estates. You can't do it by yourself. You get other people's brains involved. That's what I did. You also use the power of positive emotions. That's important. How do people handle emotions? We don't go to emotion school. There's no course, no outlines. Emotions can get hold of you and make you do things you wouldn't ordinarily do. That's in chapter 11–how to channel emotions.

"I've got the power now. Even lying here in bed, I've still got the power. I love it and that is what I can give you—the power of the Master Mind."

That night, I read chapters 10 and 11. The next day, I flipped back to the beginning and began to read the book in its entirety. I now own my own copy and return to it frequently, rereading passages for inspiration—just like Nancy taught me to do. And, because of Nancy, I have built my own version of a mastermind group.

Looking back, I still regret that Nancy and I did not get to travel together. The trip we planned to northern Virginia to visit Nancy Love's daughters and Barbara Donahue and to eastern Ohio to visit Phyllis Burchfield was to have been only the beginning. Nancy told me that when she got her Cub up and flying she would take me out west in it. We would fly out to California and visit B.J. I had visions of renewing my effort to get my pilot's license so that I could serve as her copilot. That it would mean learning to fly a taildragger was a bit daunting, but when around Nancy I believed anything was possible. Her confidence, her positive take on all things was infectious. I wonder at what I might have learned had I had the opportunity to fly with her.

I also dreamed of doing joint book signings at Ninety-Nines and EAA (Experimental Aircraft Association) meetings, at air shows and aviation conferences around the country—Oshkosh, Sun 'n Fun, Women in Aviation International—at the Air Force Museum, International Women's Air and Space Museum, Southern Museum of Flight, the Women in Military Service for America Memorial, all of them.

Thanksgiving was drawing near and it was time for me to leave. I left the unread portion of the manuscript with Nancy. Her energy level was so low, she could only read a little at a time. I planned to return the week before Christmas to make any final changes she deemed necessary. Paul would be there then. I looked forward to meeting him.

As I left, I had momentary misgivings. Dr. Jim had reminded me of the realities. There was always the chance that Nancy wouldn't live until Christmas. Mentally, she was holding her own. Hopefully her body would do the same. I left with the promise that I would see her in a month. While she finished reading the manuscript, I would begin writing the mini biographies of each of the twenty-eight WAFS, which were to go in the back of the book. That, in itself, would be a more daunting task than I expected. As it turned out, it took me four months to gather the necessary information to write them all.

Four weeks later—December 18—I returned to Alabama.

Paul and I got along well and stayed out of each other's way. He was dealing with Lake Country Estates, as he had planned to do when Nancy became physically incapacitated. I began to pull Nancy's suggestions into a revised draft of the book.

We ate dinner on trays in Nancy's bedroom, left her to sleep when she needed to, and we talked—sometimes the three of us, sometimes just Nancy and me. The ease with which Nancy and Paul communicated struck me because I knew their history. Granted, the discussions were surface, everyday matters, but I sensed no tension between them.

Knowing time was running out, I searched for unasked and unanswered questions. When I did ask them, I felt uneasy, like I was bringing the specter of the Grim Reaper into the room. Ask now before it's too late. It may have been Christmastime in the rest of the land, but I was haunted by a Halloween-like vision of a graveyard waiting at the end of the road.

Talking on the phone now sapped too much of Nancy's strength. Her breath had to be rationed. She no longer took calls—other than from the WAFS. She did talk to Teresa, B.J., Florene, Phyllis, and Gertrude when they called, but Paul told me that whenever one of them did call, both women broke down in tears.

Because Paul was out frequently during the day, he talked to me about the "A" pills in a bottle kept next to Nancy's bed. The A—in their daily jargon—stood for *anxiety* and she was to take one if she had trouble breathing and it brought on an anxiety attack. Paul also showed me how to hook up both the regular oxygen tanks and the emergency oxygen supply. Should there be a power outage, she had tanks that would work off of a generator.

During my December stay, Nancy finally agreed to my writing her story. "You know me as well as anyone does, Sarah. I can talk to you. I trust you and I like you. If you think it is worthwhile, then tell my story."

I recall two specific conversations. Nancy had not told me much about her gliding experiences. But then I hadn't asked. Both that phase of her life and the California City story were far removed from my primary focus—writing *The Originals*. But now that she was OK with me writing her story, I needed to know about those things. So we talked about gliding—a key conversation because it revealed her passion for the purity of flying, of soaring unfettered above the earth. This was the young woman who at first resisted her World

War II instructor Barry Goldwater's attempts to teach her to fly blind. Now I understood why.

And she talked to me about California City—a bad time in her life.

I wanted Nancy to write the introduction to our book. Nancy, who did not enjoy writing, preferred that I write it for her—to say what I thought needed to be said. I drafted it. She liked it and signed it, in her shaky handwriting. The date on the printout was December 22, 2000. The introduction with her signature is on page six of *The Originals*. I still have the paper with her actual signature.

I left the next day—saying good-bye for the last time.

Our parting was unemotional. This was the woman who, dry-eyed, had taken Evelyn Sharp's broken body home fifty-seven years earlier. Nancy, by nature, was not a warm, demonstrative person. Instead, she could be rather austere, but she had put up with my parting hugs in the past. I hugged her one last time as I prepared to leave—gently, because beneath her pajamas she was skin and bones and so very fragile.

Nancy had made possible *The Originals* as well as what it heralded for my future. My task was to put the finishing touches on it. I knew she would not live to see it published. And I knew I would not see her again.

Nancy's neighbor had come over to sit with her that morning as Paul was out for a couple of hours and I was leaving. As I departed, the neighbor looked me in the eye and told me she would see me in about three weeks.

Her meaning was not lost on me. I nodded, but I couldn't speak. For all my education and years of writing about people, this Alabama countrywoman knew far more about the nature of living and dying than I did.

I drove away, turned east on I-20, and headed for Atlanta and Christmas with my family. For me it was not a season for rejoicing. I was mired in my own melancholy. I could not believe it was over.

Each time I spoke with Paul after that, he told me that Nancy had sunk a little deeper inside herself. She was sleeping more and more. Periods of wakefulness were farther apart and their duration shorter. The night of January 7, 2001, Paul called. She had slipped into a coma.

Nancy Elizabeth Batson Crews—my mentor, my benefactor, my friend—died on January 14, 2001, nine years and two days from the day we first met when she came to IWASM to be on the WASP panel.

A graveside ceremony was to be held at 1 p.m. January 18 at Birmingham's Elmwood Cemetery. She would be buried beside Paul Sr., near her mother and father in the Batson plot. On January 17, I flew into the Atlanta airport, where my son picked me up. The next morning, he and I headed west on I-20 bound for Birmingham.

The day was ready-made for a funeral. Dark, heavy clouds hung low over the highway and poured rain. A mist hovered about the car. One must always consider one's blessings. Had this been Detroit, Cleveland, or Chicago, we could have been encountering snow. In Alabama, it was wet, but not freezing. In fact, the atmosphere bordered on warm for January.

As we navigated our way through streets unfamiliar to both of us, the rain subsided to a drizzle, but the mist and fog remained. Birmingham, Alabama, was weeping for one of its favored daughters.

We found the cemetery and the gathering place. Chris would not be there. She was away on the trip to the West Coast that her employer had scheduled for mid-January—the same one she and Nancy had made the year before. That impending trip had caused Chris much concern as she watched Nancy's decline after Christmas. She told me later that she went to see Nancy before she left for Des Moines—and how hard it was to say good-bye. Chris and Nancy both knew Nancy would not be there when Chris returned.

Paul and Dr. Jim were the first two people I looked for in the room that held Nancy's flag-draped casket. I met Radford and Jane for the first time.

As 1 o'clock neared, we donned our raincoats and headed for our cars to drive to the grave site. There, a procession of umbrellas wound up the hill to the waiting awning, rows of chairs, and the military color guard.

When we were all assembled, Paul stepped forward to give the eulogy. He evoked a chuckle from the gathered crowd when he recalled watching his mother rediscover flying after being grounded for more than ten years. Following Paul, the Air National Guard chaplain gave his brief remarks.

Nancy had requested that a four-man formation of J-3 Cubs fly over the grave site with her own beloved Cub, flown by her friend Ed Stringfellow, peeling off and flying west—the pilot's symbolic epitaph. But the rain and fog combined to produce a two-hundred-foot ceiling, grounding all but the jetliners that flew shrouded in the mist into Birmingham Municipal Airport. The flyover was cancelled.

Nancy's nephew Steve Batson, an Episcopal priest, spoke next. As he began to recite the Lord's Prayer, the faint drone of a jet engine pierced the fog. Several of us looked up, startled. I know it flashed through my mind that, by golly, Nancy was up there, above the low-hanging clouds, buzzing us. Discussing this later, several of us were convinced that since the weather saw fit to cancel her farewell flyover, Nancy's spirit decided to do it herself. Odds are, from Birmingham she flew on to New York for one last pass by the Statue of Liberty—like she did as a WASP P-47 ferry pilot stationed on Long Island in World War II. That accomplished, she would have begun her last flight west.

When she died, Nancy had just over forty-two hundred hours recorded in her logbooks.[1]

In 1944, Nancy had told a mourner that it was all right to place an American flag on Evelyn Sharp's coffin—even though she and all the other WASP who died in World War II were denied official military funerals with a color guard and flag.

In 2001, that military funeral and the flag on the coffin were Nancy's by right. The WASP are now officially veterans. Nancy and her fellow WASP had worked hard for that recognition. At the end of the service, two members of the color guard methodically folded the flag that had draped her casket into the familiar triangle and presented it to her elder son, Paul Crews Jr.

22

Alabama Women's Hall of Fame

Back at Nancy's house after the service, family members and friends gathered to talk and, thanks to neighborly Southern hospitality, have a bite to eat. There, I had a chance to talk at length with Jane and Radford.

Nancy's children had been going through their mother's things, deciding what to keep and what to throw. Because they knew I was interested in writing their mother's story, they offered me several boxes containing her memorabilia—scrapbooks, papers, plaques noting her achievements, a book about the 2nd Ferrying Group, some photos, and her logbooks. Her first logbook, of course, has a permanent home at the Southern Museum of Flight. All the rest were in the boxes. Now I could track where Nancy flew and when. They asked simply that, when I was finished, I put the material in the hands of a museum, library, or archive where it would be appreciated and cared for.

Before we left, I spoke briefly to Nancy's sister Amy. We had met at the WAFS reunion in 1999. In a sad turn of events, Amy also had been diagnosed with terminal cancer. She came to the visitation, the burial, and Nancy's house leaning heavily on her son Luther's arm, and accompanied as well by her daughter, Liz. She seemed worn out by the hubbub created by the funeral preparations and the psychological stress of losing her last sibling. It had been just the two of them for so long.

I wanted to talk at length to her, but didn't feel this was the time and the place.

I had been home less than a month when Amy's daughter called and told me that her mother would like to speak with me. Amy was, by then, living with Liz and her family in Auburn. "I understand you are going to write a book about Nancy," Amy said when she came on the phone. "Would you want to talk to me about her?"

The answer, of course, was yes. We did the interview in late April 2001.

It was a good interview. Amy and Liz gave me some different insights into Nancy. (Amy died in mid-September 2001.)

The official publication date of *The Originals: The Women's Auxiliary Ferrying Squadron of World War II* was July 4, 2001. I received my two advance copies on June 14—five months to the day after Nancy's death. How thrilled she would have been! That she never held a real copy in her hands still saddens me.

The hard work was just beginning. With Nancy gone, the marketing and selling of *The Originals* became my sole responsibility and I have spent the years since traveling to various aviation and other venues to sell and sign copies of *The Originals* and to speak about it, about the WAFS' story, about Nancy's role in the book, and why I wrote it.

In 2002, Disc-Us published my second book, the WASP novel *Flight from Fear*—the book for which I sought Nancy's help back in 1999. I also wrote an article about Nancy for *Alabama Heritage* magazine, published by her alma mater, the University of Alabama. "Nancy Batson Crews, Pursuit Pilot Extraordinaire" appeared in the summer 2002 issue.[1] Nancy loved it when I called her a pursuit pilot *extraordinaire*, thus the title.

It was that article that, three years later, gave me something concrete to show The University of Alabama Press when I began my initial queries in the hunt for a publisher for Nancy's story. The UA Press editors had seen the article and were interested. When I approached them, they were receptive and this book has evolved from there.

As 2003 dawned and I thought about beginning to write Nancy's biography, two things stopped me. One was that sense that something still was missing. I really didn't have closure on Nancy's story. The other? I had by then put myself in the position to write Nancy Love's biography. Love's story needed to be written first, because she was the founder and commander of the WAFS and there was no book about her. That left a huge void in the history of women's aviation. Once Nancy Love's story was out there, biographies of other WAFS would fit into the whole context of the first group of women pilots who later came to be known as WASP. I had written a one-thousand-word mini-biography of Nancy Love for *Notable American Women*.[2] That small beginning grew into the larger project.

I immersed myself in researching and writing Nancy Love's story (*Nancy Love and the WASP Ferry Pilots of World War II*, University of North Texas Press, 2008). That took nearly three years. Then, once it was finished and out looking for a publisher, I began to work on this book. In the meantime, Nancy Batson Crews had received yet another well-deserved honor.

Through *Alabama Heritage* magazine, I discovered the Alabama Women's Hall of Fame. Established in 1970 at Judson College, Marion, Alabama, the Hall of Fame "recognizes women native to, or identified closely with, the state of Alabama. Each year the Board of Directors selects two women for induction who have made significant contributions on a state, national, or international level within their personal or professional lives. Only those who have been deceased for two years or longer may be considered."

At that point, early 2003, Nancy had been gone just over two years. She was eligible. The year 2003 marked the all-important centennial of powered flight—it had been one hundred years since Orville and Wilbur Wright first flew at Kitty Hawk, North Carolina, on December 17, 1903. Nationwide celebrations already were under way. I thought it fitting to nominate Nancy in 2003, for possible induction in 2004.

Mary Chapman Mathews, an Alabama native and an alumna of both Judson College and the University of Alabama, helped with the nomination. I asked Mary if she would write a second letter of nomination for Nancy, to be included in the submission packet for the Hall of Fame committee in August 2003. She agreed.

Mary is intimately connected with aviation in Dayton, Ohio. In 2003 she was the executive director of Dayton's Carillon Historical Park, which is dedicated to the history of the development of transportation and features Dayton's own favorite sons, the Wright brothers. Mary also served on the U.S. Centennial of Flight Commission advisory board. Mary's husband, Dr. David M. Mathews, is a graduate of and a former president of the University of Alabama.

Nancy Batson Crews was selected for induction, with the ceremony to be held March 4, 2004. Joining her as an honoree that year was Rosa Gerhardt, one of Alabama's earliest woman lawyers and the first woman attorney in Alabama to be elected president of a local (Mobile Bar Association) or state bar association.[3]

The selection committee asked Paul and me to be the presentation speakers for Nancy's induction. Nancy's nephews Luther Strange and Stephen Batson came from Birmingham for the event, as did Dr. Jim and Chris and Dr. Ed Stevenson. A lovely bronze plaque of Nancy—done in bas-relief—was unveiled. The photo we used for the likeness was her favorite—her WAFS portrait, the one with the Mona Lisa smile.

It was Nancy's day, and a proud one for all of us who attended. We felt that Nancy had truly taken her place among her peers—Alabama's women of note. Past inductees whose names are well known outside Alabama include Helen Keller (humanitarian), Tallulah Bankhead (actress), and Lurlene Wallace, the first woman governor of Alabama and also the wife of Nancy's long-time friend, George Wallace, who served four terms as governor of Alabama.

Following the ceremony and the luncheon, Chris, Dr. Jim, and I made our way back to Birmingham. Paul was staying with Luther. He wanted to talk to me. Chris and I met him for dinner that evening, as he was flying back to the West Coast the following day.

What he told me was this. After being estranged from his mother for twenty years and having only minimal contact with her for another ten, coming back into her life literally to help her die as comfortably as possible had had a profound effect on him. He told Chris and me about it over dinner.

Simply said, Paul's account granted me the closure to Nancy's story that, up to then, had eluded me. It also endowed me with the inspiration I needed to write it.

I had no tape recorder with me and I wanted his exact words.

"Paul, I can't do this from memory," I told him. "We need to talk again—preferably face-to-face—when I can tape record this and then ponder its impact."

He shook his head. "I'm leaving in the morning."

"I'm coming to southern California later this month to visit B. J. London. Can we get together then?"

23

Redemption

On March 20, 2004, in the dining room of the Seal Beach (California) Inn, where I was staying, Paul related how he came to care for his mother as she prepared to die.

Beginning with Nancy's induction into the Alabama Aviation Hall of Fame in October 1989, relations between Nancy and Paul began to thaw, if only slightly. Radford had called Paul to tell him that, on the advice of her lawyer, their mother had written him back into her will and that he needed to sign some papers. Radford also told Paul about the upcoming induction and that Nancy very much wanted all three of her children there with her when she was honored. She was offering to pay for airline tickets to Birmingham for the event and to foot the bill for tuxedo rental for her two sons.

"She re-owned me again because she wanted to have us all there when she was inducted."

Paul honored his mother's wishes and attended. That trip was when he realized that one of her three children needed to be knowledgeable about Lake Country Estates.

"She showed me her housing development. I asked some questions. I realized what she had there and that a lot of money was involved, though I had no idea how much. She was about to turn seventy. I had watched what happened to my father's health. If my mother should come down with a debilitating illness, someone was going to have to take over and manage her land-development business. I decided I'd better learn what I could.

"I told her I would come visit from time to time because somebody needed to be able to take care of the business if she couldn't. She flew me to Birmingham a few times so that I could keep up with what was going on and would know whom to contact if necessary. So I did get involved, to some extent, with my mother after that, but it was because of Lake Country Estates."

The relationship still was tenuous at best. "There was no mention of my family.

"In July 2000, my mother called me and told me that she had been diagnosed with lung cancer and that she was going to have surgery. She said that this form of cancer [bronchoalveolar carcinoma] was thought only to be treatable with surgery and the doctors were confident that surgery would take care of the problem."

When Paul learned that neither Radford nor Jane could make the trip to Alabama for their mother's surgery, he felt it was up to him to go. He arrived a day early. "I drove her to the hospital and stayed there with her. When they opened her up, the doctors found the cancer had progressed much further than they expected. Dr. Pittman and her surgeon talked to me. As it turned out, they had to just sew her back up."

Dr. Jim's words in that distressing e-mail came back to me as Paul was speaking: "The surgeon actually telephoned the medical pulmonary oncologist from the OR and asked whether he thought it might help—at least psychologically if nothing else—to go ahead and remove that LLL (lower left lobe), but he said no, she had some normal lung there and this would just make her short of breath and probably hasten the end. So the surgeon just closed her up, removed nothing except the confirmatory biopsies."

"Her doctor thought she probably had had it for over a year," Paul said.

"My supposition is this. She was constitutionally so strong that the debilitating part didn't identify itself until the tumor was pretty well entrenched. A normal person her age would have manifested earlier. But she was such a physically strong individual.

"I was the guy who had to give her the bad news. I was there with her while she was in the hospital and I brought her home.

"My mother was pretty angry about this. This was not part of her plan to go down like this. I think she planned, sometime after her hundredth birthday, to go to sleep and not wake up. And she wasn't a hundred yet. The doctors gave her anywhere from three weeks to three months to live—six months at the outside. With her kind of cancer, they said, it was hard to tell how long, but that toward the end one deteriorates rapidly."

Before returning to California, Paul initiated arrangements with Hospice to come in and care for Nancy. He also made plans to return in three months—November 3—though he wasn't sure that she would live that long. When he left, he thought everything was taken care of and that his mother would have the care she needed. But Nancy had her own ideas and, after Paul was gone, she told the Hospice people she didn't need them.

During August and September, Dr. Jim tried—at Nancy's request—to get her into an experimental treatment program. Neither of the programs they tried to schedule her for panned out. Then Nancy found a cancer specialist who was willing to try her on a chemotherapy program. She was told it probably wouldn't work, but that it certainly wouldn't hurt to try. She opted for the chemo. She was to learn the results from the doctor on November 7.

"When I came back November 3," Paul said, "I found out she had made arrangements with a friend to come in and fix her meals. I asked her about Hospice and she acted like she didn't know anything about it, but she did. This was Nancy. She wanted to do it on her own. It was that 'I'm going to take care of myself' kind of mental toughness that she had.

"The doctors had said she would either die from her heart giving out from overwork when she was struggling to breathe or she would not be able to utilize enough oxygen to keep her bodily functions going and that would kill her. We elected to keep her body going. Good food was the way to do it. I would cook for her. I had learned to cook at the Forty-Niner Tavern here in southern California, so that was no problem for me. I did it for fun."

Nancy's house, at that point, had no stove. Shades of California City, she had been cooking—making do—all those years on a propane-operated camp stove and a microwave. When Paul returned in early November and assessed the situation, his first move was to buy a stove.

"I began fixing her rich, high-calorie food to build up her strength. She was eating gourmet and I served it to her on her mother's best china.

"I called Hospice to have them come back. She agreed.

"The Saturday after I got there, my mother and I were sitting in her room talking and she started in on me about my marriage—thirty years after the fact. She got angry and started sobbing. I didn't know an eighty-year-old woman with greatly reduced lung capacity and oxygen intake could get that hysterical. But we were interrupted and, fortunately, the topic never came up again.

"That coming Tuesday was the presidential Election Day 2000—November 7. It also was the day of her doctor appointment. I took her to the doctor. Luther went with us. The doctor had to tell her the chemo was not working and that there were no more medical treatments. What they could do was make her comfortable. She was so angry at the news, she asked the doctor to give her a shot and put her to sleep. The doctor said, 'no.'

"I remember the drive back to her house. It was a beautiful fall day. On the way home she said, 'well at least an airplane didn't get me.' I do think she was kind of proud to have made it without dying in an airplane accident.

"Otherwise, that afternoon, she was seething. I honestly expected her to overdose that night. But when we got home, she started watching TV with all the election news. I think the drama over who was going to be president and the build-up over the hanging chads put a spark back in her. She was a real political student.

"The next day, as I was preparing to leave, she said, 'you know, Paul, you and I have been getting along pretty well. I'd like for you to come back and take care of me until I die.'

"I didn't want a repeat of that diatribe. I could not contend with a woman that angry. I told her I'd have to check with my family, and with my boss to see if I could get the time off. I told her I would get back to her. But when I left, I had had enough of my mother's anger to last me the rest of my life. It was my intent not to come back. Then I went home and told my wife what my mother had asked me to do.

"'You have to go back and take care of your mother,' she said.

"I talked to my boss. He said I could use my sick time to take care of a dying relative. I told him it could be up to three months. He said that was OK, all I needed was a letter from her doctor. I had a faxed copy the next day. I had no excuse. No reason not to go. I went back to Alabama the day after Thanksgiving to take care of my mother and run her business."

Paul had been there for nearly a month when I arrived for our scheduled December session. Their routine was well established. Nancy and I worked on the final stages of our book. She was still very with it mentally.

After hearing Paul's description of the last few weeks of her life, I now wonder if the appointment to work with me on the book helped keep her alive that one more month. I do think Nancy marshaled her remaining strength for our time together. I've always suspected that my visit took its toll, that she was exhausted after I left. But I'm equally sure she wanted to do it. After all, she was the reason the book had been written and would be published.

Chris and Dr. Jim came for one last celebratory dinner, which Nancy seemed to enjoy immensely. That was a magical night for five very different people brought together by the overt needs of one, but also by the personal commitments the other four had made to her.

I left the morning of December 23. That night, Nancy's life—and in the process, Paul's—took one last dramatic turn.

"I love Charles Dickens's *A Christmas Carol*," Paul said. "If possible, I like to watch it a couple of days before Christmas. It's my favorite part of Christmas because it captures the spirit of the season. I saw in the *TV Guide* that it was going to be on. I made a big deal about wanting to watch it. My mother agreed. We set up to watch it on the TV in her bedroom.

"About a third of the way through, it dawns on me that the reason I like this story is that my mother clearly represents the Scrooge character. This is the not-so-pleasant part of her personality. She was very strident, very judgmental, only wanted things her way. But it was what drove her—it made her successes possible.

"I began thinking, if she catches on to this, has the same realization I've had, I'll be in trouble again. But I was *not* going to turn the TV off after I had made such a big deal of watching it. I thought, maybe if I keep quiet she won't realize . . . about that time I heard her sobbing.

"Finally, when she was able to speak, she said, 'Paul, it occurs to me that I've held a hard place in my heart for you all these years. Can you ever forgive me?'

"I was shocked. That was completely uncharacteristic of Nancy Crews! Totally unexpected, a transformation took place.

"I said, 'well I have and I do.'

"'Thank you,' she said, 'you're a bigger person than I am.'

"With that, I relaxed. After that, her countenance was much different. She, too, relaxed. There was no judgment and she seemed to be at peace. Maybe her asking me to come take care of her gave her an opportunity to do that. I don't know, but there definitely had been a change in her.

"She began sleeping more and more and after that was pretty hazy when she was awake. At this point, I had to have twenty-four-hour care for her. Someone had to be up and awake and obviously I had to sleep, so she had nurses around the clock from then on and they took care of her.

"She slowly lapsed into unconsciousness. She had requested not to be fed with an IV. She had done a living will to that effect. On January 6, she had an incident. She deteriorated that day and never came back from it. After that the only interaction was a 'yes' or 'no.' She went into a coma the next day that lasted until she died early in the evening January 14.

"She was at peace."

24
Paul Jr.

"That incident has set me on a path very different from the one I was on," Paul said.

After Nancy's death, Paul began a spiritual journey. The two months he spent with his mother to help make the process of dying easier for her deeply affected both of them. Nancy's Christmas Eve awakening made it possible for her to be at peace—with herself and with her son. For Paul, the experience as a whole—his mother asking his forgiveness and his own ability to forgive—profoundly changed him and consequently has changed his life.

"What I experienced with my mother is called by some 'the dark night of the soul.'

"The Lord's Prayer directs us to practice forgiveness, which, when done on a regular basis, is a portal to an expanded state of consciousness. This is a universal, fundamental, spiritual teaching. Expanded consciousness is possible for those who move through and beyond events like this.

"That experience with forgiveness has taught me so much. Our life—the one we make for ourselves—is based on our perception. My mother was very successful doing this with her flying adventures and her business ventures. At the end of her life my mother was able to change her perception about our relationship through the act of requesting forgiveness. I saw her change as a result. The lesson I have learned from that is that it is possible to achieve a life free of anger and guilt. And a life guided by wisdom and love is rewarding beyond description."

Epilogue

Nancy Batson Crews had a profound effect on many people's lives. Her life and her death probably had their greatest impact on her elder son. Paul now uses the special gift his mother gave him—the lessons of forgiveness he learned from living through her death—to help others. He is teaching others how to use forgiveness to bring about peace of mind and he is writing about his experience so that others can read, understand, and find guidance.

Nancy dramatically changed my life. She made possible my crowning career achievements. First she challenged me, then she helped me fulfill my dream. None of what has happen to me since 1999 would have taken place had it not been for her faith and trust in me. She was, and is, my inspiration.

Nancy also possessed the gifts of "risk-taking," of "planning ahead," and of "follow through." She was willing to draft a long-range plan to build a subdivision and risk her money, her land, and her future against possible loss and failure. But she had her "Master Mind" plan and team in place. She did *not* fail and Nancy lived to derive pleasure from fulfilling her dream. Her children and grandchildren are now the beneficiaries of who she was and what she accomplished.

People are living in houses Nancy built. Craftsmen and laborers had jobs during the building phase. A community of homes exists because of her foresight. And she fulfilled the dream she and her father shared.

Nancy taught a lot of people to fly—both powered aircraft and gliders. She showed her students by example what it was like to soar like an eagle and look down at the marvel that is the earth. Surely some of her passion rubbed off.

Nancy has helped keep a small but important piece of World War II history alive in her telling and retelling of the WAFS experience. And the larger organization, the WASP, owes her its organizational structure, dating back to her presidency, 1972 to 1975.

Fellow pilots like Joe Shannon, Jim Pittman, Ed Stevenson, Chris Beal-Kaplan, and Ed Stringfellow revere her and are richer for having known her. The foreshortened lives of Evelyn Sharp, Helen McGilvery, Cornelia Fort, and Charlie Miller were enhanced by their brief wartime brush with her.

Nancy didn't think of herself as a role model. She felt her privileged upbringing—by well-to-do parents who were exceptionally receptive to their children's dreams—made it easy for her to achieve. But she took what she was given and, on her own, forged an enviable personal, aviation, and business record of achievement that can be an inspiration for women and men.

Notes

1. To ferry an airplane is to fly it from one place to another.

2. Kay Gott Chaffey, *Women in Pursuit* (self-published, McKinleyville, CA, 1993), pp. 96, 120, 140, 168, 198.

3. On May 29, 1941, the Air Corps Ferrying Command was established as part of the Army Air Corps (an arm of the U.S. Army). Its mission: to ferry Lend-Lease airplanes to the British and also to train more pilots for ferrying duties. On June 20, 1941, the Army Air Forces was created. The Air Corps continued to exist as a combat arm of the Army (similar to the Infantry), but was no longer an administrative organization; rather, it became a subordinate element of the Army Air Forces. All this was prior to the United States' entry into World War II.

In June 1942, after the United States had entered the war, the Air Corps Ferrying Command was reorganized and renamed the Air Transport Command (ATC). Its primary arm—the one responsible for ferrying aircraft worldwide—was named the Ferrying Division, which was charged with ferrying aircraft across the United States and abroad. A total of 303 women pilots (members of the WAFS/WASP) were, at some point, assigned to the Ferrying Division, Air Transport Command, between September 1942 and December 1944. Most of them referred to their service as "the Ferry Command." William H. Tunner (Lieutenant General) with Booton Herndon, *Over the Hump* (New York: Duell, Sloan and Pearce, 1964), pp. 11, 18, 28; "United States Army Air Corps," Wikipedia, http://en.wikipedia.org/wiki/United_States_Army_Air_Corps#Lineage_of_the_United_States_Air_Force Site, accessed January 2, 2009; and random interviews with women pilots who served in the Ferrying Division.

4. The term *check out* was used widely in the Ferrying Division, Air Transport Command, U.S. Army Air Forces, during World War II. It means to be deemed qualified to fly a given airplane as Pilot in Command.

WASP ferry pilot Iris Cummings Critchell (Class 43-2) gives the following explanation: "*Check out* is a quick, colloquial expression for the completion of required training—either the initial phase or a later currency check—on a specific airplane. The record of each 'check out' was carefully recorded on your Flight Record Form 5 and listed as 'checked out' next to the make and model on your qualification card, which you carried with you as you ferried airplanes from base to base or location to location."

Critchell was stationed with the women's squadron, 6th Ferrying Group, Long Beach, California, from June 1943 through December 1944.

Chapter 1

1. Information in this chapter comes from interviews with Nancy Batson Crews dated May 1999 and June, August, November, and December 2000; from Chapter 34 in the author's book about the WAFS, *The Originals: The Women's Auxiliary Ferrying Squadron of World War II* (Sarasota, FL: Disc-Us Books, Inc., 2001), pp. 321–325; and from an article by the author in the *Birmingham Aero Club Newsletter*, February 2001.

Chapter 2

1. Except where otherwise noted, the information in this chapter comes from a series of interviews conducted by the author with Nancy Batson Crews in January 1992 and May 1999 in Centerville, OH, and between June and December 2000 in Odenville, AL.

2. Interview by the author with Amy Batson Strange, Nancy's sister, April 18, 2001, Auburn, AL.

3. Katherine Price Garmon and Virginia Pounds, *Winnataska Remembered* (Birmingham, AL: Brown, Beechwood Books, 1992; sponsored by the Camp Winnataska Advisory Committee).

4. Ibid.

5. "Grade of the Grader," undated and otherwise unidentified news clipping, in Nancy Batson Crews's scrapbook, private papers, in the author's possession. An accompanying article, also unidentified, is headlined "Council Rates Capstone Clubs."

6. Interview with Amy Batson Strange.

Chapter 3

1. Letter to Nancy from Fred R. Maxwell Jr., Director, University of Alabama—C.A.A. [Civil Aeronautics Authority] Flight Training Program, dated October 31, 1939, in Nancy's scrapbook.

2. Patricia Strickland, *The Putt-Putt Air Force: The Story of the Civilian Pilot Training Program and the War Training Service, 1939–1944* (Department of Transportation, Federal Aviation Administration, Aviation Education Staff, GA-20-84, ca. 1970), p. iii. The Civilian Pilot Training Program (it became the War Training Service after Pearl

Harbor) originated in the mind of Robert H. Hinckley, a member of the newly created (1938) Civil Aeronautics Authority. It used facilities already in existence. The ground training was handed over to colleges and universities; the flight training to established flight operators. The CPT Program began with 13 colleges and 330 students. By the time it ended in 1944, 1,132 educational institutions had been involved and 1,460 contractors had qualified 435,165 trainees, including several hundred women.

3. "Four Jills in Jodhpurs," *Alabama Heritage* (The University of Alabama and the Alabama Department of Archives and History, Tuscaloosa), Number 67, Winter 2003, pp. 8–9.

4. "Birmingham Dawn Patrol Here," *Chattanooga [TN] Press*, September 29, 1941. Clipping found in Nancy's scrapbook along with membership cards from the Civil Air Patrol and the Aeronauts Club, dated January 1, 1942.

5. Nancy Batson, pilot's logbook. In Nancy Batson Crews private papers.

6. "Three Local Girls Are Making Good in Aviation Jobs," *The Birmingham News*, April 8, 1942, clipping in Nancy's scrapbook.

7. "Controls Air Traffic," *The Toledo [OH] Blade*, August 1, 1942, clipping in Nancy's scrapbook.

8. "Blonde Tomboy Joins Teaching Staff at Embry-Riddle School," *The Miami Herald*, August 7, 1942. Also, photo of three women flight instructors with caption, *The Miami Herald*, August 23, 1942, clipping in Nancy's scrapbook.

9. Nancy Batson, logbook. She got her rating in a Waco A50 with a 225-horsepower Wright engine.

10. Rickman, *The Originals*, pp. 77–79.

Chapter 4

1. Rickman, *The Originals*, pp. 156–157. The original source for this story is an interview with Nancy Batson Crews in 1999.

2. "WAFS to Fly in Gray-Green Slacks, Jackets," *Times Herald*, September 16, 1942 (exact newspaper unknown; possibly that serving Norristown and Montgomery County, PA). Article in Nancy Harkness Love collection, International Women's Air and Space Museum, Cleveland, OH.

3. Rickman, *The Originals*, pp. 80–81. The original source for this material is "Catch a Shooting Star," an unpublished memoir written by WAFS Delphine Bohn, ca. 1980s.

4. Interview with Nancy Batson Crews, January 1992.

5. Rickman, *The Originals*, pp. 91–92.

6. Ibid., pp. 96–98.

7. Interview with Nancy Batson Crews, June 2000.

8. Rickman, *The Originals*, pp. 107–118.

9. Author has either listened to personally or read the accounts of five of the six. Only Thompson's account is missing.

10. Army Air Forces historian Lt. Col. Oliver La Farge, "Notes on Interview with Mrs. Nancy H. Love, October 3, 1945." Nancy Love collection, the WASP Collection, the Woman's Collection at Texas Woman's University, Denton.

11. Betty Gillies, "The When-Why-Who-Where of the WAFS," a talk presented at the Southern California WASP Meeting, Laguna Hills, CA, June 14, 1987. The Betty Huyler Gillies collection, International Women's Air and Space Museum, Cleveland, OH.

Chapter 5

1. Adela Riek Scharr, *Sisters in the Sky*, Vol. 1, *The WAFS* (St. Louis: Patrice Press, 1986), p. 240.

2. Nancy Batson's orders, Air Transport Command, Ferrying Division, January 1943. In Nancy Batson Crews private papers.

3. Taped interview with Nancy Batson Crews by the author, August 13, 2000.

4. Nancy Batson Crews oral history done by Dawn Letson of the Woman's Collection at Texas Woman's University, Denton, June 11, 1997, in Odenville, AL. Transcript and tapes in the WASP Collection, the Woman's Collection at Texas Woman's University, Denton.

5. Nancy Harkness Love, logbooks. In Nancy Harkness Love private collection, in the possession of her daughter, Margaret Campbell Love.

6. Rob Simbeck, *Daughter of the Air: The Brief Soaring Life of Cornelia Fort* (New York: Atlantic Monthly Press, 1999), pp. 226–229.

7. Lt. Col. Oliver La Farge, for the Historical Branch, Intelligence and Security Division, Headquarters, Air Transport Command, "Women Pilots in the Air Transport Command," prepared in accordance with ATC Regulation 20-20, AAF Regulation 20-8, and AR 345-105, as amended; 1946, pp. 82–84. Copies in author's possession and at Texas Woman's University, Denton.

8. Ibid., pp. 84–85.

9. Ibid., pp. 73–75.

10. Ibid., p. 85.

11. Rickman, *The Originals*, pp. 165–166.

12. Ibid., pp. 167–171. This story was told to me by Nancy Batson Crews, was used in my first book, *The Originals*, and is repeated here.

13. Capt. Walter J. Marx, "Women Pilots in the Ferrying Division, Air Transport Command," an unpublished history written in accordance with AAF Regulation No. 20-8 and AAF Letter 40-34; 1945, pp. 114–115. In Nancy Harkness Love private collection; a copy of the Marx manuscript is also in the author's hands. See also La Farge, "Women Pilots in the Air Transport Command," pp. 85–86.

14. La Farge, "Women Pilots in the Air Transport Command," pp. 86–87.

15. Col. William H. Tunner, letter of April 26, 1943, Nancy Harkness Love private collection.

16. Nancy Batson's orders, Air Transport Command, Ferrying Division. In Nancy Batson Crews private papers.

Chapter 6

1. Tunner, *Over the Hump*, pp. 12, 27-28.

2. Rickman, *The Originals*, pp. 217-219. Material originally taken from interview with Nancy Batson Crews, August 12-13, 2000, in Odenville, AL.

3. Rickman, *The Originals*, p. 221. The Ferrying Division, Air Transport Command, U.S. Army Air Forces was responsible for ferrying the pursuit airplanes. To train pilots for this specialized task, the Army decided to bring trainees—male and female—to one location and train them to fly all four single-engine pursuits in one intensive four-week course. Pursuit transition school was born December 1, 1943. Twenty to nearly fifty men trained at one time, along with two to twelve women. The facility was located first in Palm Springs, California, and then in Brownsville, Texas. The letter *P* was used to designate pursuit planes.

4. Rickman, *The Originals*, p. 232. Material from a phone interview with Nancy, September 9, 2000.

5. Tunner, *Over the Hump*, pp. 27-28.

6. Louise Thaden, *High, Wide and Frightened* (New York: Air Facts Press, 1973), p. 150.

7. Rickman, *The Originals*, pp. 273-275. Material from an interview with Nancy, June 18, 2000.

8. For Evelyn Sharp's story, see Diane Ruth Armour Bartels, *Sharpie: The Life Story of Evelyn Sharp–Nebraska's Aviatrix* (Lincoln, NE: Dageford Publishing, 1996).

9. Rickman, *The Originals*, p. 275.

Chapter 7

1. Marx, "Women Pilots in the Ferrying Division," pp. 295-297.

2. Ibid., p. 298.

3. Ibid., pp. 296-298 (full text of the Costello Bill, H.R. 4219, 78th Congress, 2nd Session).

4. Ibid., pp. 298-300.

5. Rickman, *The Originals*, pp. 280-281, and interviews with Nancy, August and December 2000.

6. Marx, "Women Pilots in the Ferrying Division," pp. 336-337.

Chapter 8

1. J. Merton England (CWO), for the AAF Historical Office, Headquarters, Army Air Forces, *Women Pilots with the AAF, 1941-1944*. Army Air Forces Historical

Studies No. 55 (1946), p. 99. Document is on file both at the WASP Collection, the Woman's Collection at Texas Woman's University, Denton, and at the Dwight D. Eisenhower Presidential Library, Abilene, KS.

2. Rickman, *The Originals*, pp. 347–348, and interview with Nancy, June 18, 2000.

3. "First Squadron of Girl Pilots Here to Fly P-47s," *Republic Aviation News* (Indiana Division), September 15, 1944, photograph and article. In Nancy Batson Crews private papers.

4. Rickman, *The Originals*, pp. 306–307, and interview with Nancy, August 2000.

5. Marx, "Women Pilots in the Ferrying Division," pp. 352–353.

6. England, *Women Pilots with the AAF*, p. 101.

7. Rickman, *The Originals*, p. 310.

8. Nancy Batson Crews photographs, in her private papers, and interviews with the author.

CHAPTER 9

1. Interview with Amy Batson Strange.

2. Phone interview by the author with Elizabeth Simpson, Amy's daughter and Nancy's niece, February 24, 2007.

3. Nancy Batson Crews oral history done by Dawn Letson.

4. Bernt Balchen was a Norwegian-American aviation pioneer. He flew across the Atlantic Ocean with Richard E. Byrd in 1927 and was the chief pilot on Byrd's first Antarctic expedition. He piloted the first airplane over the South Pole on November 29, 1929. Balchen and his men constructed the Army Air Forces base Bluie 8 West in Greenland in 1942. "Bernt Balchen," Wikipedia, http://en.wikipedia.org/wiki/Bernt_Balchen, accessed December 22, 2008.

5. "Memphis Lieutenant Dies in Air Crash." Newspaper article dated January 27, 1945; newspaper not identified, but believed to be the Memphis *Commercial Appeal*. In Nancy Batson Crews private papers.

6. Newspaper articles, unknown newspapers, datelined August 25 and August 26, 1948. Helen E. McGilvery private collection, in the hands of her nephew, Eduardo Escallon; copies in the hands of the author and the WASP Collection, the Woman's Collection at Texas Woman's University, Denton.

CHAPTER 10

1. Nancy Batson Crews, logbooks.

2. Twenty-six licensed women pilots, including Amelia Earhart, gathered at Curtiss Airport, Valley Stream, New York, on November 2, 1929, and founded what became known as the Ninety-Nines, the International Organization of Women Pilots. The purpose of the fledgling organization was established as "good fellowship, jobs

and a central office and files on women in aviation." Membership was open to any woman with a pilot's license. The twenty-six present that day were representative of America's 117 (at that point) licensed women pilots, all of whom received an organizational letter announcing the meeting and an invitation to attend. The name Ninety-Nines was decided on later when the charter membership grew to, and was established at, ninety-nine. Earhart became the group's first elected president in 1931.

Information on the Ninety-Nines's founding is from *The Ninety-Nines Yesterday–Today–Tomorrow*, researched and written by the Ninety-Nines History Book Committee: Lu Hollander, Gene Nora Jessen, and Verna West (Paducah, KY: Turner Publishing Co., 1996), pp. 11–12. Information on the women's air races is found in *The Ninety-Nines Yesterday–Today–Tomorrow*, pp. 26–27. Copies of the book are held at the Ninety-Nines Inc. Headquarters, 4300 Amelia Earhart Road, Oklahoma City, OK 73159, and at the International Women's Air and Space Museum, Cleveland, OH. Information also found at "Who Are the Ninety-Nines?" The Ninety-Nines Web site, http://www.ninety-nines.org/99s.html, and "Women in Air Racing," The Ninety-Nines Web site, http://www.ninety-nines.org/racing_women.html, both accessed December 17, 2008.

3. Nancy Batson Crews, logbooks.

4. Interview with Elizabeth Simpson.

5. Family information in this chapter is taken from interviews by the author with Paul Crews Jr., March 2004 through March 2007; with Radford Crews, April–June 2006; and with Jane Tonarely, September 10, 2005. Further information from *Times of Our Lives*, a home video compiled by Radford Crews using movie film taken by his parents, 1940s–1960s, and video interviews with his mother, brother, and sister filmed by Radford in the 1980s. Copy in author's possession.

6. Interviews by the author with Nancy.

7. Stephen Lesher, *George Wallace–American Populist* (New York: Addison-Wesley, a William Patrick Book, 1994).

8. Interviews by the author with Nancy.

9. Interviews by the author with Paul Crews Jr.

10. Interviews by the author with Radford Crews.

Chapter 11

1. Interviews by the author with Nancy; also transcript of Nancy Batson Crews oral history done by Dawn Letson.

2. "San Gabriel Mountains," Wikipedia, http://en.wikipedia.org/wiki/San_Gabriel_Mountains, and "San Gorgonio Mountain," Wikipedia, http://en.wikipedia.org/wiki/San_Gorgonio_Mountain, both accessed December 18, 2008. Pilots flying in mountainous terrain are advised to maintain a minimum one-thousand-foot clearance above the terrain. Colorado Department of Transportation, Division of Aeronautics, 5126 Front Range Parkway, Watkins, CO 80137.

CHAPTER 12

1. Sarah Byrn Rickman, *Nancy Love and the WASP Ferry Pilots of World War II* (Denton: University of North Texas Press, 2008), p. 215.

2. Phone interview by the author with Mary Martin "Marty" Wyall, May 4, 2006. Wyall's oral history done by Dawn Letson can be found in the WASP Collection, the Woman's Collection at Texas Woman's University, Denton.

3. Col. Paul Crews, letters to Jacqueline Cochran, February and March 1969, Cochran Collection, Dwight D. Eisenhower Presidential Library, Abilene, KS.

4. Leoti "Dedie" Deaton was the Chief Establishment Officer, Women Airforce Service Pilots, first at Houston and then at Avenger Field in Sweetwater. Her oral history can be found in the WASP Collection, the Woman's Collection at Texas Woman's University, Denton.

5. Mary Regalbuto Jones's oral history done by Dawn Letson can be found in the WASP Collection, the Woman's Collection at Texas Woman's University, Denton.

6. Interview by the author with Marty Wyall.

7. Bee Falk Haydu's oral history can be found in the WASP Collection, the Woman's Collection at Texas Woman's University, Denton.

8. Rickman, *Nancy Love*, pp. 272–273.

9. *WASP Newsletter*, December 1976, Nancy Harkness Love private collection.

10. Marianne Verges, *On Silver Wings* (New York: Ballantine Books, 1991), p. 235.

11. Verges, *On Silver Wings*, p. 234.

12. Sally Van Wagenen Keil, *Those Wonderful Women in Their Flying Machines*, 2nd ed. (New York: Four Directions Press, 1990), p. 344.

13. Ibid., pp. 347, 348.

14. Ibid., p. 348.

CHAPTER 13

1. Interviews with Radford Crews, April–June 2006.

2. Interview by the author with Nancy's daughter, Jane Tonarely, and Nancy's logbooks.

CHAPTER 14

1. Nancy Batson Crews, logbooks.

2. Judy Barras, "Southern Belle Now Rules Eastern Kern City," *The Bakersfield Californian*, May 2, 1980.

3. "Mayor Crews Denounces City's 'Bad Management,'" *The Enterprise* (Kern County, CA), October 30, 1980; "City Hall Mayor's Office Approved," *Mojave Des-*

ert *News,* June 19, 1980. These are among several articles in a scrapbook that Nancy kept, Nancy Batson Crews private papers.

4. "Sabotage Attempt on Mayor's Airplane," *Mojave Desert News,* August 7, 1980.

5. "Police 'Eliminating Suspects' in Sabotage," *Mojave Desert News,* September 25, 1980.

6. "Mayor Crews Turns in Resignation," *The Enterprise* (Kern County, CA), July 8, 1981; and "Resident Upset with Council over Budget," *The Enterprise* (Kern County, CA), July 8, 1981.

7. "Crews Explains Her Resignation," *The Enterprise* (Kern County, CA), August 5, 1981.

CHAPTER 15

1. Napoleon Hill, *Think and Grow Rich* (North Hollywood, CA: Wilshire Book Company, 1999). This book, originally published in 1938, has been reprinted several times.

2. Hill, *Think and Grow Rich,* pp. 249–258.

3. The Birmingham Aero Club Web site is at www.aeroclub.tv/ (accessed December 28, 2008).

4. Southern Museum of Flight Web site, www.southernmuseumofflight.org, accessed December 16, 2008.

5. Alabama Aviation Hall of Fame Web site, www.southernmuseumofflight.org/AAHOF.html, accessed December 16, 2008.

6. "Daniel 'Chappie' James, Jr., General, United States Air Force," Arlington National Cemetery Web site, www.arlingtoncemetery.net/djames.htm, accessed December 16, 2008.

7. "Daniel 'Chappie' James Jr.," Alabama Aviation Hall of Fame, www.southernmuseumofflight.org/AAHOF_James.html, accessed January 24, 2009.

CHAPTER 16

1. Keil, *Those Wonderful Women,* author's note.

2. Bartels, *Sharpie,* pp. 1–4.

3. Ibid., pp. 252–255.

4. "The Forest and How It Came To Be," in the official booklet from the 2005 annual celebration of the International Forest of Friendship, Atchison, KS, June 17–19, 2005, p. 4; The Ninety-Nines, "International Forest of Friendship," www.ninety-nines.org/fof.html, accessed December 18, 2008.

5. The Ninety-Nines, "International Forest of Friendship," www.ninety-nines.org/fof.html, accessed December 16, 2008.

6. The International Forest of Friendship official booklet, June 2005, in the author's possession. The map in the centerfold indicates that the white pine is number 35. Thanks to Kay Baker, Executive Director, Forest of Friendship, P.O. Box 99AE, Atchison, KS 66002, for additional information.

7. Onas P. Matz (Colonel, USAF retired), *The History of the 2nd Ferrying Group, Ferrying Division, Air Transport Command* (Seattle, WA: Modet Enterprises, Inc., 1993), pp. 273–274.

CHAPTER 17

1. The museum has a new name. It is now known as the National Museum of the United States Air Force.

2. *Women in Aviation: Nancy Batson Crews,* a video produced by John Moraites for Miami Valley Cable Council, Centerville, OH, May 1999.

CHAPTER 18

1. Fannie Flagg, *Fried Green Tomatoes at the Whistle Stop Café* (New York: Random House, 1987).

2. "Eternal Word Television Network," Wikipedia, http://en.wikipedia.org/wiki/EWTN#Mother_Angelica.27s.first_television_series, accessed December 22, 2008.

3. Irondale Cafe Original WhistleStop Web site, www.whistlestopcafe.com/hist.html, accessed December 6, 2008.

4. Abiola Sholanke, "High-Flying Women of Second World War Gather at Museum," *Birmingham Post Herald,* June 24, 1999.

CHAPTER 19

1. Interview by the author with Nancy and Christine Beal-Kaplan, November 14, 2000, in Odenville, AL.

CHAPTER 20

1. *Ladies Courageous,* directed by John Rawlins (Paramount Pictures, Hollywood, CA, 1944).

2. Ann Hamilton Tunner and WASP (Class 43-2) Margaret Ann Hamilton are the same person. Mrs. Tunner entered the WASP in 1942 as Margaret Ann, but has gone by Ann since the war.

CHAPTER 21

1. Nancy Batson Crews, logbooks.

Chapter 22

1. Sarah Byrn Rickman, "Nancy Batson Crews, Pursuit Pilot *Extraordinaire*," *Alabama Heritage* (The University of Alabama and the Alabama Department of Archives and History, Tuscaloosa), Number 65, Summer 2002.

2. Sarah Byrn Rickman, "Nancy Harkness Love," in Susan Ware, editor, *Notable American Women*, vol. 5 (Cambridge, MA: Belknap Press, 2004), pp. 397–399.

3. The Alabama Women's Hall of Fame Web site, http://www.awhf.org, accessed December 6, 2008.

Bibliography

ARCHIVES AND UNPUBLISHED SOURCES

Batson (Crews), Nancy. Private papers including pilot's logbooks; orders, Air Transport Command, Ferrying Division; scrapbooks; and photographs. All currently in the hands of the author.

Bohn, Delphine. "Catch a Shooting Star." Unpublished WAFS memoir, ca. 1980s. Copies available in the Woman's Collection at Texas Woman's University, Denton, and in the author's hands.

Crews, Col. Paul (USAF retired). Letters to Jacqueline Cochran, February and March 1969. Cochran Collection, Dwight D. Eisenhower Presidential Library, Abilene, KS.

England, J. Merton (CWO), for the AAF Historical Office, Headquarters, Army Air Forces. *Women Pilots with the AAF, 1941–1944.* Army Air Forces Historical Studies No. 55 (1946). Copies available in the Woman's Collection at Texas Woman's University, Denton, and at the Dwight D. Eisenhower Presidential Library, Abilene, KS.

Gillies, Betty. "The When-Why-Who-Where of the WAFS." Transcript of a talk presented at the Southern California WASP Meeting, Laguna Hills, CA, June 14, 1987. The Betty Huyler Gillies collection, International Women's Air and Space Museum, Cleveland, OH.

International Women's Air and Space Museum, Cleveland, OH. Collections.

La Farge, Lt. Col. Oliver (AAF historian). "Notes on Interview with Mrs. Nancy H. Love, October 3, 1945." Nancy Love collection, the WASP Collection, the Woman's Collection at Texas Woman's University, Denton.

Love, Nancy Harkness. Private papers including pilot's logbooks; WASP Newsletter, December 1976; Col. William H. Tunner letter of April 26, 1943. Nancy Harkness Love private collection, in the possession of her daughter, Margaret Campbell Love.

Marx, Capt. Walter J. "Women Pilots in the Ferrying Division, Air Transport Command" (a history written in accordance with AAF Regulation No. 20-8 and AAF

Letter 40-34). Unpublished manuscript, 1945. Nancy Harkness Love private collection. A copy of the Marx manuscript is also in the author's hands.

Articles

Barras, Judy. "Southern Belle Now Rules Eastern Kern City." *The Bakersfield Californian*, May 2, 1980.

"Birmingham Dawn Patrol Here." *Chattanooga [TN] Press*, September 29, 1941.

"Blonde Tomboy Joins Teaching Staff at Embry-Riddle School." *The Miami Herald*, August 7, 1942.

"City Hall Mayor's Office Approved." *Mojave Desert News* (Kern County, CA), June 19, 1980.

"Controls Air Traffic." *The Toledo [OH] Blade*, August 1, 1942.

"Crews Explains Her Resignation." *The Enterprise* (Kern County, CA), August 5, 1981.

"First Squadron of Girl Pilots Here to Fly P-47s." *Republic Aviation News* (Indiana Division), September 15, 1944.

"Four Jills in Jodhpurs." *Alabama Heritage* (The University of Alabama and the Alabama Department of Archives and History, Tuscaloosa), Number 67, Winter 2003.

"Mayor Crews Denounces City's 'Bad Management.'" *The Enterprise* (Kern County, CA), October 30, 1980.

"Mayor Crews Turns in Resignation." *The Enterprise* (Kern County, CA), July 8, 1981.

"Memphis Lieutenant Dies in Air Crash" (Charlie Miller obituary). Newspaper unknown, but presumably the Memphis *Commercial Appeal*, dated January 27, 1945. Nancy Batson Crews private papers.

The Miami Herald. Photo of three women flight instructors with caption. August 23, 1942.

"Police 'Eliminating Suspects' in Sabotage." *Mojave Desert News* (Kern County, CA), September 25, 1980.

"Resident Upset with Council over Budget." *The Enterprise* (Kern County, CA), July 8, 1981.

Rickman, Sarah Byrn. "Nancy Batson Crews, Pursuit Pilot *Extraordinaire*." *Alabama Heritage* (The University of Alabama and the Alabama Department of Archives and History, Tuscaloosa), Number 65, Summer 2002.

———. "Nancy Harkness Love." In *Notable American Women*, vol. 5, edited by Susan Ware, 397–399. Cambridge, MA: Belknap Press, 2004.

———. Untitled article about Nancy Batson flying ailing P-38 over Pittsburgh, excerpted from Chapter 33 of *The Originals*. *Birmingham Aero Club Newsletter*, February 2001.

"Sabotage Attempt on Mayor's Airplane." *Mojave Desert News* (Kern County, CA), August 7, 1980.

Sholanke, Abiola. "High-Flying Women of Second World War Gather at Museum." *Birmingham Post Herald*, June 24, 1999.

"Three Local Girls Are Making Good in Aviation Jobs." *The Birmingham News,* April 8, 1942.

Books

Bartels, Diane Ruth Armour. *Sharpie: The Life Story of Evelyn Sharp–Nebraska's Aviatrix.* Lincoln, NE: Dageford Publishing, 1996.

Churchill, Jan, with Teresa James. *On Wings to War: Teresa James, Aviator.* Manhattan, KS: Sunflower University Press, 1992.

Flagg, Fannie. *Fried Green Tomatoes at the Whistle Stop Café.* New York: Random House, 1987.

Garmon, Katherine Price, and Virginia Pounds. *Winnataska Remembered.* Sponsored by the Camp Winnataska Advisory Committee. Birmingham, AL: Brown, Beechwood Books, 1992.

Hill, Napoleon. *Think and Grow Rich.* North Hollywood, CA: Wilshire Book Company, 1937. Multiple printings.

Keil, Sally Van Wagenen. *Those Wonderful Women in Their Flying Machines.* 2nd ed. New York: Four Directions Press, 1990.

Lesher, Stephen. *George Wallace: American Populist.* New York: Addison-Wesley, 1994.

Makanna, Philip, and Jeffrey Ethell. *Ghosts: Vintage Aircraft of World War II.* Charlottesville, VA: Thomasson-Grant, Inc., 1987.

Matz, Onas P. (Colonel, USAF retired). *History of the 2nd Ferrying Group, Ferrying Division, Air Transport Command.* Seattle, WA: Modet Enterprises, Inc., 1993.

Rickman, Sarah Byrn. *Flight from Fear.* Santa Fe, NM: Disc-Us Books, Inc., 2002.

———. *Nancy Love and the WASP Ferry Pilots of World War II.* Denton: University of North Texas Press, 2008.

———. *The Originals: The Women's Auxiliary Ferrying Squadron of World War II.* Sarasota, FL: Disc-Us Books, Inc., 2001.

Strickland, Patricia. *The Putt-Putt Air Force: The Story of the Civilian Pilot Training Program and the War Training Service, 1939–1944.* Department of Transportation, Federal Aviation Administration, Aviation Education Staff, GA-20-84, ca. 1970.

Scharr, Adela Riek. *Sisters in the Sky.* Vol. 1, *The WAFS.* St. Louis: Patrice Press, 1986.

Simbeck, Rob. *Daughter of the Air: The Brief Soaring Life of Cornelia Fort.* New York: Atlantic Monthly Press, 1999.

Thaden, Louise. *High, Wide and Frightened.* New York: Air Facts Press, 1973.

Tunner, William H. (Lt. General), with Booton Herndon. *Over the Hump.* New York: Duell, Sloan and Pearce, 1964.

Verges, Marianne. *On Silver Wings.* New York: Ballantine Books, 1991.

Personal Interviews

Nancy

Crews, Nancy Batson. Series of interviews by the author, January 12–13, 1992, and May 24, 1999, in Centerville and Fairborn, OH, and June 11–15, August 12–13,

November 13–15, and December 19–22, 2000, in Odenville, AL. Tapes in author's possession.

Crews, Nancy Batson. Oral history done by Dawn Letson of the Woman's Collection at Texas Woman's University, Denton, June 11, 1997, in Odenville, AL. Transcript and tapes in the WASP Collection, the Woman's Collection at Texas Woman's University, Denton.

Family

Crews, Paul Jr. Interviews by the author, March 20, 2004, Seal Beach, CA, and May 26, 2006, by phone. Tapes in author's possession.

Crews, Radford. Series of phone interviews by the author, April 22, May 13, and June 24, 2006. Tapes in author's possession.

Simpson, Elizabeth (Nancy's niece, Amy Batson Strange's daughter). Phone interview by the author, February 24, 2007. Tapes in author's possession.

Strange, Amy Batson (Nancy's sister). Interview by the author, April 18, 2001, Auburn, AL. Tapes in author's possession.

Tonarely, Jane Crews. Interview by the author, September 10, 2005, suburban San Diego, CA. Tapes in author's possession.

Friends

Beal-Kaplan, Christine, with Nancy. Interview by the author, November 14, 2000, Odenville, AL. Tapes in author's possession.

Shannon, Lt. Col. Joseph L. (USAF ret.), Dr. Ed Stevenson, Dr. Jim Pittman, and Christine Beal-Kaplan. Interview by the author, September 19, 2001, Southern Museum of Flight, Birmingham, AL. Tapes in author's possession.

WASP/WAFS (Interviews/Oral Histories)

Deaton, Leoti "Dedie" (Chief Establishment Officer, WASP, at Houston and then at Avenger Field, Sweetwater). Interview by Ziggy Hunter, March 18, 1975. Deaton's oral history can be found in the WASP Collection, the Woman's Collection at Texas Woman's University, Denton.

Fulton, Phyllis Burchfield (WAFS). Several phone interviews by the author, January 2001 to present. No tapes.

Haydu, Bee Falk (WASP 44-7). Phone interview by the author, June 6, 2006. Tapes in author's possession. Haydu's oral history can be found in the WASP Collection, the Woman's Collection at Texas Woman's University, Denton.

James, Teresa (WAFS). Interviews by the author, March 2–5, 2000, Lake Worth, FL. Tapes in author's possession.

LeValley, Gertrude Meserve Tubbs (WAFS). Interview by the author and oral history, December 2, 2004, Bradenton, FL. Tapes and transcript in the WASP Collection, the Woman's Collection at Texas Woman's University, Denton.

London, Barbara Erickson (WAFS). Tapes and transcript of the March 18–19,

2004, Long Beach, CA, interview/oral history done by the author, located in the WASP Collection, the Woman's Collection at Texas Woman's University, Denton; also, unrecorded phone conversations and one-on-one interviews, 2000 through 2008.

Jones, Mary Regalbuto (WASP 44-9). Oral history done by Dawn Letson can be found in the WASP Collection, the Woman's Collection at Texas Woman's University, Denton.

Ross, Barbara Donahue (WAFS). Interview by the author and oral history, May 17, 2006, Warrenton, VA. Tapes and transcript in the WASP Collection, the Woman's Collection at Texas Woman's University, Denton.

Wyall, Mary Martin "Marty" (WASP 44-10). Phone interview by the author, May 4, 2006. Tapes in author's possession. Wyall's oral history done by Dawn Letson can be found in the WASP Collection, the Woman's Collection at Texas Woman's University, Denton.

Video and Film

Ladies Courageous. Directed by John Rawlins. Paramount Pictures, Hollywood, CA, 1944.

Times of Our Lives. Home video compiled by Radford Crews using movie film taken by his parents 1940s–1960s and video interviews with his mother, brother, and sister filmed by Radford in the 1980s. Copy in author's possession.

WAFS videotaped interviews done jointly by the author and military aviation historian H.O. Malone with Barbara Erickson London, Barbara Poole Shoemaker, Gertrude Meserve Tubbs LeValley, and Teresa James, June 23–24, 1999, Birmingham, AL. The interview with Florene Miller Watson, June 24, 1999, in Odenville, AL, was done by the author only. Original tapes are located in the WASP Collection, the Woman's Collection at Texas Woman's University, Denton; copies in author's possession.

Women in Aviation: Nancy Batson Crews. Produced by John Moraites for Miami Valley Cable Council, Centerville, OH, May 1999. Features Nancy Batson Crews touring the National Museum of the U.S. Air Force, Dayton, OH, with the author, Sarah Byrn Rickman.

Web Sites

Alabama Aviation Hall of Fame
Located at the Southern Museum of Flight, Birmingham, AL
www.southernmuseumofflight.org/AAHOF.html

Alabama Women's Hall of Fame
Judson College, Marion, AL
www.awhf.org

Forest of Friendship (The Ninety-Nines)
Atchison, KS 66002
www.ninety-nines.org/fof.html

Greater Birmingham Convention and Visitor Bureau
www.bcvb.org

Irondale Café
www.whistlestopcafe.com/hist.html

Southern Museum of Flight
Birmingham, AL 35206
www.southernmuseumofflight.org/aboutmuseum.html

Index

Index of Airplanes that Nancy Flew